The Library as Literacy Classroom

A Program for Teaching

Marguerite Crowley Weibel

Foreword by Senator Paul Simon

AMERICAN LIBRARY ASSOCIATION

■ *Chicago and London 1992* ■

Project Manager, Joan Grygel

Cover and text designed by Harriett Banner

Composed by Publishing Services, Inc.
in ITC Caslon No. 224 and ITC Leawood
on Xyvision/Cg8600.

Printed on 50-pound Finch Opaque, a pH-neutral
stock, and bound in 10-point C1S cover stock
by Braun-Brumfield, Inc.

The paper used in this publication meets the minimum requirements of American National Standard for Information Sciences—Permanence of Paper for Printed Library Materials, ANSI Z39.48-1984.

Library of Congress Cataloging-in-Publication Data

Weibel, Marguerite Crowley.
   The library as literacy classroom / by Marguerite Crowley Weibel.
      p.   cm.
   Includes bibliographical references and index.
   ISBN 0-8389-0596-X (alk. paper)
      1. Public libraries—Services to the illiterate.   2. Public libraries—Services to adults.   3. Libraries and adult education.   4. Libraries and new literates.
   5. Literacy programs.   I. Title.
   Z716.45.W44   1992
   027.6—dc20   92-24275
                                                                            CIP

Printed in the United States of America.

96 95 94 93 92   5 4 3 2 1

To the memory of my parents,
Nellie and Michael Crowley

Contents

Sample Activities and Lessons

Credits

"Winter Moon" from *Selected Poems* by Langston Hughes. Copyright 1926 by Alfred A. Knopf, Inc. and renewed 1954 by Langston Hughes. Reprinted by permission of the publisher.

"Dust of Snow" from the *Poetry of Robert Frost* edited by Edward Connery Lathem. Copyright 1923, © 1969 by Holt, Rinehart and Winston. Copyright 1951 by Robert Frost. Reprinted by permission of Henry Holt and Company, Inc.

"Young Woman at a Window" by William Carlos Williams: *The Collected Poems of William Carlos Williams, 1909–1939, vol I.* Copyright 1938 by New Directions Publishing Corporation. Reprinted by permission of New Directions Publishing Corporation.

"Because" from *Cotton Candy on a Rainy Day* by Nikki Giovanni. Copyright © 1978 by Nikki Giovanni. By permission of William Morrow & Company, Inc.

"Response" by Bob Kaufman: *Solitudes Crowded with Loneliness.* Copyright © 1965 by New Directions Publishing Corporation. Reprinted by permission of New Directions Publishing Company.

"The Party" by Reed Whittemore copyright by Reed Whittemore, 1982. Reprinted by permission of the author.

"Good Night, Willie Lee, I'll See You in the Morning," copyright © 1975 by Alice Walker, from *Good Night, Willie Lee, I'll See You in the Morning* by Alice Walker. Used by permission of Doubleday, a division of Bantam Doubleday Dell Publishing Group, Inc.

"Those Winter Sundays" is reprinted from *Angle of Ascent, New and Selected Poems,* by Robert Hayden, by permission of Liveright Publishing Corporation. Copyright © 1975, 1972, 1970, 1966 by Robert Hayden.

"This Is Just to Say," "Complete Destruction," and "The Great Figure" by William Carlos Williams: *The Collected Poems of William Carlos Williams, 1909–1939, vol I.* Copyright 1938 by New Directions Publishing Corporation. Reprinted by permission of New Directions Publishing Corporation.

"Juke Box Love Song" by Langston Hughes from *Montage of a Dream Deferred* by Langston Hughes. Copyright 1951 by Langston Hughes. Copyright renewed 1979 by George Houston Bass. Reprinted by permission of Harold Ober Associates Inc.

"Scaffolding" from *Poems, 1965–1975* by Seamus Heaney. Copyright © 1980 by Seamus Heaney. Reprinted by permission of Farrar, Straus & Giroux, Inc.

"He Said," from *Good Night, Willie Lee, I'll See You in the Morning* by Alice Walker. Copyright © 1979 by Alice Walker. Used by permission of Doubleday, a division of Bantam Doubleday Dell Publishing Group, Inc.

Gunning Fog Index from *Using Readability: Formulas for Easy Adult Materials* by Robert S. Laubach and Kay Koschnick, copyright 1977 by New Readers Press, the publishing division of Laubach Literacy International. Reprinted by permission of New Readers Press.

"The New Instant Word List" by Edward Fry, *The Reading Teacher,* December 1980, pp. 284–289. Reprinted with permission of Edward Fry and the International Reading Association.

Foreword

by Senator Paul Simon

Illiteracy is a great weight that keeps this country and millions of our citizens from being all that they can be. Unfortunately, it is largely a hidden problem: Those afflicted are embarrassed to talk about it. This attitude makes illiteracy more difficult to confront. Twenty-three million Americans cannot address an envelope, fill out an unemployment form, or—perhaps worst of all—help their children with their school work. Tragically, there are many more who can address an envelope but cannot read a book, magazine, newspaper article, or the words I am now writing.

Not being able to read and write is a tremendous obstacle to success. Illiteracy prevents many from being productive members of society. Most who are illiterate have low self-esteem and a low income. But virtually all adults who cannot read and write have access to a library.

My conviction that libraries are logical focal points for fighting illiteracy led me in 1984 to introduce an amendment to the Library Services and Construction Act that facilitated the use of libraries as tutoring centers. I did it because I knew no one in our society has as great an appreciation for what reading and writing mean to personal enrichment as librarians do. I also did it because literacy efforts must take place where people feel no embarrassment when they walk into a building. People who cannot read and write do not want to walk into a grade school or a high school—that embarrasses them. But they can walk into a library with pride. Libraries provide a place for volunteer tutors to meet with students; they welcome everyone. No social stigma is attached to walking into a library.

In 1991, the federal government enacted the National Literacy Act, a landmark law designed to eliminate adult illiteracy from our nation by the year 2000. This law includes the Library Literacy Programs provision, which encourages libraries to serve as literacy tutoring centers. Congressional support for this important provision demonstrates that Marguerite Crowley Weibel and our nation's leaders have reached the same conclusion: libraries are an invaluable resource for literacy students and tutors.

In *The Library as Literacy Classroom,* Ms. Weibel explores in detail how people can creatively and effectively use the materials found at the local library to help teach adults to read and write. This book is a resource designed for teachers and librarians working with adult literacy programs.

The rich and diverse materials found within a library can be used imaginatively and effectively to help teach adults to read. Ms. Weibel's creative suggestions, including extensive lists of specific materials that have been helpful to her in tutoring her students, will help literacy tutors. She offers sample lessons and suggests specific methods for using them, including language experience, that have proven successful.

Although beginning literacy students cannot read and write complex sentences, they can and do think complex thoughts and feel mature emotions. It is easy to understand why many students and tutors dislike the simplistic and often patronizing style of many tutoring manuals, which resemble books written for young children. All too often, tutoring materials fail to recognize and reinforce that adult learners are intelligent and capable. Finding appropriate materials—that are interesting and mature in content yet use simple language—presents a major challenge to tutors. Librarians can play a pivotal role in helping adult learners meet this challenge by encouraging libraries to acquire such materials and by assisting students and tutors in locating these materials.

The Library as Literacy Classroom is geared toward librarians and literacy tutors, but it should interest all of us. Whether paying higher taxes to support those unemployed due to the inability to read and compete in the job market, paying higher prices for goods and services when companies must use resources to train employees lacking basic skills, or being the victim of a crime committed by someone who lacks the skills necessary for employment, all Americans are affected by illiteracy. Solving the illiteracy problem is a critical step toward addressing other societal problems, and libraries can be an invaluable resource in the solution.

How can literacy tutors best use libraries to help teach their students to read and write? In *The Library as Literacy Classroom* Ms. Weibel creatively answers this important question.

July 9, 1991

Acknowledgments

This book has been long in the making, and many friends and colleagues have contributed to its development and final form. In 1977 I began working as the educational coordinator of the Ohio State University Right to Read Program, a federally funded reading academy for adults. Paula Schneiderman was the director of the program and together we developed an instructional program using language experience, information reading, and other methods discussed in this book. Peggy Scantland, secretary and tutor, contributed many ideas and insights that helped make the program more responsive to the students who sought our help as well as countless hours preparing teaching materials for tutors and students. Burt Cantrell, who became director after Paula, continued to steer our efforts toward a student-centered curriculum and guided my early explorations of poetry for new readers. I am grateful to Paula, Peggy, and Burt. I also thank the many students and tutors whose persistence, generosity, and dedication made working in that program more a privilege than a job.

In the summer of 1981, Professor Ron Carstens, director of the humanities program at Ohio Dominican College, invited me to participate in a faculty seminar on teaching the humanities. It was in that seminar, studying the epic poetry of ancient Greece, that I began to understand the power that stories of personal and ancestral history hold for all cultures, and so I began to look for ways to use oral history and the stories and poetry of our contemporary culture with adult literacy students. I am deeply grateful to Ron for his generous invitation.

In the fall of 1981, Angela Fasone, director of the Columbus Literacy Council, invited me to teach a class to students, using poetry and works of art as stimuli for reading and writing activities. I thank Angela and also Barbara Fellows, assistant director of the Main Library of Columbus Metropolitan Library, for making it possible for us to use the library's facilities and resources.

I also thank Kathy Frank, adult services coordinator of Columbus Metropolitan Library, whose leadership and support of my work led to a grant from the Library Services and Construction Act, administered by the State Library of Ohio, to establish five library learning centers in inner-city branches of the Columbus Metropolitan Library. An additional grant from the Ohio State Department of Education, administered by Jim Bowling, supported the writing of an earlier book, *The Library Literacy Connection*. Jim Bowling, as well as Sandra Scott and Mike Jaugstetter of the State Library of Ohio, read and offered advice for that original manuscript, which was the seed for *The Library as Literacy Classroom,* and I am grateful to them.

Floyd Dickman and Tom Szudy of the State Library of Ohio have supported my work and offered references when I needed them. Tom Szudy also read the entire manuscript. Burt Cantrell read specific chapters of this book, as did Leslie Pearse and Nancy Campbell. I thank them all for their time and encouragement.

I used the resources of many libraries in preparing this book: the Bexley (Ohio) Public Library, the Columbus Metropolitan Library, the Upper Arlington (Ohio) Public Library, and, most particularly, the many libraries of Ohio State University. At OSU, I particularly thank Lucy Caswell of the Cartoon, Graphic, and Photographic Arts Research Library and Tom Hubbard of the School of Journalism for help in locating the photographs in

Chapter 5, and all the librarians and staff at the Health Sciences Library for their continued support as well as help in making copies and sending manuscripts.

I thank Herbert Bloom, senior editor at ALA Books, who was always a patient and enthusiastic supporter of this project, and Joan Grygel, who edited the manuscript for typesetting and offered many thoughtful insights that have strengthened the book's message.

Finally, I thank my family: my husband, Stuart, who was the first to say, "You should write a book," and who has been my most perceptive critic and advisor throughout this much-longer-than-expected project; and my sons, Mathias and Brendan, who learned to read themselves during the course of my writing this book, and who taught me many wonderful things about learning and about life.

Introduction

I asked myself, "Why the public library?" And then I realized, that is where you go to read.[1]

A Literacy Student

My student has mastered the first workbook in his reading program. He is very proud of himself, but he is also getting restless. He asks me when he will be able to read "real books."

I have heard many tutors describe situations similar to this one. They have taught their students the beginning skills of reading, and the students are pleased with their first steps into the world of literacy. But just as babies who have taken their first steps want to explore the world beyond their living rooms, so new readers are eager to apply their newly learned skills to all aspects of their everyday lives. Experienced tutors know that this is a pivotal point in any student's literacy program. Indeed, many students drop out at just such a time. They cannot see how the skills they've learned to date will ever enable them to read books or newspapers or job orders with security and ease.

This is the time to take literacy students to the public library. Most public libraries house collections of books and other materials written specifically for adult new readers. These collections are substantial and getting better as publishers recognize the need for books written about adult subjects at easy reading levels.

But special collections of books for new readers are not all the library has to offer literacy students. In fact, the general collection of any public library contains many books and other materials that will appeal to new readers, although their usefulness in literacy instruction may not be immediately apparent. Let me give a few examples.

Literacy students need to read works that are short and use simple language, but ones that are rich and mature in content. Much poetry, written specifically for adults, fits that description. Poetry describes feelings we recognize in ourselves but can't express, and suggests ideas that spur a reader's thoughts in new directions. Poetry also uses rhyme, repetition, and vivid imagery to convey meaning, elements that make the language of poetry engaging and readable.

Like most adults, literacy students are interested in contemporary social issues, although they lack the skills to read about them. In the library, students will find numerous photodocumentaries that present ideas in pictures. Reviewing such a book with a tutor or with other students, new readers can "read the picture" by explaining its theme, inferring relationships among people pictured, noticing specific details, or expressing a personal reaction, all skills they will later apply to the written word.

Photodocumentaries can also be used to extend the language experience technique, a teaching method that records the student's own language to create reading material. Language experience stories initially derive from the student's retelling of a personal experience, but they can also result from discussions about the pictures in photodocumentaries, in art and photography books, or in picture biographies.

Students also come to literacy instruction with many information needs. The library houses the resources to provide that information, but the students have no access to it because they can't read. However, tutors can use a variation of the language experience technique, called the information reading technique, to help students acquire the information they need. Using this method, tutors find books in the library that contain information that students want or need to know, then read to the students from those books and discuss the information with them. Tutors then write down the students' understanding of the material in the students' words. Tutor and students thus create a written version of information that is important to the students—one that the students can learn to read.

Using books from the public library offers adult literacy students the opportunity to practice their developing skills on a wide range of reading material. It also connects new readers to a world of information and ideas outside their immediate circumstances. But using library books as a primary source of reading material for literacy students presents a particular challenge to tutors. Not only must tutors find books to engage their students' interests, they also have to teach the basic skills that will help students progress to new reading tasks. Since library books don't come equipped with skill-building exercises, the tutor must create practice exercises to reinforce those basic skills. *The Library as Literacy Classroom* addresses this challenge. It promotes a library-based curriculum for teaching reading and suggests a wide variety of books to use with new readers. It provides an outline of basic skills—including reading, spelling, writing, and critical thinking skills—that literacy students must master to become good readers. It also suggests numerous skill-building activities for teachers to develop using the words and ideas derived from whatever library books or other materials the students are reading.

This book is intended for both literacy teachers and librarians. Each will read it from a different perspective, as each has a specific role to play in the promotion of literacy; however, those roles need not be mutually exclusive. Librarians can choose to be tutors as well as readers' advisors, but even if they function in a more traditional library role, they are essential partners in the literacy team. Tutors teach adult literacy students how to read by developing instructional plans that teach the basic skills students need to master to become independent readers, linking the process of reading with the particular needs and interests of each student's everyday life, and motivating literacy students to continue to read and learn throughout their lives. To do this complex job effectively, tutors need to introduce their students to the world of knowledge and information—the world of books—available in any public library. But first, tutors need to become familiar with the variety of resources the library has to offer new readers and to consider how to incorporate those resources into their students' instructional programs.

Librarians, on the other hand, know those resources, and it is their job to link tutors and students with the wealth of material the library has to offer. Just as a school library provides books and other materials to supplement and extend whatever students are learning in their classes, a public library can provide a similar service to the literacy programs in its community. To do this effectively, librarians need to understand adult literacy students and to know what motivates them, what difficulties they face, and what reading needs they have. Librarians also need to know how literacy students are taught and what basic skills they learn in their literacy classes. Knowing the background as well as the educational experience of literacy students, librarians can look at their library's entire collection from the point of view of adult new readers. They can identify materials currently available that new readers can use, either independently or with the assistance of tutors. Librarians can also determine what additional purchases—for the new readers' collection as well as for the general collection—will increase the number of materials accessible to new readers.

The Library as Literacy Classroom is divided into four sections. Part One, The Library and the Adult New Reader, discusses the role of the library in promoting literacy and presents a profile of adult new readers.

Part Two, Teaching Adults to Read, examines several methods used to teach adults to read, emphasizing the methods of language experience, information reading, and assisted reading. These methods enable even beginning level readers to learn to read using adult level materials that engage their interest and teach them things they need to know. Part Two also outlines the basic skills that literacy students need to master and suggests activities to teach those skills. Anyone who chooses to tutor can apply this basic skills curriculum to the library resources discussed in Part Three. Librarians can read this section to better understand the teaching process and apply that understanding to an examination of the books in their collections that will support reading instruction.

Part Three, A Library-Based Reading Program, is the heart of this book. It describes how to extend the language experience approach and other learner-centered methods described in Part

Two using a wide variety of library resources. In particular this section describes lessons using poetry, photodocumentaries, art and photography books, how-to manuals, literature, books from the children's collection, and audiovisual materials. It discusses family literacy programs and special collections of materials written specifically for adult new readers. And it suggests lessons to help adult literacy students learn to use the library themselves as they progress toward reading independence. Several chapters contain significant annotated lists of resource materials suggesting sample titles of books appropriate for adult new readers. In this section, tutors will find many practical suggestions for building a library-based literacy program. Librarians will find numerous examples of books already in their collections that they can recommend to literacy tutors. Even if libraries do not have the specific titles suggested, they will undoubtedly have other similar books.

Part Four, Bringing It All Together, suggests how libraries, literacy programs, and other community organizations can work together to build a broad-based literacy coalition for their community.

Throughout this book the terms *adult new readers* and *adult literacy students* are used interchangeably, as are the words *tutor* and *teacher.* The term *literacy program* can refer to a one-to-one tutoring relationship, a small group session, or a classroom arrangement as found in many Adult Basic Education (ABE) programs. Methods described in one setting can be adapted to fit other situations. While the methods and materials described generally are intended for use with English speaking adults who are learning to read, many of them can also be adapted for use with students of English as a foreign language.

Literacy is one of the pivotal issues of our time. The economic vitality of our nation depends on the availability of an educated workforce. The strength of our democracy rests with an informed, thoughtful citizenry. Our ability, as individuals, to lead fulfilling, happy lives grows with our understanding of the world around us and our place in it. To achieve the level of literacy that will ensure our economic, political, and personal security, we must do more than teach people how to read. We must help them to become readers. It is the purpose of this book to show literacy teachers and librarians how to work together to accomplish that task.

Part One

THE LIBRARY
AND THE ADULT
NEW READER

The Role of the Library in Promoting Literacy

> Knowledge will forever govern ignorance, and a people who mean to be their own governors must arm themselves with the power which knowledge gives.[1]
>
> James Madison

I remember clearly the day I first began to think of the library as a resource for adult new readers. I was tutoring a literacy student, using a workbook that presented a brief story about an adult followed by some comprehension questions. The questions asked simple facts such as the name of the man in the story, where he lived, where he worked, and why he was traveling from one place to another. We were sitting side by side at a table, the student to my right. As he read a question, then stopped to remember the correct information, I found myself lifting up the left-hand page to check back in the story. I couldn't remember the answer either.

I was embarrassed and irritated by my own lack of attention. But the more I thought about this incident, the more I understood that the material itself was at least partly to blame. It was boring. It was written in the kind of flat, simplistic language found frequently in texts for new readers but never heard in real speech. Neither the story nor the language engaged the reader's interest in any way. It was an exercise in reading, not the real thing.

I wanted to find books to read with my student that would engage his interest, that would have him really reading, so I went to our local public library. Initially I found a small collection of books written for reluctant readers. This was the late 1970s, when few such books were available and the quality of those books varied, but some were both simple and interesting enough for my student to enjoy.

But I wasn't really satisfied. I knew the collection was neither large enough nor varied enough to sustain my student's interest for very long. I began to look beyond the collection of high interest/low reading level books to the general collection. In my literacy program, we frequently used the language experience technique for teaching reading. This technique produces its own reading material from conversations between tutor and student. I found some adult "picture" books in the library: photodocumentaries, collections of photographs, travel books—what some might call "coffee table" books—that I thought might inspire some interesting language experience conversations. I also discovered the poetry of writers such as Langston Hughes, whose poems talked of adult ideas, experiences, and feelings, but in language that was simple, yet rich and rhythmical, language so engaging that lines and phrases stayed with my student and me for weeks after reading a poem.

This experience taught me that *what* adult literacy students read is of paramount importance, and that learning to read requires more than just mastering a set of skills. Reading is, in part, a matter of skill, and, like any other skill, it needs to be practiced frequently. But reading is so much more than a skill. Reading is a means of acquiring information we need, of learning about our past and preparing for our future, of escaping everyday life into imaginary worlds, of thinking about and changing the way we live our lives. Students need to be exposed to books that offer such opportunities from the very beginning of literacy instruction. At every lesson, they need to read—or at least listen to—real books. To do this, teachers and students need to use the books and resources they will find in the public library.

The Library as Literacy Classroom

When I speak of the library as a literacy classroom, I use the word *classroom* in its broadest sense: as a place where learning occurs, or a place that fosters learning. In its long history, the public library has been a classroom to many—"the people's university" that serves immigrants and scholars, writers and entrepreneurs, businesses and families.

In this literacy classroom, librarians are educators, not in the limited sense of teachers instructing a group of students but in the broader sense of professionals who prepare a rich environment for learners, introduce the learners—in this case, both literacy students and their tutors—to the varied collections of materials available to them, and help those tutors and students find and use materials that are particularly appropriate to each student's needs and interests. In fact, for the library to become a classroom for adult literacy students simply means extending the library's traditional services to a new user group, adult new readers, and actively promoting the role of the library in the community's literacy efforts. Let's look more closely at those traditional services: providing access, advising readers, offering facilities for learning, and promoting the public debate about issues of importance to the communities libraries serve.

Providing Access

Public libraries provide access to the information and knowledge so necessary for active participation in an economy and a culture that are based on learning. Equally important, they provide access to our collective human culture as preserved in our written heritage, access that is crucial to our understanding of ourselves, our community, and our global neighbors.

They provide this access by collecting books and other sources of information over a wide range of subjects, by maintaining these collections long after most of the books are out of print and no longer in popular memory, and by opening their collections to everyone. In fact, the Public Library Association states:

> The public library is unique among our American institutions. Only the public library provides an open and nonjudgmental environment in which individuals and their interests are brought together with the universe of ideas and information. The ideas and information available through the public library span the entire spectrum of knowledge and opinions. The uses made of the ideas and information are as varied as the individuals who seek them. Public libraries freely offer access to their collections and

services to all members of the community without regard to race, citizenship, age, education level, economic status, or any other qualification or condition.[2]

Working together with literacy tutors and students, librarians can open this treasure of knowledge to adult new readers. In any library's collection are books covering virtually every subject, books written on a wide range of reading levels and in varying formats, books intended to appeal to readers from many different backgrounds and with many different interests. Some of these books are already accessible to adult new readers because they are written at easy reading levels. Others can be made accessible to new readers through use of teaching techniques such as language experience, information reading, and assisted reading, techniques described in this book.

Advising Readers

Since the inception of public libraries, librarians have served as readers' advisors, skilled professionals who know the books in their collections and link those books to the patrons who come to the library seeking information, intellectual growth, and entertainment. Librarians can extend this traditional role to new readers and their tutors by recommending the materials to support the library-based curriculum outlined in Parts Two and Three of this book. Specifically, they can recommend books to meet the particular needs of individual students and tutors, give workshops to tutors describing the range of materials available in the library to support a library-based curriculum, choose books from the general collection to label for new readers or add to the new readers' collection, prepare bibliographies of available materials to share with local literacy programs and other libraries, give book talks to students at local literacy programs, and purchase additional materials for the library to support local literacy programs.

Offering Learning Facilities

Libraries offer literacy students a place to learn. Many students and tutors meet in public libraries across the country. As tutoring sites, however, libraries offer more than tables and chairs—libraries are welcoming places. They are not perceived as part of the educational establishment in the same way that schools are. Rather, libraries are community centers that invite all comers, regardless of any economic, social, or educational standing, to participate in learning activities of their own choosing.

Promoting Public Debate

All libraries contribute to the public debate on important social issues by buying and maintaining a collection of books that discuss those issues from varying perspectives. Libraries can extend the reach of the public debate about literacy by serving as clearinghouses for information about literacy programs, both local and national; by building comprehensive collections of teacher education materials related to literacy; by inviting authors and educators to speak about literacy and related issues; and by sponsoring forums and other community education projects to discuss the issue of literacy.

Adult literacy students stand at the center of a serious national dilemma. On the one hand, newspapers, magazines, and television and radio commentaries frequently decry the declining competence of our educational system and the related problem of adult illiteracy. On the other hand, we are continually reminded, in the media and in virtually every task we must perform, that technology brings swift and extensive change to our way of life and that, as individuals and as a nation, we need more information, more knowledge, and more understanding to fulfill our appointed tasks as well as our aspirations. The gap between an ill-informed and poorly educated populace and a society based on quick and efficient access to information is widening. If that gap is to be narrowed and literacy students are to become active participants in the learning society we hope to build, then they need no less than the treasury of ideas and information contained in the public library as their literacy classroom.

Beyond Functional Literacy

Improving the literacy standards of our citizens is a national goal that most of us support wholeheartedly. There is considerable debate, however, about what it actually means to be literate in today's ever-changing society.

Functional literacy is a term commonly used in discussions about literacy. It has been the focus of many adult education programs since 1975 when the Texas Adult Performance Study was published. The Texas study measured the ability of adults to read such items as bus schedules, product labels, job applications, TV schedules in the newspaper, and apartment leases, and it concluded that perhaps as many as 20 percent of our adult population were functionally illiterate. That is, some 27 million adults were unable to read well enough to perform the tasks that define modern American life.[3] In response to this study, many Adult Basic Education and literacy programs began to concentrate on teaching what are called "life-coping" skills, and publishers produced many workbooks aimed at improving students' ability to read while also teaching them to balance checkbooks and compare items in the grocery store.

While improving the level of functional literacy among our citizens is clearly necessary, it is not sufficient. Attaining functional literacy may enable new readers to succeed in their current circumstances, but those circumstances can change quickly and unpredictably. A student who is transferred to a new job requiring new skills can easily slip back into functional illiteracy at the workplace. We want our students to go beyond functional literacy so they will be prepared for the fluctuations and changes that will inevitably occur in their lives. We want our students to be able to do more than read grocery labels; we want them to be able to make informed decisions about whether or not to buy a particular product. We want them to be able to do more than read a newspaper; we want them to be able to agree or disagree with what they see in print. We also want our students to recognize the power that reading can bring to their lives: the power to learn new things, the power to change the circumstances of their personal lives, and the power to become active participants in the world of commerce, government, and ideas.

To achieve this level of literacy, we need to use our public libraries and their rich resources as literacy classrooms. When literacy students discuss the pictures in a photodocumentary, such as Betty Medsger's *Women at Work,* then read the resulting language experience stories, they not only learn to read their own words in print but, more importantly, they learn to formulate and express their own ideas about an important social issue. When literacy students read, or listen to, a poem such as Alice Walker's "Good Night, Willie Lee, I'll See You in the Morning," they learn how a writer can tell a family story in a few simple words and make a profound statement about how human beings struggle to love each other. Or when literacy students read, or listen to, the letters, diaries, speeches, sermons, and other words presented in Milton Meltzer's *The Black Americans: A History in Their Own Words,* they learn about American history and about the strength, perseverance, and courage of so many people struggling to achieve a goal, and perhaps they begin to see their own place in that history. By engaging the words and ideas written in the books the library offers them, adult literacy students will have the opportunity to gain access to the records of history, to engage in an active exchange of ideas and knowledge across space and time, and to pursue their own interests to any depth and in any direction, even as they are learning to read.

In many of his writings Daniel Boorstin, the former Librarian of Congress, promotes a vision of America as a nation of readers. He observes that people who read widely and are well informed about important civic issues will strengthen our democracy and promote the economic health of our nation.[4] It is equally true that when we read, we are personally enriched because we have the opportunity to understand our present by learning about our past and because we can exercise both our knowledge and our imagination in creating the future. By inviting adult literacy students into the public library and helping them use the resources found there, librarians and literacy teachers will enable adult literacy students to become a part of this Nation of Readers.

Resources on the Role of the Library in Adult Literacy Efforts

Alliance for Excellence: Librarians Respond to a Nation at Risk. Washington, D.C.: U.S. Dept. of Education, Office of Educational Research and Improvement, 1984.

A Nation at Risk was an alarming federal report on the status of our national educational system; it did not mention libraries. *Alliance for Excellence* discusses the need for libraries to take a leadership role in forming the new learning society.

Bayley, Linda. *Opening Doors for Adult New Readers.* Syracuse, N.Y.: New Readers Press, 1980.

This small, but practical, book discusses selecting, organizing, displaying, and promoting materials for adult new readers.

Johnson, Debra Wilcox, and Jennifer A. Soule. *Libraries and Literacy: A Planning Manual.* Chicago: American Library Assn., 1987.

Intended for libraries deciding whether or in what way to participate in literacy activities in their communities, the manual gives an overview of the problem of illiteracy and discusses all aspects of a library's involvement, including building collections, working with literacy providers, publicizing literacy activities, and evaluating programs.

————, Jane Robbins, and Douglas L. Zweizig. *Libraries: Partners in Adult Literacy.* Norwood, N.J.: Ablex Publishing Corp., 1990.

While exploring the many facets of the library's role in adult literacy, the authors include a review of the literature, 1979–1988, a survey of various types of libraries regarding their involvement in literacy, and case studies of model programs.

Libraries and the Learning Society: Papers in Response to a Nation at Risk. Chicago: American Library Assn., 1984.

Several writers address the omission of libraries from *A Nation at Risk* and place libraries squarely in the forefront of educational reform movements. Among the most notable chapters is Douglas Zweizig's "Public Libraries and Excellence."

Lyman, Helen Huguenor. *Literacy and the Nation's Libraries.* Chicago: American Library Assn., 1976.

Written primarily for librarians, this book discusses the problem of illiteracy and the role that libraries can play in eliminating it. It contains many specific suggestions for developing literacy programs and establishing contact with other agencies.

Salter, Jeffrey L., and Charles A. Salter. *Literacy and the Library.* Englewood, Colo.: Libraries Unlimited, 1991.

The authors provide a comprehensive review of the topic of libraries' involvement in literacy, the problems of illiteracy, and the many ways in which libraries can help. Almost half of the book consists of extensive, but not annotated, bibliographies covering various aspects of the literature on literacy.

A Profile of Adult Literacy Students

Without reading you ain't nothing. You just another
human being walking around this earth being wasted.[1]

A Literacy Student

Much of what is written about education pertains to children. While some of this information is useful to adult educators, teaching adults requires a significantly different perspective than that of teaching children, as well as different materials. Furthermore, teaching adult literacy students requires a sympathetic understanding of this unique group of adult learners.

A perusal of the numerous statistics gathered to describe adult literacy students reveals great diversity. Literacy students range through all ages and ethnic groups. They are both men and women. While many have received little or no formal schooling, others have high school diplomas. They come from rural and urban environments throughout the country and from the ranks of the employed as well as the unemployed. Many are poor and living on the margins of society, but others are reasonably successful as workers and middle-class citizens, and a few are financially well-off.

Literacy students also share certain characteristics. The following profile examines some of the circumstances common to many adult new readers. Of course, no such profile accurately describes all students, nor should it. Individual students will always present a unique combination of abilities, problems, and needs that shapes their particular instructional program. But understanding those characteristics common to many literacy students helps us choose teaching methods and materials appropriate for adults who are learning a skill usually taught to children. As we profile the adult literacy student in this chapter, we also discuss the implications that the social and psychological circumstances of new readers bring to bear on the teaching program.

The Importance of Self-Direction

The years of adulthood are years in which we strive to achieve as much independence and self-direction as possible.[2] Adults want to be in control of situations that affect their lives. They want to make their own decisions whenever possible. When that is not possible, as in many work situations, adults want to be consulted for their ideas, valued for their contributions, and respected for the talents they have, even as they perform tasks imposed by someone else. The business pages of major newspapers and news magazines frequently report on the improved productivity of companies that offer employees some participation in the creative process and some control over the way in which they spend their working days.

Adult literacy students also strive for independence and self-direction. Many achieve it in some aspects of their lives; others not at all. In the world of knowledge and information, however, all adult literacy students feel out of control.

Just as increased participation leads to increased productivity in business, so active involvement in learning activities increases students' chances for success. Therefore, give your adult literacy students the opportunity to make decisions regarding their own learning. Discuss their long-range goals, and help them set intermediate goals that will advance them toward their individual objectives. Reassess those goals with the students as learning progresses. Encourage them to bring reading materials to class from their work or home environment. Help them select other materials from alternatives you offer. Talk openly with them about what is helpful and what is not, what they feel good about learning, and what they think they should be learning.

To become directors of their own learning, adult literacy students will need much help and encouragement. Initially, students will look to you for direction. They assume you are the expert. Encourage the students' active participation right from the start. Even offering a simple choice between two books you've selected will help establish a pattern of making choices. Students may be reluctant at first, but if you gain their trust, they will gradually make more choices on their own, greatly enhancing their prospects for success.

The Significance of Students' Other Social Roles

Adult learners are also workers, parents, spouses, church members, and citizens involved in their communities in numerous and varied ways. Their motivation to learn often stems from their desire to improve their performance in one or more of these social roles or a desire to develop a new one.[3] As Ginny, a mother and student in a Vermont Adult Basic Education program, explained: "I can't read to them [her boys], and, of course, that's leaving them out of something they should have. It bothers you if you can't read, and if you can't read to your boys, it bothers you more."[4]

Keep your instructional program student centered, not subject centered. Use materials that pertain to the various roles of the students' lives. For example, teach students who are parents of young children to read children's books that they can then read to their children. (See Chapter 9 for a discussion of family literacy programs.) Teach students with minimal skills to read and write the names of family members so they can send greeting cards. Teach a student who wants to be a clerical worker the sequence of the alphabet by having her alphabetize word cards or lists of personal names. If your student was born in another state or country, find travel and geography books in the library that describe her home, and ask her to bring items from her country to class to share. Because their desire to learn to read is rooted in their performance of so many everyday tasks, adult literacy students need to realize right from the beginning that the skills they are learning in their reading instruction will have a direct, immediate, and positive impact on their everyday lives.

Remember too that many literacy students are actually very successful in some of their social roles. Some have learned to hide their illiteracy in order to succeed, often developing elaborate coping mechanisms to circumvent their inability to read. Others are honest about their reading problem and solicit help from a network of family, friends, or service providers. Help your students identify the particular characteristics of their successful activities and apply those characteristics to the process of learning to read.

The Contribution of Life Experience

Adults bring to all learning endeavors a wealth of experience gained over time from the events in their lives. These experiences, both good and bad, are part of each student's identity, of what makes each individual the person he or she is. Not only do these experiences define each adult, they also provide the foundation on which each student will build all future learning.[5]

Depth of experience, in living and in language, is the one advantage in learning to read that adults have over children (who clearly have more time and leisure to master this difficult task). Students don't always realize this, so you must convince them that their experiences, accomplishments, and skills are valuable resources for learning to read. Using reading materials from the home or workplace, creating stories based on students' experiences or ideas, reading poems that describe events or feelings recognizable to students, and other methods described in this book are all ways to use the wealth of students' life experiences to teach them to read. Doing so honors the students, who they are and what they have done, and capitalizes on the wealth of resources they bring to their task of learning.

Over the course of a tutoring relationship, learn as much as possible, as much as the students will allow, about their life experiences and their feelings about those experiences. Armed with this knowledge, you can help students build new learning on the foundation of what they already know and gain the self-confidence that comes from learning new things.

The Burden of Past School Experiences

Of course, not all experience has a positive effect on learning. Many adult literacy students, for example, have had negative, even disastrous, experiences in school. Some students didn't learn to read because they left school early to fulfill family responsibilities. Others didn't attend regularly, especially in the early grades, and fell far behind their classmates in reading skill. Some students had learning disabilities or sight or hearing problems that were not detected and addressed. Others were labeled as "slow learners" and placed in special classes where no one expected them to learn to read. Some adult students enroll in, then drop out of, literacy classes more than once in their adult lives. For students who have known failure in the past, school, or anything remotely resembling school, evokes feelings of inadequacy, anger, defeat, frustration, and embarrassment.

The best antidote to the memory of past failure is the experience of current success. Structure every lesson so students succeed quickly and often. Build lessons that capitalize on students' verbal language skills and their knowledge of life outside the reading classroom. Use materials that connect reading to the everyday tasks students must perform. Praise their successes—not excessively, but honestly. When students read, supply words they don't recognize easily, since meaning, not word recognition, is the first objective. Then note the words that cause difficulty so you can build practice exercises using those words. Mistakes are inevitable, even frequent, in the beginning. Students may view their mistakes as confirmation of their low opinion of themselves. Remind your students that even good readers make mistakes. The difference is that accomplished readers know how to differentiate between little mistakes that don't affect the sense of their reading and more significant errors that indicate a need for rereading or learning new words. With time and practice, students will develop that confidence as well. Most importantly, at the end of each lesson, review what the students have learned. However minor their success may seem, it is one step in the right direction.

Encourage students to choose materials, subjects, and activities from suitable alternatives that you offer. Active participation in the development of their own instructional program will help convince students that this time around, "school" is here to serve them, not to require them to fit into a predetermined mold.

Consider, too, that the physical environment where students meet affects their attitude toward the place and what they do there. Libraries are wonderful tutoring places because they provide so many resources, are generally pleasant and comfortable, are used by many different people at all levels of education and reading ability, and are neutral, which is to say they are not school buildings. But even if you have to meet in a school building or the kind of drab public buildings that often house Adult Basic Education or literacy programs, make it as different from a traditional schoolroom as possible. Hang posters or reprints of artwork wherever possible. Not only will they make the space more attractive, they may also spark stimulating conversations or impromptu reading lessons. Furnish the rooms as comfortably as possible. Literacy and ABE programs operate with very limited budgets, but buying from surplus stores or soliciting donations of used or handmade items from students and staff is an inexpensive way to furnish an attractive, comfortable learning place. Even one cozy easy chair and lamp in the corner of a classroom or literacy center can go a long way toward breaking the connection in students' minds between the school buildings of their past and the place of their current learning. If possible, involve students actively in arranging and decorating their learning place. These are tasks that students can easily succeed at, and the resulting sense of ownership may well facilitate their active participation in learning activities.

Mistrust of Institutional Programs

Some adult literacy students fear or distrust institutions. They may have to deal with several—the welfare office, the unemployment office, schools their children attend, etc. They may have experienced disrespect and poor treatment and may harbor suspicions about the literacy program. Will teachers and students treat them with respect? Will teachers try not only to teach them to read but to be different people as well, more traditional or "middle class"? Such fears are often unspoken; sometimes they exist unrecognized by the students themselves. Teachers and program administrators may sense some reluctance on the part of the student but not recognize its source.

George Eyster of Morehead State University in Kentucky has described Adult Basic Education students according to their perceptions of their own place in society and the role education might play in helping them achieve a better life. Looking at individual literacy students as members of one of the four groups identified by Eyster can help us understand how they might be looking at us. Eyster divided these educationally disadvantaged adults into the following four service groups:

Group 1 This group includes many adults who have not completed high school but are, nevertheless, both economically and personally secure. They believe in education and in public services such as libraries. If they know that services exist, they are likely to seek them out.

Group 2 This group includes persons who suffer from undereducation and underemployment, but they too believe in the value of services and are willing to use them.

Group 3 Persons in this group are sporadically employed or severely underemployed and far from the mastery of basic skills. They still believe in returns from public services, although with some skepticism. They usually need individualized help from such services.

Group 4 Persons in this group have the severest problems and the greatest need. They don't believe they have any control over their lives, and they pass on that hopelessness to their children. They must spend all their energy on getting along from day to day. They are the unemployed and the unemployable.[6]

There are two important implications here. The first is that the focus of all instruction must be on the learner and his or her needs and interests, not on the literacy program's definition of the needs of students. The more the students are involved in the program—choosing reading materials, helping to decorate the space, making suggestions for promoting the program, inviting speakers, participating in discussion groups—the more they will feel that the program is their own and not to be feared.

The second implication concerns motivation and recruitment. Students from Eyster's groups 1 and 2 can be recruited by relatively simple means such as billboards and public service announcements on radio and television. They will need to experience success to continue in the program, but with sufficient support they can weather the ups and downs they will inevitably experience. Persons in groups 3 and 4, on the other hand, need to be personally invited to the literacy program or into the library by a friend or a professional whom they trust. They need continuous and personal support at all phases of their learning, especially when they experience difficulty or disappointment.

The Fear of Being Treated Like Children

Adults are obviously not children, and no tutor wants to treat an adult student as a child. Yet teaching adults a skill normally taught to children can make it hard to maintain an adult-to-adult perspective. Similarly, we can make the mistake so prevalent in our society of assuming that since the students don't know how to read, they don't know much of anything else. Either of these attitudes can deal a fatal blow to a student's attempts to learn or a teacher's attempts to teach. As one of the students in the Vermont program explains, "After I tell my friends, the next thing I know, they go out of their way to explain things to me, they start pointing this out to me that they didn't use to point out to me. . . . Before you know it you're being treated as a kid, as half what you used to be treated."[7]

The materials used in teaching reading will have a major effect on the students' perception of themselves. Materials taken from their everyday lives—job manuals, recipes, food labels—certainly reflect their adult activities. Library books such as poetry, photodocumentaries, art books, and how-to manuals also reflect their adult interests and sophistication. These materials are also obvious reminders to you that your students, despite their lack of reading skill, are experienced adults.

Facing a Difficult Task

Learning to read is hard work. Children spend five hours a day, five days a week, nine months a year learning reading and related tasks, and they don't have to go home to cook supper or to work to pay the rent. Most adult students spend two or three hours a week with a teacher. Though many want to practice reading at home, it is very difficult for them when work and family responsibilities compete for their time.

Hard as it may be for students to summon the courage to admit their difficulties and enroll in a literacy program, it is still easier for them to enroll than it is for them to stay with it. Drop-out rates in all literacy programs are high; students are easily discouraged. For those whose confidence is shaky to begin with, one frustrating session can convince them that the task is impossible. Often the pressures of responsibilities from family, work, and community life impinge on literacy work, sometimes crowding it out altogether. Even students who are initially enthusiastic and optimistic reach a time, or several times during the long-term course of instruction, when they must face the enormity of the task. Given this, students must feel some success, however small, right from the start. They also must recognize early on that what they are doing in reading class will have direct application to their everyday lives.

Acknowledging the true difficulty of the task at hand is the first step toward coping with it. Both students and tutors must know from the outset that the challenge is a formidable one. Once they recognize this fact, many students will not be able or willing to commit themselves to the task. Drop-out rates are particularly high in the initial weeks of instruction. Those who do continue beyond those first lessons need to be continually reinforced for every success, however small. Even when the success of one lesson is simply perseverance, students need to be reminded that their progress, though slow, is moving them toward their goal and that learning to read is indeed possible, despite its difficulty.

Accommodating to Change

Adult students worry about whether they can accommodate to the changes literacy can bring to their lives. A mechanic who is hoping to pass the qualifying test for a new job may worry about what will happen if he is successful and gets the job. Will he be able to handle it? Will he like it? Will he find friends and colleagues like the ones he has now? A woman who wants to read so she can learn to drive and get a job may worry that her husband, on whom she now depends for transportation and support, will resent her growing independence from him. And success can give rise to uncomfortable questions. A student who learns to read, after years of convincing himself he couldn't, can become depressed wondering what his life would be like if he had learned to read earlier.

These uncertainties may be unspoken and perhaps even unrecognized, but they can have enormous impact on students' ability to concentrate and to learn. Literacy tutors are not psychological counselors, but they need to find a way to help students focus on learning without ignoring the many personal questions that arise. Here again, the instructional approach used can help to expose some of these fears. Language experience lessons, in which the student dictates a story based on personal experience, can offer insights into the student's feelings about learning to read. Discussions or writing exercises developed from materials the student brings to tutoring sessions can expose some hidden fears. Consider asking experienced students who have weathered some of these personal upheavals to play an advocacy role, offering support and advice to newer students. Once these feelings are out in the open, tutor and student can talk about them—to the extent that they both feel comfortable. These discussions may not solve the student's particular dilemma, but they can at least help her recognize the problem she is facing and consider some resolutions. Underlying this is a relationship of trust built over time between the tutor and student.

Being the Outsider

"You never know what's going on unless someone tells you."[8] These words of a student from the Vermont Adult Basic Education program convey the sense of being an outsider, of being "out of the loop" of knowledge and information that many adult literacy students experience. They can't read the information pamphlets at the welfare office or the doctor's office, so they must rely on the verbal information given them by the clerks they encounter. Sometimes that leaves them with a vague sense of uncertainty. Have they been told the correct information for their particular situation? Have they been told all they need to know?

Building a literacy program around the information needs of the students gives them the sense that they are working on real life problems and that learning to read will help them end their isolation and become more active participants in the affairs of their own lives.

Literacy and Other Social Problems

Illiteracy exists in a social context. Students' reading problems may be intertwined with problems of poverty, unemployment or underemployment, poor housing conditions, and unstable personal relationships. Illiteracy is not necessarily the cause of those problems; indeed, it may be the result. But illiteracy exacerbates the difficulties students must contend with every day. Attaining a higher level of literacy, however, will not automatically cure the social ills afflicting students' lives. Literacy will not bring miracles, and tutors, students, and librarians must recognize this to avoid unrealistic expectations. But improved reading ability can contribute to a better life: a life lived with pride in the accomplishment of one goal and the confidence to set and achieve other goals.

Improved literacy skills will have a real impact on the quality of students' lives only if students can see a clear connection between what they are doing in class and the everyday events of their lives. Learning to fill out a job application can give a student the confidence necessary to perform well in a job interview. Reading a poem that describes the feelings of a mother looking at her children may help a new reader think about herself as a parent from a new perspective.

The many difficult problems adult literacy students face can interfere with their attempts to learn to read. Tutors sometimes complain that students, once they become comfortable with their tutors, want to talk about their problems more than they want to work on reading. While most tutors want to be understanding and helpful, they are not social workers or counselors and feel uncomfortable being cast in such a role. Using the experiences, thoughts, and feelings of students' lives as the raw material for reading practice enables tutors to recognize those problems while keeping the focus of the tutoring sessions on reading.

A successful literacy program recognizes that teaching adult students to read is very different from teaching children. Adults bring a different set of strengths and weaknesses to the classroom, as well as highly individualized learning needs. Literacy providers and the librarians who work with them need to build a student-centered instructional program that recognizes the social and psychological difficulties students face, capitalizes on students' knowledge and accomplishments, and addresses individual students' needs for information and learning that will directly and immediately relate to the everyday events of their lives. Literacy providers and librarians also need to understand the process of teaching reading so they can build an instructional program to suit each student. In the next two chapters, we will examine methods used to teach students to read, as well as the specific skills they need to master to become independent readers.

Resources for Understanding the Adult New Reader

Draves, William A. *How to Teach Adults.* Manhattan, Kans.: The Learning Resources Network, 1984.

Draves presents a highly readable overview of techniques for teaching adult students. Although he does not focus on adult literacy students, the circumstances described and the teaching methods suggested are appropriate for and adaptable to the literacy student population.

Eberle, Anne, and Sandra Robinson. *The Adult Illiterate Speaks Out: Personal Perspectives on Learning to Read and Write.* Washington, D.C.: The National Institute of Education, 1980.

This invaluable book offers eloquent testimony from adult literacy students about their fears and their experiences in learning to read. Written by the directors of the Vermont Adult Basic Education program, a unique program that offers homebound instruction and other services to suit Vermont's rural and isolated population, the book also presents a compelling argument for building programs to fit the particular needs and circumstances of the students they hope to serve.

Eyster, George W. *Recruiting Disadvantaged Adults*. Morehead, Ky.: Morehead State University, 1975.

Eyster's extensive study of adults in the Appalachian area of Kentucky provides valuable insight into the perceptions and behaviors of adults needing help from educational and social services.

Fingeret, Arlene, and Paul Jurmo. *Participatory Literacy Education*. San Francisco: Jossey-Bass Inc., 1989.

Part of a series, "New Directions for Continuing Education," this book emphasizes the importance of looking at the skills and coping strategies of adult literacy students and encouraging them to put their skills and experiences to work as they learn to read.

Harman, David. *Illiteracy: A National Dilemma*. New York: Cambridge Book Co., 1987.

Harman's comprehensive study of illiteracy includes definitions of various kinds of illiteracy, a historical review of the problem, a study of the social contexts of illiteracy, and a review of various types of programs with comments about their effectiveness.

Hunter, Carmen St. John, and David Harman. *Adult Illiteracy in the United States*. New York: McGraw-Hill Book Co., 1979.

The book provides a comprehensive review of the problem of illiteracy and details what has been done and what should be done to bring about a higher level of literacy. It remains among the most important contributions to the literature of adult illiteracy.

Knowles, Malcolm S. *The Modern Practice of Adult Education*. New York: Association Press, 1970.

This comprehensive textbook on adult education gives particular emphasis to the theory separating andragogy, the teaching of adults, from pedagogy, the teaching of children.

Rose, Mike. *Lives on the Boundary: The Struggles and Achievements of America's Underprepared*. New York: The Free Press, 1989.

Rose, himself an underachieving student who was "rescued" by a few conscientious and perceptive teachers, became a teacher and director of the writing program at UCLA. He writes with insight, compassion, and extraordinary grace about what it is like to be a failing student and what kinds of educational intervention can really make a difference. This is an exceptional book.

Part Two

TEACHING
ADULTS
TO READ

3

Methods of Teaching Reading

I hungered for books, new ways of looking and seeing.[1]

Richard Wright

The adult new reader is one who is "progressing from beginning literacy to an increasingly mature use of print,"[2] according to librarian Helen Lyman. That description recognizes that learning to read is not a finite goal, but a lifelong process. All of us, good readers and beginners alike, are developing "an increasingly mature use of print." For some of us that means learning to identify a writing style or to evaluate the power of an argument, but for others it means learning to recognize in print those words that are familiar in speech.

Edward Jones helps us see that progression more graphically by explaining that all readers exist somewhere along a continuum that moves from learning to read to reading to learn.[3] Here again, new readers are part of a process in which *all* readers participate. Obviously, new readers are at the beginning of this continuum, spending most of their time and efforts learning to read. But just as those of us who are accomplished readers must occasionally step back along that continuum to grapple with new vocabulary or complex ideas, so those who are beginning readers need to step forward along the continuum to experience the satisfaction of reading materials that will teach them something they want to know.

The reading process is a dynamic one. Students' eagerness to learn how to read is reinforced by their interest in what they are reading. Reading frequently and over a wide range of material expands those interests as it requires students to improve their skills. The tutor's challenge is to establish a balance between teaching students the skills they need to become independent readers and providing a variety of reading materials that will match students' interests, satisfy their immediate information needs, and inspire them to use their developing reading skills to explore an ever-growing world of knowledge and ideas.

A library-based literacy program helps tutors and students establish that balance between content and skills. Building an instructional program around the rich and varied resources of a public library ensures a wealth of meaningful materials for students to read. But it also presents many challenges. Library books don't come supplied with skill-building exercises. Using library books and student-teacher–created materials requires tutors to identify books that are appropriate for students, use those books in creative ways to make them accessible to students, and then develop original exercises from the books in order to teach students the basic skills they need to become good readers. Tutors who are volunteers and not professional teachers may be understandably wary of such a task.

Chapters 3 and 4 of *The Library as Literacy Classroom* respond to those challenges by providing the volunteer tutor with the information necessary to build a library-based instructional program for adult literacy students. Chapter 3 discusses various methods used to teach reading to adults, emphasizing those most useful in a library-based literacy program: language experience, information reading, and assisted reading. It describes briefly how these techniques can make a wide range of library resources accessible to new readers, a discussion continued in more detail in later chapters. Chapter 3 also describes four stages of literacy development through which new readers progress and suggests some general principles for teaching new readers. Chapter 4 discusses the specific skills students need to master to become mature readers. Specifically, it discusses word recognition, spelling, writing, and thinking skills, and suggests numerous exercises to reinforce those skills.

The discussion that follows speaks directly to tutors, since it is the tutors who teach the students. But it is also important for librarians to know the methods that are used to teach adult new readers. The more the librarians understand the tutoring process, the more they will be able to identify the materials in their collections that support and extend that instruction.

Comparison of General Teaching Methods

There are many methods used to teach adults to read. Generally speaking, these methods can be divided into two groups. One group includes those teaching methods that emphasize the importance of reading for meaning right from the start of reading instruction, even with students who can't read at all. These methods, which include language experience, information reading, and assisted reading, are rooted in a belief that students learn best when they are reading from materials that relate to their everyday lives and their information needs.

The second group includes teaching methods that stress word recognition skills in the early stages of instruction, teaching basic skills in a particular sequence. Using these methods, which include sight word, phonetic, and linguistic approaches, students read from stories and texts written with a controlled vocabulary that reflects only the words and skills learned to date.

There are advantages and disadvantages to both approaches. Teaching methods that emphasize reading for meaning from the beginning establish a direct link between students' life experiences and the reading process. Such methods invite students to use their knowledge of the world as well as their extensive oral vocabularies to support their efforts to read. Students use books and other reading materials that engage their interests and satisfy their information needs. But these methods also present a significant challenge to tutors who must develop their own curriculum and exercises for teaching the word recognition skills necessary for independent reading.

On the other hand, the sight word, phonetic, and linguistic methods of reading instruction teach students the word recognition skills necessary to read independently, to "break the code."

The graded workbooks also provide students a way of measuring their progress according to the number of workbooks or pages completed. For volunteer tutors, many of whom lack confidence—at least initially—in their ability to teach reading, commercially produced workbook series provide numerous directions for reading lessons as well as a structured outline of skill development to guide their instructional program.

But teaching methods that emphasize word recognition skills also have disadvantages. Most students don't see an obvious connection between mastering the consonant sounds and filling out a job application. They have difficulty transferring isolated skills to reading matter outside their workbooks. Many students tire of doing exercises and want to read "real books." Most seriously, a heavy emphasis on mechanical skills deprives students of what Mike Rose calls "the real stuff of literacy," namely: "conveying something meaningful, communicating information, creating narratives, shaping what we see and feel and believe into written language, listening to and reading stories, playing with the sounds of words."[4]

While most teachers rely more on one set of methods than another, good teachers are also what Frank Smith calls "intelligently eclectic."[5] They recognize that most teaching methods have advantages and disadvantages, and they use whatever works best in a given situation.

Teaching methods that emphasize reading for meaning from the outset are best suited to a library-based literacy program. But teachers who use these methods clearly need to incorporate skill-building exercises from the phonetic, linguistic, or sight-word methods into their instructional program. On the other hand, teachers who rely primarily on structured approaches to teaching reading need to supplement and expand their curriculum with resources from the public library.

Methods That Emphasize Meaning

The Language Experience Technique

The language experience technique for teaching reading is widely used in adult literacy programs. Language experience uses the actual words of the student as the reading text. To use the language experience technique:

Talk to the student about a topic of personal interest. If he is willing, let him choose the topic. If he is reluctant to do so, suggest ideas based on what you know of his interests or circumstances.

Write down what the student says, using his words and speech patterns as much as possible, but with correct spelling.

Read the sentences you have written to the student, first reading the piece as a whole, then one sentence at a time.

Ask the student to read the sentences, perhaps with your assistance at first.

Use words, phrases, and ideas from the language experience story to teach basic skills. (Chapter 4 and related Appendixes offer examples of skill-building exercises.)

Once students have mastered the story they have created, they see the connection between the words on the page and the ideas in their own minds. Words and ideas are two halves of one whole. Now students are ready to separate that whole into parts, into individual words from which they can learn the word recognition skills necessary to becoming independent readers.

Based on your student's specific abilities and needs, choose words from the story she has created to teach specific skills. For example, choose words to teach as sight words, find words that exemplify initial consonant sounds, or choose words that teach variant plural endings. Use the word lists in Appendixes A–D and exercises suggested in Chapter 4 to help you decide what to teach. It isn't necessary to teach skills in the order in which they appear in Chapter 4, other than to go from easier skills to more difficult ones. Explain the particular skill you wish to teach your student, show her the words from the story that exemplify a skill, then give her several other words that fit that pattern but that are not found in the language experience story. Following is an example of a language experience story as dictated by a student at the Ohio State Right to Read program.

SAMPLE LANGUAGE EXPERIENCE STORY ACTIVITIES _____

Sample Language Experience Story

There's a woman at work that's a salesman. She is fifty years old, and she tries to dress like young girls. She is some salesman. A woman stopped in to say "Hi," and she talked her into buying a necklace. She seen she didn't have a necklace. She took one the woman was looking at and put it around her neck. She brought a mirror and said, "Look how lovely it is. Be good to yourself, buy it." The woman bought the necklace. It was a little gold cross.[6]

Choose activities, such as the following examples, based on your student's skill level.

1. Several words begin with the consonant *s*. Use some of the following activities with your student:

   Ask your student to select words that begin with the letter *s*. As he says them, write each on an index card to practice as sight words.

   Say three words, one of which begins with the letter *s*. Ask your student to tell you the word that begins with *s*.

   Describe some object the name of which begins with the letter *s*. Ask the student to guess what you are thinking of.

2. Two compound words in this story are *salesman* and *yourself.* Here are some exercises for studying compound words:

   Point out the compound words in the story. Give the student a few others to be sure he understands the concept. Then describe some objects, the names of which are compound words, and ask him to name the objects you are describing.

   Give the student a list of about fifteen words, some of which are compound words. Ask him to find all the compound words.

   Once he has learned several compound words, ask him to list them all, writing each word twice, once as a whole word and once separated into its two parts.

3. Have the student begin to work on writing by copying his own language experience stories. As the student advances in skill, read the story to him so he can write from your dictation rather than by copying from the printed page.

The great virtue of language experience is its immediate relevance and familiarity to the student: his or her own words and ideas become the reading material. But some teachers worry that when students read from language experience stories they are simply memorizing what they've said or what they've heard the teacher read. For readers with minimal skills, this is often true, but it is not cause for concern. Literacy students who have memorized language experience stories are doing exactly what preschool children do who "read" from well-loved books they've memorized from repeated hearings. Parents and teachers are delighted to see a child attempt to read in this manner because they recognize the child's behavior as an important step toward literacy. The child is associating particular words she's heard with the pictures and print of a particular book. Even if the association is not a one-to-one correspondence between spoken word and written word, it establishes an important link in the child's mind.

The same is true for literacy students. Even if beginning readers memorize the first language experience stories they read, they are still moving their eyes across a printed page matching spoken word to written word; they are still seeing their own language and thought made permanent in print. These are essential first steps toward mastering reading. As their skill and confidence improve and as they create longer and more detailed stories based on sources outside their own experience, literacy students come to rely more on reading skill than on memory.

Tutors also wonder about the wisdom of writing students' words verbatim, even if the students speak nonstandard English. It is best to use the student's own language at the beginning stages of literacy instruction since you are emphasizing the link between spoken and written language. Always use standard spelling, however. You can gradually shift toward a more standard form of speech by offering students the choice of saying something exactly as they said it or in a way that you rephrase. As students grow in confidence and in familiarity with written language, they recognize the difference between their speech and the more formal language of most books. Usually, they want to learn that more formal language, not as a replacement for the comfortable language they speak, but rather as an additional language they can use for reading and writing.

Language Experience and Library Books

The language experience technique can be adapted and extended in many ways. Sometimes the stories are based on the student's own words as spoken in simple conversation with a tutor, sometimes they are the retelling of an experience or event from the student's life experiences. Language experience stories can also develop from a student's reaction to such things as a work of art, a poem or a story read by the tutor, or a book of photographs perused by tutor and student. Many books found in any public library can inspire language experience stories. Photodocumentaries, picture biographies, travel books, and collections of art and photography are a few examples of the kinds of books that can entertain and instruct your student as well as spark many language experience stories. Chapter 5 offers a number of language experience activities developed from library books as well as a bibliography of suggested titles.

The Information Reading Technique

The information reading technique is a variation of the language experience technique. It helps students make the transition from reading their own words to reading the words of others. To use the information reading technique:

Read from some material of personal importance to the student, a driver's manual or an instructional manual from work, for example.

Read a paragraph or section at a time, then discuss the material with the student.

Ask the student to explain the information learned in his or her own words.

Write the student's version of the information, using the student's words, but suggesting changes if necessary to ensure accuracy.

Read the student's version aloud.

Ask the student to read the simplified version of the information, with your assistance if necessary.

Develop word recognition and critical thinking activities based on the text the student has written. (Use Chapter 4 and related Appendixes as a guide to creating skill-building activities.)[7]

SAMPLE ACTIVITY USING THE
INFORMATION READING TECHNIQUE

In the following example, a beginning level student brought a pamphlet on social security disability benefits to a tutoring session and asked her tutor to help her understand the information provided.

Original Text

Your disability checks generally will be paid for as long as your impairment has not medically improved and you cannot work. They will not necessarily continue indefinitely. Because of advances in medical science and rehabilitation techniques, an increasing number of disabled people recover from serious accidents and illnesses. Also many individuals, through determination and effort, overcome serious conditions and lead productive lives in spite of them.

As explained on page 11, your case will be reviewed periodically to make sure you meet all requirements for disability checks. In addition, you are responsible for promptly reporting to Social Security anything that could affect your status as a disabled person. You must tell us if your medical condition is better, if you believe that you can work, or when you actually do return to work.[8]

What follows is the student's version of this information in her own words (as written by the tutor).

Rewritten Text

You will receive your check as long as a doctor says you are not able to work. If you recover from your illness or injury and go back to work, your payments will stop.

The government will review your case periodically. You are responsible for reporting any changes. If your health improves, if you think you can work, or if you do go back to work, you must tell the government.

Using the information reading technique, you and your student generate reading material that teaches her something she needs to know. The process of discussing the information in her own words, then reading her words as you have written them, will help her understand and retain that information. As you did with language experience stories, develop skill-building exercises based on the words and content of the text you have created together, using the exercises in Chapter 4 and related Appendixes as examples.

Information Reading and Library Books

Cookbooks, craft books, how-to manuals, and numerous other nonfiction works found in any library are good examples of books that can be read by tutors and students using the information reading technique. Chapter 6 describes some specific examples of this technique and suggests types of books useful for this method and several specific titles.

The Assisted Reading Technique

As described by Edward Jones, assisted reading is another method that helps students make the transition from reading their own language experience stories to reading directly from the text of another author, a necessary step toward literacy. With this technique, even beginners have the opportunity to read and interact with the words and ideas of many other people. To use the assisted reading technique:

> Together with your student, choose a text of interest to him and within range of, or slightly above, his reading ability.
> Read the text aloud, in meaningful phrases, pointing to each word as you go.
> When the student feels comfortable, ask him to join in by reading the words he knows and skipping over the others. You keep reading at the pace established.[9]

Eventually, the student will assume the leader's role in reading, with the tutor joining in only when help is needed. Reading together establishes a comfortable pace and rhythm, and helps the student read for meaning without worrying about identifying every single word. This technique is highly transportable. Students who are comfortable in doing so can ask family or friends to read along with them until they are able to read a particular piece on their own.

Some tutors may feel that assisted reading gives students too much help, depriving them of the chance to practice word recognition skills. But practicing fluid reading is equally important. Think of how young children learn to ride a two-wheeled bicycle. In the beginning, the child rides along with training wheels or with an adult running behind holding on to the seat of the bike. The child is gaining a feel for riding without needing to worry about keeping the bike in balance. As the child becomes more comfortable, as this feel for the balance of the bike becomes ingrained, the training wheels come off and the adult lets go, providing only an occasional steadying hand. The child is now skilled enough to steer and maintain balance at the same time. A similar principle applies to learning to read. Students need many chances to experience fluent, meaningful reading—to ride along with the tutor—without having to worry about figuring out the unknown words. As their skill and confidence increase, they will gradually take over more of the reading and the tutor will "drop out," providing only the occasional word needed to maintain fluency.

Assisted Reading and Library Books

Obviously, the assisted reading technique can be used with many kinds of text, including language experience stories, work-related materials and other reading matter the students bring to class, or any library books that are within range of their reading abilities. This technique can be particularly useful for students who are reading selected books from the children's collection of the library, a concept discussed in more detail later in this chapter.

Methods That Emphasize Word Recognition

Many literacy tutors, especially those operating in volunteer literacy programs, use methods of teaching reading that are more structured and formalized than those just described. These approaches rely on commercially produced skill books that emphasize word recognition skills in the early stages of literacy instruction. Word recognition methods can generally be categorized as one of three types: phonetic, linguistic or pattern, or sight word methods.

Phonetic Methods

The Laubach method, used by many volunteer literacy programs, is a good example of a phonetic method of reading instruction. Using the Laubach skill books, tutors teach students specific sounds such as short *i* as in *hit,* short *a* as in *cat,* long *e* as in *team,* etc., in an ordered sequence. Students learn a set of words containing a specific sound, then read sentences using those words. All exercises and related stories use a strictly controlled vocabulary that includes words containing the sounds already taught. The following example from *Skill Book 2* of *Laubach Way to Reading* comes in a lesson on the short *i* sound.

> This is Miss Jill Hill.
> This is Miss Kim Hill.
> Jill is the big sister.
> Kim is the little sister.[10]

Linguistic or Pattern Methods

A similar but slightly different approach, sometimes called the "linguistic approach," teaches students to recognize spelling and sound patterns of words or syllables rather than isolated sounds such as short *i*. In this method, the grouping of words into lists of word families makes the patterns obvious. Students do not need to memorize phonetic rules or identify sounds. Rather, they learn words in groups such as *tan, pan, ran, sand,* and *plan,* and read numerous sentences using words that exemplify the patterns taught. The following sentences come from a lesson teaching the pattern *en* in *Building Word Power:*

> Pay the ten men.
> May the ten men pay.
> Send ten men.
> I sent ten men then.
> Open the tent.[11]

Sight Word Methods

Yet another approach relies more on the repetition of words to be learned than on phonetic rules or rhyming patterns. This approach emphasizes the skill of developing sight vocabulary. Words are usually presented in the context of a story considered relevant to adult students. Consider the following example from *Practice in Reading:*

> My name is Jim Davis. I want to read. I want to write. I want to read my name. I want to read and write my name.[12]

Combining Teaching Methods

Teaching methods that focus initially on word recognition and those that emphasize reading for meaning right from the start are not mutually exclusive. They can support and extend each other. If you rely primarily on structured approaches to teaching reading, incorporate some aspects of a library-based literacy program into your routine. Use language experience, information reading, and assisted reading in addition to workbooks. Take your students to the library frequently. Browse the collection of materials for new readers with your students, showing them fiction and nonfiction titles as well as reading skill and life-coping skill workbooks available. With students, find books and other resources to answer specific questions they have raised. Introduce them to other materials as well, such as poetry, art and photography books, travel books, sports and hobby books, how-to manuals, pamphlets, and audiovisuals. Use the language experience, information reading, and assisted reading techniques to help the students read and learn from materials they select.

If at all possible, make trips to the library a regular occurrence, and use the materials you have borrowed as part of all tutoring sessions, even if you read to a student from a poem or work of literature for only the last few minutes of your time together. If you are working with students who can read books on their own, consider adopting a practice now common in many elementary classrooms called "sustained silent reading." This will be especially useful in an Adult Basic Education classroom. *Sustained silent reading* means that for a specified length of time, perhaps ten or fifteen minutes, everyone in the classroom, including the teacher, reads from any material he or she chooses. Set ground rules that support a quiet environment. For example:

Students write down words they don't know rather than ask for help during the silent reading time. Later they may ask for assistance with words they didn't know.

Although no assignments are made, informal discussions about the readings are permissible after the reading time is over.

The teacher reads, too. No planning or grading of papers allowed!

On the other hand, if your instructional program is based on language experience and other methods that employ meaningful reading material not specifically written for literacy students, you can use the more structured materials to strengthen the skill-building component of your program. For example:

Use commercially prepared workbooks as an outline for your own skill development plan.

Use the exercises in the structured workbooks as examples and develop similar ones for your student, using words and concepts taken from the student's language experience and information reading texts.

After your student has learned a particular skill from doing exercises using the vocabulary of his or her language experience stories, provide exercises from structured workbooks as additional practice.

Incorporating Other Library Resources into Reading Instruction

In addition to the methods and materials described previously in this chapter, other kinds of books and library resources are particularly well-suited to use with adult literacy students.

Poetry

Poetry is a form of literature that expresses ideas using rhyme, rhythm, and descriptive and succinct language. Much poetry written for adults is short and uses simple language, yet is rich in ideas and content. Reading poetry to students, helping them to read poetry themselves, and teaching them to write poetry of their own are all ways to use this rich literature to teach adults to read. Chapter 7 explores the use of poetry with adult new readers and suggests several anthologies of poems suitable for adult new readers.

Books from the Children's Collection

Literature-based reading instruction is a teaching method currently influencing the way elementary school children learn to read. Using this approach, teachers select works of children's literature to teach reading rather than traditional basal readers and workbooks. It is an exciting development that recognizes that the quality of the language and the depth of meaning found in works of literature have captivated children—and their parents—for generations, while the repetitiveness and controlled language of basal readers can turn children against reading.

A literature-based approach to teaching reading can be adapted for use with some adult new readers. For example, many picture books, although intended for young children, are beautiful works of art and literature that appeal to readers of all ages. Selected works of fiction written for students in upper elementary grades or in high school may also appeal to some adult new readers, especially younger ones. In addition, numerous nonfiction books found in the children's section explain a wide range of topics in clear, precise, and easy-to-read language, often in a format that never identifies children as its intended audience. In fact, in some public libraries, adult and juvenile works of nonfiction are interfiled on the shelves, removing any stigma some readers may experience choosing books from a children's collection. In other libraries, librarians purchase multiple copies of titles they consider "crossover" books that can be shelved in both the children's and adult departments.

Clearly, not all books written for children are suitable for adults, and not all students will be willing to read from children's literature. While some adults will try anything that may help them read, others may object strenuously to reading children's books. Consider your students before broaching the subject of children's literature. Students who have young children of their own might be interested in learning to read specific books that they can then read to their children. Students who are interested in learning about a particular subject matter may appreciate the simple but authoritative text found in good nonfiction titles for children. Take your cue from your students; if they are willing, explore the range of children's literature with them. Both you and your students will be surprised by the depth, variety, and simple beauty of the books you will find. Chapter 9 examines possibilities in this area more fully, and suggests titles of picture books, works of literature, and nonfiction that are appropriate for adult new readers.

Special Collections for New Readers

Many stories and nonfiction books have been written specifically for the adult new reader audience. The best of these books (and they have gotten better over the years) recognize that good writing and interesting subjects are more important than strictly controlled vocabulary in creating readable books for new readers. Chapter 10 discusses qualities to look for in choosing books written for new readers and lists some good bibliographies that recommend specific titles.

Resources Other Than Books

In today's high-tech world, even the smallest library is likely to offer information in several formats. Audiotape, videotape, books on tape, and computer software allow tutors and students to find information using several different media and to supplement books with materials that reinforce visual and auditory skills. Libraries also keep files of pictures and pamphlets on a variety of topics. Pictures from a picture file can be used to spark a discussion or a language experience story, while pamphlets often provide succinct information on topics of interest to the student. Chapter 11 suggests ways to incorporate audiovisual materials and other resources into the literacy classroom.

Four Stages of Literacy Development

As suggested at the beginning of this chapter, literacy instruction is a process of helping students progress along a continuum that leads from learning to read to reading to learn. It is fairly easy to imagine students at the very beginning of this continuum as well as at the end. But what about all those students somewhere in the middle? Tutors and students using a graded series of workbooks can easily chart students' progress through those books. Charting progress is not so easy to do if you are using language experience, information reading, and library books as sources of reading material.

To help mark the progression of students along the continuum toward reading to learn, consider the following four stages of literacy through which students pass as they become independent readers. These four stages are adapted from discussions of reading levels in Herbert Kohl's *Reading, How To* and Helen Lyman's *Reading and the Adult New Reader*.[13]

The four stages of literacy are beginning new readers, intermediate new readers, advanced new readers, and mature readers.

1. *Beginning New Readers*. Students at this level cannot use reading and writing in their daily lives without significant help, although they may have sophisticated oral language skills. They need to master basic sound-letter correspondence, build a good sight vocabulary, and learn to incorporate their knowledge about language and the world in which they live into the task of learning to read. The beginning new reader stage corresponds generally with reading grade levels 1–3.

2. *Intermediate New Readers*. At this level students read some everyday materials, such as road signs, food labels, and simple menus, but often have difficulty reading job orders or reading the newspaper. For the necessary tasks of their everyday lives, they are still functionally illiterate. The intermediate new reader stage corresponds generally with reading grade levels 4–6.

3. *Advanced New Readers*. At this level students are functionally literate; they can read well enough to get by in current circumstances. But if those circumstances change—a new job, beginning a vocational class—they can easily slip back into functional illiteracy. They still need to improve their reading to pass the General Education Development (GED) test or to move on to advanced schooling of any kind. The advanced new reader stage corresponds generally with reading grade levels 7–8.

4. *Mature Readers*. At this level readers are mature users of print. They read for personal and professional fulfillment, but

they also recognize the need to continue to grow and develop their reading ability.

Not all literacy students will become mature readers. Not all will reach advanced new reader level either. We must be realistic and accept this fact. But too often the reading programs we design for our students fall far short of this goal. We teach students word recognition skills, but don't spend sufficient time reinforcing thinking skills. We help students learn to read, but don't take them far enough along the continuum to enable them to read to learn. We teach students the skills of reading, but don't help them become readers.

In the beginning stages of literacy instruction, the emphasis will always be more on word recognition than on thinking, but even students who are just mastering consonant sounds can express sophisticated opinions about the mood of a poem read to them or about the message conveyed by a photograph. In every lesson, give your students some opportunity to practice skills at all ends of the continuum, even if the activity is based on something they hear or see rather than on something they read themselves.

Keeping the ideal of mature literacy in view as our long-range goal for all students will help us direct all our instructional efforts toward the kind of active engagement with the written word that characterizes readers at this level. Like the proverbial rising tide that lifts all boats, a broadly defined understanding of literacy will stretch the potential and increase the possibilities for all students.

General Principles for Good Teaching

Most literacy tutors are volunteers. While some are also trained teachers, many are not. If teaching is a new experience for you, remember that time and practice will help you develop confidence and skill. Remember, too, that whether you call it a science or an art, good teaching is highly individualized. There is no magic formula, so be yourself. Don't be afraid to admit your uncertainties or mistakes. Your honesty, enthusiasm, and commitment will contribute greatly to your chances of success.

Following are some general principles to help you develop your skills as a teacher.

Be prepared, but be flexible. Come to class prepared with a clear plan for that lesson, and tell your students what your plan is. But also be prepared to abandon your plans in response to a student's question or to the reading material he brings to class. Seize the "teachable moment."

When you first meet a student, discuss her long-range goals, or help her establish them, and then help her choose short-range goals she can accomplish frequently. Periodically review those goals and discuss how various activities in your lessons are leading toward those goals.

Encourage your students' active participation in planning and carrying out your lessons. Invite them to bring reading materials to the lessons, to choose between alternative books or activities, and to suggest topics for discussion and writing.

Use words familiar to your students as examples of specific skills. Take words from language experience stories, books the students are reading, or from everyday reading materials such as coupons, job orders, menus, or newspapers.

In general, proceed from the easier to the more difficult skills, but let the student's particular needs or interests guide your choice of skills to teach in each lesson. Do not confine your lessons to the order of skills listed here or in any other workbook.

Give your students many chances to see, hear, say, and write the words they are learning. When appropriate, involve the students' motor skills as well by having them trace letters, write letters in the air, or move letters written on cards. A set of Scrabble letters, or something similar, would work nicely. Any physical movement of letters or words always enhances learning.

In all tutoring sessions, while remembering the need to be flexible and to allow your students opportunities to shape the course of their literacy instruction, include the following elements as much as possible:

Review skills learned in the preceding lesson.

Begin something new: an experience story, an information reading lesson, a writing exercise based on a previous lesson, or whatever is appropriate.

Develop skill building activities based on the words and content of the new lesson.

Allow time for the student to write, whether it is a beginning student copying a language experience story or a more advanced student writing in a journal or in response to something you suggest.

Take the time to read something to your students. It can be a poem you like or something you read in the newspaper or something you think they might enjoy. Tell them why you chose to read it.

Suggest a plan for the next lesson as well as some "homework" for the student to reinforce what was learned. Be realistic, though—literacy students have limited time outside class to practice reading. Try to think of activities that can easily fit in with the students' daily routines, such as writing words they see in their work environments or charting the week's temperature variations as listed in the newspaper.

In this chapter, we have examined the common methods used to teach adults to read, described four stages of literacy development, and reviewed some basic principles of good teaching. The following chapter reviews the basic skills literacy students need to learn to become mature and independent readers. A bibliography that suggests additional reading about teaching methods and basic skills follows Chapter 4.

4

Teaching Literacy Skills

> "Very well," thought I. "Knowledge unfits a child to be a
> slave." I instinctively assented to the proposition, and
> from that moment I understood the direct pathway from
> slavery to freedom.[1]
>
> Frederick Douglass

To help adult literacy students progress as quickly and efficiently
as possible along the path toward lifelong reading, we need to
teach them several basic skills: Preliminary skills familiarize students with the sounds represented by letters in words and with
the look of letters and words in print; word recognition skills help
students decipher new words they encounter in print; comprehension and critical thinking skills help students understand and
learn from what they read; and spelling and writing skills help
students express their own ideas, sharpen their thinking, and
share their thoughts with other readers. Each of these skill areas
is discussed in detail in the material that follows, along with
suggested activities to help reinforce the skills.

The basic skills curriculum outlined here supports an instructional program that relies on library books and student-teacher
created reading materials. You can supplement and extend this
basic skills curriculum by adapting skill building exercises found
in commercially available workbooks to the particular circumstances of your own students. In addition, several books mentioned in the resources at the end of this chapter contain skill

building exercises you can use with your students. The important point is that skill building exercises are not ends in themselves. Rather, they support an instructional program that fits the needs and interests of individual students and—most importantly—gives them access to information and ideas contained in a wide range of books as they are learning to read.

Preliminary Skills

There are three basic skills that form the foundation for learning to read: familiarity with the sound of formal written language, auditory and visual discrimination, and the ability to concentrate. Although these skills are often referred to as "readiness skills" in elementary school reading texts, students do not need to master them before learning to read. Rather, you can incorporate opportunities for students to practice these skills at all stages of the tutoring process, along with word recognition and thinking skills.

Familiarity with the Sound of Formal Written Language

Adult literacy students usually have strong oral language skills. They use substantial vocabularies, and they express many different ideas through speech. However, they are not used to listening to the more formal structure of written language. This is a handicap for anyone learning to read. By contrast, children who learn to read easily in kindergarten or first grade are children who have listened to numerous stories, poems, and nursery rhymes read to them. They have been imbued with the sound of written language. Adult literacy students need to have similar experiences, however abbreviated they must be at this stage of their lives.

SAMPLE ACTIVITIES TO FAMILIARIZE STUDENTS WITH THE SOUND OF FORMAL WRITTEN LANGUAGE

1. Read to your students during every class or tutoring session, even if only for a brief time. You can read from any printed material students bring to class or from books of poetry or stories that you choose.

2. Encourage students to talk about what they hear by recalling specific facts or discussing their reactions. Discussing the written language they hear is a preliminary step to discussing the written language they will eventually read for themselves.

3. Suggest that students borrow books on tape from the library's audiovisual collection to listen to in the car or at home. Ask the librarian to suggest some good titles. Consider listening to the same books on tape as the students so you can discuss them together.

Auditory and Visual Discrimination

Students need to hear the discrete sounds made by specific letters and groups of letters to learn to recognize rhyming words, consonant sounds, and various vowel patterns. They also must learn to differentiate visually between letters such as *p* and *q* or *d* and *b* and between words such as *was* and *saw.*

Many new readers have trouble with auditory and visual discrimination. That is to be expected; don't let your students become overly frustrated if they confuse the sound or the sight of letters and words in the early stages of reading. For most students, mistakes of visual or auditory differentiation result from unfamiliarity with reading more than from any specific learning disability. Their skills will improve with practice.

Give students a chance to practice auditory and visual discrimination skills frequently, but be careful not to spend too much time practicing these skills in isolation, using individual letters or words read outside a meaningful context. Instead, choose letters and words from poems, language experience stories, or reading materials the students bring to class.

SAMPLE AUDITORY AND VISUAL DISCRIMINATION ACTIVITIES

1. Have students match letters, words, or combinations of letters. Vary activities to give students practice in seeing letters and combinations, listening to the sounds represented by the letters, or moving letters written on cards or blocks. For example:

   Circle the word that is the same as the first.

   pan   pin   pen   pun   pan

Circle the word with the same vowel sound as the first word.

pot   bat   bin   lot

Circle the letters that are the same as the one on the left.

b   tab   fba   pbf   trab

Circle the letter combination that is different from the other three.

sidron   siodrn   sidron   sidron

2. Give students a large-print newspaper headline, an advertisement, or a cartoon with few words. Ask them to circle every occurrence of a particular letter or letter combination.

3. Give students words and letters formed with yarn, sandpaper, or other tactile material that is raised from the surface of the paper. Have students trace their fingers over the letters while saying the names of the letters.

4. Have students match a set of scrambled alphabet cards with a set of cards arranged in proper sequence, or use Scrabble letters to match any letter sequence you suggest.

5. Show students a word, then turn it over. Then show them the same word, but with some letters covered. Have them supply the missing letters.

6. Show students a list of words from their sight vocabulary in which letters have been scrambled. Have them unscramble the words.

7. Say four words, including two that rhyme. Ask students to pick out the rhyming pair.

8. Get a copy of the words to a song known to the students. Read the words known to them and ask them to note all the rhyming words.

9. Say four words, and ask students to pick out the two with the same beginning sound, ending sound, or middle sound.

10. Have students arrange a set of flash cards in the same order as the words are spoken or dictated on tape.

Be aware that some students may be particularly strong in one area, but not in the other. Students who have strong auditory skills, for example, will be able to hear rhymes, phonetic patterns, and consonant sounds easily. On the other hand, students with strong visual skills will learn well from an approach that emphasizes sight words and visual patterns. Observe your students closely. Their successes and difficulties with various exercises and their comments about what does and does not come easily and about what they do and do not like to do are important clues to help you devise exercises that take advantage of their natural skills and preferences.

Be aware, too, that some students have more than the usual difficulty with auditory or visual discrimination. These students may, in fact, have a learning disability. Such students can learn to read; many often have developed ingenious methods of coping with their particular difficulty. But they need additional assistance. If you suspect your student has a learning disability, consult an expert in your local community Adult Basic Education program, community college, elementary school district, or state department of education. Professionals in the field of learning disabilities can help you locate appropriate resources for your student.

Ability to Concentrate

Concentration is necessary at all reading levels. Adult literacy students can be easily distracted. Sometimes the problem is one of short attention span; at other times it is one of interference from the concerns and worries of everyday life. If students need a chance to talk about what is bothering them, give them some time to do so. Talking often enables students to get past the worry and concentrate on reading.

SAMPLE ACTIVITIES TO STRENGTHEN
STUDENTS' CONCENTRATION _____

1. Whenever possible, turn your student's account of a problem into a language experience story or find some material in the library that will address the problem. By incorporating the student's

problems into the reading lessons, you have recognized the significance of the problem even as you turn it into a positive motivation for learning.

2. Read aloud to students for progressively longer periods to help them develop concentration.

3. Read to students about something familiar or of particular interest—an account of yesterday's football game, for example. Then ask them specific questions based on what you read. (Remember that the more interested students are in the subject matter, the easier it will be for them to concentrate.)

4. Ask a question students probably can't answer, then tell them you are going to read something that contains the answer. Ask them to listen for the answer to your question.

5. Teach students to ask questions themselves before reading something—to predict what will be said—and then try to answer their own questions based on what they read.

6. Have students listen to a taped story and then answer questions about it.

7. Give students a map, then give them oral directions for finding a specific place on the map.

Word Recognition Skills

To become independent readers, adult literacy students must be able to recognize many words on sight or be able to figure out those words not immediately familiar. All readers, even mature ones, encounter words they don't recognize immediately. Think about what you do when you come across an unfamiliar word. Do you skip over it? Do you figure it out from the context of the material you are reading? Do you try to sound it out or examine it to determine if the word is plural or past tense or contains a prefix? Do you go to the dictionary? If you are like most readers, you probably employ all those strategies at one time or another, depending on the circumstances. Adult literacy students need to learn to use the same strategies with confidence.[2] Specifically they need to develop a sight vocabulary, use context intelligently, recognize phonetic patterns, and use word analysis skills.

Develop a Sight Vocabulary

Fluent readers recognize most words by sight. To succeed at initial reading tasks, new readers must also master a growing vocabulary of words they can read by sight.

Many reading texts provide lists of common sight words for new readers. One such list, containing 300 frequently used words, appears in Appendix A. Use this list as a guide as you help your students build their own lists. Teach words from the list not in order as they appear but rather as they come up in language experience and other reading materials. Add words from the students' reading materials that are not on the list. Each student's list will then be individualized, containing many words that are personally significant as well as some of the more general words found on the textbook lists.

Many words must be learned by sight simply because they do not follow any phonetic rules. Words such as *of, where, were, been, was*, etc., fall into this category. These words are actually very hard to learn because they are irregular, many look and sound quite similar, and, by themselves, they offer no meaningful association to jar the learner's memory. Be sure to give your students many opportunities to practice these words, especially in the context of meaningful sentences.

SAMPLE SIGHT WORD ACTIVITIES _____

1. Give students a sentence with a word deleted. (With beginning students, read the sentences to them if necessary.) Have them choose the missing word from two similar words.

   _____ time is it?
     What   Want   When

   John _____ to the store.
     went   when   why

2. Give students sentences containing sight words from which some letters have been deleted. Have them try to complete the word.

Wh_____ of these two houses do you live in?

John and Peter w_____ having breakfast when I saw them.

3. Take a flash card containing a study word, such as *when*. Hold it before the student for a few seconds, then take it away. Ask the student to recall the word. Ask the student to spell it.

4. Say a word, such as *when*. Then hold up two flash cards, one containing the word you have said and the other a similar word. Have the student select the word you said.

5. Write new words on index cards and keep them in an alphabetical file for continuous review. Have students build sentences using words from the file or match sentences you have written for them.

6. Have students keep a notebook containing new words. Suggest that they arrange the words in a modified alphabetical order, grouping all the words beginning with the same letter on one page. With this arrangement, students will add new words in their appropriate places, creating a list of sight words that also illustrate the sound or sounds of their initial letters. (This will be useful when the students are learning phonetic patterns.)

7. Have students look for sight words in newspaper articles, grocery ads, and TV commercials and list those they find.

8. Have students look at a sight word, study it, then close their eyes to get a mental picture of the word. Have them try to write the word from memory. If that is too difficult, show them the word with one or more letters covered. Ask them to supply the missing letters.

Use Context Intelligently

Skipping an unknown word may initially strike you as an inefficient, even lazy, approach to reading. But skipping an unknown word is often the first strategy used by many good readers.[3] While such a statement may provoke a lively debate among reading teachers, it reminds us that reading is not just a process of word recognition, but of extracting meaning from printed words. New readers need to be convinced that it is acceptable not to know every word. Of course, knowing which words are essential and which ones are not is a matter of judgment, and the ability to make those judgments grows along with other reading skills. If the entire sentence leaves you puzzled, then you need to go back to that unknown word and try to figure out the word from its context, the meaning of the rest of the sentence. New readers may do this already, although many of them will consider it guessing and, therefore, not acceptable. However, making informed guesses based on an understanding of the sentence or paragraph as a whole is a mark of sophisticated reading skill. If you can make a good guess, then you are thinking about what you are reading, and that is the whole idea behind reading—to understand what you read.

An exercise known as the *cloze procedure* strengthens students' ability to make intelligent guesses for unknown words. This exercise requires students to supply words deleted from a sentence or a paragraph. In some cases, a clue to the word is given; in others, the student is free to make any reasonable choice.

SAMPLE CONTEXT ACTIVITIES

1. Using materials appropriate to the students' reading level and interests, delete one or more words from a sentence. Have students choose the correct word from a choice of two.

   Just as _____ have fur, birds have _____.
        (coats, animals)   (feathers, wings)

2. Delete every sixth word from a paragraph appropriate to the students' reading level. Supply one or two letters of the correct word and have the student complete the word.

   My favorite flavor of ice cream is ch_____.

3. Delete every sixth word, but give no clue. Accept any reasonable synonym for the missing word, so long as it is grammatically appropriate.

4. Play a game of Twenty Questions, in which one person may ask up to twenty questions to figure out what another is thinking about. This games helps sharpen students' skills in using clues to decipher words.

Recognize Phonetic Patterns

If the context of the passage does not yield the word, then students need to "sound it out"; that is, to use their knowledge of linguistic patterns or phonetic rules to determine the word. Most letters and letter combinations fit into recognizable patterns—"families," as they are often called in elementary reading texts—or make phonetically predictable sounds. Since English is a language noted as much for its phonetic irregularity as for its conformity, it is best to help students recognize as many phonetic patterns as possible and teach them selective phonetic generalizations that are useful and easy to apply, such as the predictable sounds of initial consonants or the vowel/consonant/ silent-*e* pattern.

Context and phonetic analysis skills reinforce each other. Students who are reading a paragraph about a familiar subject, baseball for example, and who have learned the blend *sl* and the phonetic pattern *ide* can easily combine context with a recognized pattern and read the sentence, "He knew he had to slide into third base."

The following discussions suggest ways to teach consonant sounds and vowel patterns.

Consonants That Represent a Single Sound

The consonants are easier to hear than the vowels, so single consonant sounds should be taught first. Among the consonants, some always sound the same, while others have two sounds. The consonants that always sound the same are:

b as in *bat*	*k* as in *kite*	*r* as in *rug*
d as in *dog*	*l* as in *land*	*t* as in *toy*
f as in *five*	*m* as in *mop*	*v* as in *vase*
h as in *hand*	*n* as in *nose*	*w* as in *wig*
j as in *jar*	*p* as in *pig*	*z* as in *zero*

The order in which you teach the consistent consonant sounds is not so important as the words you choose to represent the sound. Choose words that the student easily recognizes as examples of the letter/sound combination you want to teach.

SAMPLE INDIVIDUAL CONSONANT SOUND ACTIVITIES

The activities suggested here deal with initial consonants. They can easily be adapted to test students' ability to hear or see medial or final consonants as well.

1. Tell students that *Tim* begins with the sound /t/. Ask them to tell you which word in the following group of words you say also begins with the sound /t/.

   dog   father   taper   baby

2. Tell students you will say four words. Explain that three begin with the sound /t/ and one doesn't. Have students tell which word doesn't begin with the sound /t/.

   team   tire   baby   tangerine
   ticket   dark   turn   torn

3. Tell students you will say two words. Have them tell if both words begin with the /t/ sound.

   tin toad   tank torque   car task   tense paste

4. Say that you are thinking of a word that begins with the sound of /t/ and means a drink with sugar and lemon. Ask them to tell you the word.

5. Ask students to name words beginning with the letter *t*.

6. Make a list of all words from experience stories and other reading beginning with the letter *t*.

7. Ask students to look for words beginning with the letter *t* on billboards, store signs, in newspapers, etc. Have them keep lists of those words. Accept any "th" words on the list, but have students put them in a separate group. Explain that the *th* combination usually makes a difference in sound and that you will discuss it later in the reading program.

8. Choose words students are familiar with and write them by deleting the initial consonant. Remind students that these are words they know very well, then ask them to supply the missing consonant.

More Difficult Consonant Sounds

After your student has learned all the consonants that are sounded consistently, teach those that are associated with more than one sound.

soft c (/s/) as in *cent*	s (/s/) as in *salt*
hard c (/k/) as in *cake*	s (/z/) as in *plays*
soft g (/j/) as in *gem*	x (/ks/) as in *six*
hard g (/g/) as in *garden*	x (/z/) as in *xylophone*
q (/kw/) as in *quake*	y (/y/) as in *yellow*
q (/k/) as in *torque*	y sometimes acts as a vowel

To teach a pair of sounds, it is a good idea to introduce examples of both sounds. Students may be able to infer the general rules governing each.

SAMPLE MORE DIFFICULT CONSONANT SOUND ACTIVITIES ___

1. Teach the initial sound of *c* as you did with the consistent consonants. After students are familiar with the sound of the "hard" *c*, introduce the "soft" *c*. Then write out two lists, one for each *c* sound. Read the words to students, pointing to each as you read.

Hard c (/k/)	Soft c (/s/)
cake	city
cookie	civilian
candy	cent
container	center
cutlet	certain
cute	citizen
carburetor	celery
candle	Celsius
contract	citation
costume	circus

As the students listen to each word, ask them to make a note of the vowel following each letter *c*. Ask them if they recognize any pattern. They should notice that the "hard" *c* is followed by either *a, o,* or *u,* while the "soft" *c* is followed by *e* or *i.* If they don't notice the pattern, show it to them. To reinforce this pattern, show students additional words to see if they can apply the pattern. (The primary goal here is to pronounce the correct sound for *c.* If students say the correct sound but cannot say the rest of the word, tell them what it is.) Now add these words to the "hard" and "soft" *c* lists for further practice.

2. Repeat a similar sequence of activities for words beginning with "hard" *g* and "soft" *g.* Again the pattern is similar: "Hard" *g* is followed by *a, o, u* as in *gate, goat,* and *gut.* "Soft" g is followed by *e* and *i* as in *germ, gender,* and *giraffe.* (Note: There are a few exceptions here, however. Words such as *girl* and *give* have a "hard" *g* sound. If these words come up during the exercises, simply point out that they are exceptions to the general patterns and must be learned as such. If these exceptions do not arise, you might mention them since they involve common words.)

Don't be discouraged by exceptions to general patterns or allow your students to be. There are numerous such exceptions in the English language, so they cannot be avoided. The best approach is the direct approach. Discuss with your students the fact that many patterns have exceptions and you will help them recognize and learn those patterns as they come up during the course of instruction.

Appendix B contains lists of words representing initial consonant sounds.

Vowel Sounds

Vowel sounds are difficult for new readers to hear. The sounds of particular vowels are highly dependent on the speaker's accent and the differences between similar vowel sounds are almost impossible to distinguish in some cases.

Spelling variations also abound. The English language contains 26 letters that represent 44 different sounds. Thus, we have some situations in which two or more letters must represent a particular sound, others in which one letter or group of letters represent more than one sound, and still others in which one sound can be represented by more than one spelling.

Given this situation, learning to read and spell the English language can loom as a nearly insurmountable problem to many—especially if the phonetic variations are viewed as many exceptions to a few basic rules. Therefore, it is better to teach vowels as patterns represented by word families rather than as isolated sounds. Using this approach, students can employ their knowledge of rhyming patterns, a good visual memory for the look of words, or their facility with contextual clues to help them read and spell vowel patterns. Students have a choice of strategies, depending on the words and their own particular learning strengths.

Lists of words containing short vowel sounds, long vowel sounds, and other vowel patterns appear in Appendix C. Following are some exercises to help students learn the vowel patterns.

SAMPLE SHORT VOWEL SOUND ACTIVITIES

1. Write a word, for example *job.* Have students say the word, then spell it. Write additional words that rhyme with *job,* and ask students to read them. If this is difficult, tell students the words, pointing out the same ending sound but different beginning sounds. Have students make lists of the rhyming words, underlining the common ending: j<u>ob</u>, m<u>ob</u>, l<u>ob</u>.

2. Have students make new words by changing the ending consonant or the vowel.

bat	bad	not	nod
bat	bet	not	nut

3. Give students riddles in which the final (or initial or middle) letter of the answer is omitted.

   You take a bath in it. tu__.

   The color of strawberries is re__.

   You use a __ap to find your way on the road.

4. Write a list of words and have students find rhyming pairs.

man	job
pet	tan
sob	pup
cup	let

SAMPLE LONG VOWEL SOUND ACTIVITIES _____

1. Say a word with a long *a* sound, *ate* for example. Then say several other words and ask students to tell the word or words that have the sound of long *a*.

   peak   gate   tame   cart
   same   team   land   fate

2. Write words with the same spelling pattern as *ate* and ask students to pronounce each word.

   gate   date   fate

3. Say some words with the *a-t-e* spelling pattern and ask students to spell them.

   hate   late   mate

4. The emphasis in Activity items 2 and 3 is on the vowel sound and the word's spelling pattern rather than the rhyme. Reinforce the spelling pattern by introducing other words that fit the general consonant-vowel-consonant-silent *e* (cvce) pattern. Change only one consonant each time.

   If *ate* is *a-t-e,* then *ape* is *a-p-e.* How would you spell the following words?

   cape   cane   came   name   tame   tape

   When the students are ready, ask them to spell words in which two consonants differ, again reinforcing the vowel sound.

   rate   wave   fade   wage   pace

SAMPLE ACTIVITY FOR TEACHING THE EFFECT OF SILENT *e* _____

When students are familiar with the cvce pattern, show them how the addition of an *e* at the end of a syllable often changes the vowel sound from short to long. (This is one of those phonetic rules that is very useful to learn.) List pairs of words that illustrate the cvce rule. Ask students to describe the effect that adding the *e* to each word has on the base word. Tell them that this rule is prevalent and helpful in sounding out new words, although there are some exceptions.

   rob   robe   pal   pale   hat   hate   rat   rate

The *r*-Controlled Vowel Sounds

Vowel patterns that are *r*-controlled present particular problems because it is difficult, if not impossible, to distinguish certain sound/spelling combinations. Consider *fir* and *fur* or *berm* and *bird*, for example. As such examples arise, point them out and explain the difficulty of spelling these vowel patterns. The following exercises will help students develop the visual memory needed to learn to spell these words.

SAMPLE *r*-CONTROLLED VOWEL SOUND ACTIVITIES

1. When students practice writing new words, have them underline the part of the word that represents the vowel pattern they are learning.

   bi<u>r</u>d   <u>fur</u>
   be<u>rm</u>   <u>fir</u>
   Octob<u>er</u>   <u>fur</u>ther

2. Create a jigsaw-type puzzle with study words. Write the words on index cards or heavy-stock paper. Using irregular cuts for each word, cut the word cards into component syllables or parts. Students will know they have rejoined the words correctly when the parts of the cards fit together.

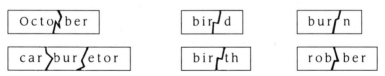

3. Show your students similarities among words. For example, the final syllable of the last four months of the year is the same:

   Septem<u>ber</u>   Octo<u>ber</u>   Novem<u>ber</u>   Decem<u>ber</u>

As students build word lists representing the phonetic patterns they have learned, they gain confidence in their control over the written language. They recognize that spellings are not totally random, and that most words fit into some pattern. They begin to see relationships and common elements among the words. They also see their lists of known words growing. What's most important, they are learning to read and spell words that are already part of their oral language—words that are familiar and meaningful to them. They are building on the considerable language skills they already have.

Consonant Blends and Digraphs

Consonant blends are combinations of two or three consonant letters whose sounds blend together to form a sound in which the individual letters are still audible. Examples include *bl, cr, spl, str*, etc. In a consonant digraph, the two consonant letters represent a unique sound that is unrelated to the sound associated with each individual letter: *ng, sh, wh, th, ch, nk, gh, ph*. A list of consonant blends and digraphs appears in Appendix D.

Consonant blends and digraphs are most successfully taught after students have learned to recognize and to pronounce the sounds of the single consonants as well as several common vowel patterns. As in the teaching of consonants, consonant blends are best taught in the context of words meaningful to the students.

The major difficulty for students will probably arise with the digraph *wh*. For most people, *wh* (/hw/) doesn't represent a sound that is any different from that represented by *w*. To most people, *which, wind, whether,* and *weather* have the same initial sound, even though the spelling of that sound varies. This is another case where visual observation and visual memory must be stressed, especially when emphasizing the spelling of these words.

SAMPLE VISUAL MEMORY OF *w* AND *wh*
SPELLING ACTIVITIES _____

1. Choose several *wh* and *w* words the students have learned. Put these words into simple sentences and accent the spelling by outlining the configuration of the words.

   The $\boxed{w\,e\,a\,t\,h\,e\,r}$ is cloudy.

   We will have the picnic $\boxed{w\,h\,e\,t\,h\,e\,r}$ or not it rains.

   John ate at $\boxed{w\,h\,i\,c\,h}$ restaurant?

   The Halloween $\boxed{w\,i\,t\,c\,h}$ rides on a broom.

2. Draw block outlines of words being studied and have the students fit the words into the configurations.

whether   wind   when

Silent Letters

Several fairly common spelling patterns in English contain silent letters. This fact may seem puzzling and a bit intimidating to beginning adult readers. "How do I know which letters are silent and which are pronounced?" is a typical question. However, this initial concern can be overcome by helping students recognize that most words containing silent letters actually fit into a number of easily learned and recognizable patterns.

b	g	h	k	w
comb	gnat	hour	knife	write
doubt	sign	rhyme	knit	two

Use Word Analysis Skills

Finally, as readers become more sophisticated in their understanding of written language, they can begin to decipher words by analyzing them. That is, they can look at a word and recognize individual parts such as endings for plurals, endings indicating tense, and suffixes or prefixes, which carry meaning.

SAMPLE WORD ANALYSIS SKILL ACTIVITIES

1. Have students generate lists of words that contain similar word parts.

   same prefix: predict   prevent

   same suffix: handful   wonderful

   same ending: played   acted

2. Give students the following list of prefixes, suffixes, and root words. Add others if you wish. Then have students construct as many real words as possible.

Prefixes	Root Words	Suffixes
ad- (to)	cede (to go or	-able (able to, able to be)
con- (together)	withdraw)	-al (of, pertaining to)
de- (down,	ceed (to go)	-ance (quality or state of being)
away)	duc, duct	-ant (performing a specific
dis- (apart, not)	(to lead)	action or being in a specific
e-, ex- (out)	ject (to throw)	condition)
in- (into, not)	mit, miss	-ed (past tense, having)
inter- (between)	(to send)	-ent (in a condition of, doing)
mis- (badly,	rupt (to break)	-er (a person who, a thing that,
opposite)	scribe, script	more than)
per- (through)	(to write)	-est (most)
pre- (before)	vene, vent	-ful (full of, abundance)
pro- (forward)	(to come)	-ive (belonging to, having the
re- (again)	vert (to turn)	quality of)
sub- (under)		-ly (in a particular manner)
un- (not)		-ment (state of being,
		something done)
		-ness (condition of being)
		-ous (full of)

3. Give students sentences that are meaningless because the wrong prefixes are substituted in certain words. Have students correct the words.

   Black smoke came from the inhaust pipe.

   Mac played subfessional football.

4. Have students look in a dictionary to find a word they know beginning with a prefix. Then ask them to look up and down the column from their word and tell how many other words they recognize with the same prefix.

Spelling Skills

As students learn to read individual words, they use many of the techniques and learn many of the skills that also teach spelling. Have students begin to practice spelling at the very early stages of reading instruction by writing the sight words and examples of phonetic patterns they are learning. Such practice will help new readers develop the visual memory and the familiarity with the forms and sounds of words that are necessary for spelling.

Spelling a word is actually more difficult than reading it. Some words are hard to spell because similar sounds often have different spellings, for example, *October* could easily be *Octobur*. How does one remember that in *siege* the *i* comes before the *e,* while in *seize* the *e* comes before the *i*? For some words, sound patterns offer no clues to correct spelling. For example, choosing the correct number of *c*'s and *s*'s in the words *necessary* and *occasion* is often a matter of knowing what looks right.

Most good spellers, and even those among us who are just adequate spellers, have developed this ability to judge what looks right. Because we read frequently, we see millions of words in print. Therefore, we have some familiarity with words; we have a frame of reference with which to compare our spelling. New readers don't have this measuring stick. They don't see words in print often enough to develop a sense of what looks right.

Hearing sounds distinctly and recognizing familiar sound/letter patterns are also important factors in good spelling. But here again, new readers are at a disadvantage. They don't have a written reference to rely on, so they often mispronounce words. They leave off endings, omit syllables, transpose syllables, and change consonant or vowel sounds. Even students who speak fluently are not accustomed to considering the phonetic elements of words. They reproduce each word as a unit, not as a sum of specific letters or syllables. Think of what happens when you hear a new or strange word such as an unusual name or a word in a foreign language. Usually, you must see it written before you are confident of your pronunciation. You must establish the connection in your mind between what you hear and what you see, between the spoken word and the written word. Literacy students can't do this because of their lack of familiarity with their own language in its written form.

Developing a Strategy for Spelling

There are many ways good spellers remember how to spell certain words. Think about what you do when you try to remember a particular spelling. Do you:

> Try to visualize the word?
> Say it to yourself and consider each sound or syllable separately?

Write it several different ways, then choose the version that
looks right?

Think about the meaning of the word, particularly any prefixes or suffixes it contains?

Think of other words that have similar sounding parts?

These are all spelling strategies that good spellers use. Literacy
students must learn to use these same strategies. In fact, an
important rule of thumb to remember when teaching spelling is:
don't ask students to learn to spell a word without showing them
a way of doing so. Remember, too, that some students have strong
visual skills so they can rely on visual memory, while other students rely more on the sounds of words. Help students identify
and use strategies that work for them.

Many of the techniques used to teach word recognition skills
can also be used to teach spelling. As students learn to read
phonetic patterns, have students practice writing and spelling
them, too. As students learn to read words by recognizing parts of
words such as endings, prefixes, and suffixes, show them how to
apply that knowledge to spelling words as well. In addition, students who reach the intermediate reader level can begin to practice listening for syllables and learning the rules of syllabication.
These rules are listed in Appendix E.

SAMPLE SPELLING ACTIVITIES _____

1. Have students learn to spell words on their sight word lists or
   phonetic pattern lists as they learn to read them.

2. Have students collect examples of words that do or do not follow
   certain patterns.

   Words that fit into a sound pattern but are not spelled the same:

   care   bear   pair

   Words that sound the same but have different spellings and meanings:

   bear   bare   pair   pear   pare

   Words that look the same, but don't fit into a sound pattern:

   bough   cough   home   come

3. Show students an index card containing one spelling word. Then show them the same word with one or more letters missing. Ask them to supply the missing letters.

4. Write words your students are learning in large letters on index cards. Hold up each card for 5 seconds and have individual students try to "photograph" it with their eyes. Then ask them to write the word, or at least as much as they can remember. Show them the card a second time if necessary.

5. Choose one word. Have students change just one letter at a time to spell a new word.

6. Have students practice writing all spelling words in syllables.

7. Write a word in large letters on an index card, then cut it up into its component syllables. First, ask students to match the syllable cards to a copy of the whole word. Then have them put the cards in proper order without referring to a copy. Finally, have them write the word from memory.

8. Encourage your students to arrive at each lesson with a word they have seen on the way to the lesson which they want to add to their spelling vocabularies. This could be a street name, a word from a billboard or shop, etc.

9. As a homework assignment, give students individual words they are likely to see in their everyday travels and ask them to note the number of times they see the words.

10. Use the following teaching technique that involves the students' visual, auditory, motor, and tactile senses.

   Write a word.

   Have students copy the word.

   Have students spell the word out loud.

   Ask students to trace the letters of the word with a finger.

   Repeat the preceding steps as necessary.

   Erase the word and have students spell it from memory.

   Have students write it.

11. Teach students to use the dictionary. Of course, to use the dictionary as a spelling tool, students must have some idea of how to spell a word in the first place. But you can introduce the dictionary even to beginning students by looking up any words encountered in a tutoring session that are new to them or to you. As you look up a word, talk about what you are doing, about the alphabetical arrangement, about the many definitions for some words, and so on. Ask higher level students to look up specific words. If students are unsure of the spelling, tell them to write down possible spellings, then look up each spelling until they find the correct one.

Comprehension and Critical Thinking Skills

Learning phonetic patterns and word recognition skills enables students to read individual words. But the ultimate aim of reading is not identifying individual words, it is understanding the meaning those words convey. The most important basic skill, and the aim of all reading, is comprehension.

Sometimes a new piano player will struggle through a piece playing every note carefully, but losing the sense of melody and rhythm, a sense of the piece as a whole. In a similar way, new readers often read each word correctly, but fail to comprehend the flow and meaning of a sentence or paragraph. Helping adult literacy students understand and think about what they read is perhaps the greatest challenge facing literacy tutors. But unless we teach our students the skills necessary to comprehend what they read, we will relegate them to a permanent place at the wrong end of the reading continuum, always learning to read, but never reading to learn.

Frank Smith's explanation of the process by which we understand what we read, in his book *Reading without Nonsense*, is among the most clear and compelling in the literature of reading instruction. He reminds us that as readers we come to the printed page with a wealth of information that we apply, almost unconsciously, to understanding the text we are reading. We have large speaking vocabularies, we know how language works, and we have an understanding of how the world works—an understanding that, for adult literacy students, encompasses many years of experience. When we are reading, according to Smith, we are continuously using our knowledge of language and of the world to predict what will be said next or what will happen next, then determining whether our predictions are correct. Comprehension, then, is a process of continually asking questions about what we've read so far and building expectations about what is to come.[4]

We comprehend, or understand, what we read at several levels. At the most basic level, we learn certain facts. We comprehend the weather forecast in the newspaper if we know what the day's temperature range will be and what the chances for rain are. At a deeper level, we understand that it may rain because a storm front that brought rain to Missouri yesterday is going to pass over Ohio today.

But true comprehension requires more than knowing what we have read. It asks us to integrate what we have learned into the body of knowledge already acquired. It leads us to act, make decisions, or look at a given situation in a different way according to our new understanding. It requires us to examine and evaluate the information we have gained. These higher level skills are generally referred to as *critical thinking* skills. These skills are developed, "by reading materials which challenge ideas, present alternatives, and recognize that adults have life experiences to draw upon."[5] By using materials that reflect students' life experiences or contain information important to their everyday lives, and by drawing from the wealth of resources available at the library, you will provide your students challenging and meaningful reading materials that will develop the critical thinking skills so essential to mature literacy.

Specifically, comprehension and critical thinking skills can be described as follows[6]:

1. *Knowledge.* By knowledge we simply mean knowing the facts. To test a student's knowledge, for example, you might ask him to recall names or dates, to summarize what has been read, to identify characters or places, to explain how to do a task, or to repeat an author's ideas about the issue being discussed.

2. *Comprehension.* Comprehension requires us to understand the facts we have learned. Activities that strengthen

students' comprehension include asking them to estimate the length of a trip given facts about mileage and driving conditions, to predict the outcome of a story, or to interpret the actions of a character in a story in light of facts known about that character.

Critical Thinking Skills

3. *Application.* The skill of application requires the reader to use information in a new way, to apply what has been learned to a different setting. Students use this skill when they can recognize actions and their consequences in a fictional story, then apply that knowledge to a circumstance in their own lives, or read about conditions in a culture unlike their own, yet recognize the commonality with their individual situation.

4. *Analysis.* To analyze an idea or a piece of writing means to take it apart and examine its basic elements in order to better understand the whole. For example, students can analyze a story by differentiating between major and supporting characters, by comparing the way events in the story affect different characters, by determining cause or effect relationships not directly stated, by stating an implied main idea, or by contrasting two methods of doing a particular task.

5. *Synthesis.* Synthesis requires the reader to use information to create something new and unique. Exercises that ask students to create floor plans for a house based on a description of efficient energy use, or write an advertisement for a product based on their knowledge of how that product is used, would require them to synthesize what they learned from their reading.

6. *Evaluation.* The ability to judge the effectiveness, quality, and value of what we read is crucial to "a mature use of print." It is a skill good readers continue to perfect throughout their reading lives. Asking students to evaluate the effectiveness of an advertisement, to decide if a writer has achieved his or her goal, or to judge the value of one book against another similar one are exercises in evaluating information.

SAMPLE COMPREHENSION AND
CRITICAL THINKING SKILLS ACTIVITIES

1. Teach students strategies for predicting the content of articles or books they read. These strategies include:

   Reviewing what they already know about the subject

   Reading the first and last paragraphs of an article

   Turning subheadings into questions

   Examining the table of contents and the index

   Previewing any illustrations, including charts and graphs

2. Teach students to reflect upon works of nonfiction that they've read by asking questions such as:

   How did the book or article you read match or differ from your expectations?

   Did the material answer your original questions?

   Did the material change your opinion or extend your own knowledge?

   What do you think the writer's attitude about the subject is?

3. Teach students to examine works of fiction by asking such questions as:

   How did you feel after reading this story? What in the story made you feel that way? Why?

   Did any of the characters remind you of people you know? Why?

   Have you had any experiences similar to those described in the story? Explain.

   Did the characters seem real to you? Could you imagine meeting them? Would you enjoy meeting them?

   What parts of the story did you like best or least? Why?

   Did the story change your attitudes about any subject or affect the way you look at certain people or certain circumstances? How?

   If you were writing this story, is there anything you would change? What?

4. One of the best measures of the impact of a story is how much it stays with us over time. Every so often, ask students to think back over what they have read and relate what stands out in their minds. Responses could include a particular character, one scene, or even certain words.

5. Have students read a newspaper editorial and select specific words or phrases that express the opinion of the writer.

6. Have students read newspaper articles and look for examples of bias, or have them compare two different articles about the same subject.

7. Have students read advertisements, then discuss the tone, the actual message, and any subliminal messages. Have them identify particular words used to attract the reader and to convey the message.

8. Devise exercises, based on activities and interests important to the students, that require them to carry out a task according to written directions. For example, have students prepare a recipe, order something from a catalog, complete an application, or set up a game according to what they have read.

9. Have students read a newspaper review of a TV show they've watched or a concert they've attended. Ask such questions as:

   Why do you agree or disagree with the reviewer?

   Is the review positive or negative, or mixed?

   Is it fair? Was the reviewer open-minded? Why do you think so?

Remember that it is important to do activities such as these with beginning new readers, too. Simply read brief stories, poems, newspaper columns, and other materials to them, then ask questions such as those previously suggested. With intermediate and advanced new readers, ask them to write the answers to the questions as much as possible. Writing actually forces us to think more clearly, so the more students write about what they are reading, the sharper their critical thinking skills will become.

Sample lessons in Chapters 5, 6, and 7 also suggest questions to help students understand and think about what they read.

Writing Skills

Writing and reading are intimately related language activities; they involve skills that support and extend each other. As students gain facility in reading and read from a widening range of books and writing styles, their own facility in writing and use of language grows. Similarly, as students gain more confidence and skill in writing, they become increasingly observant and discerning readers.

Incorporate writing activities into your instructional program right from the start. At the beginning level, most writing activities call for students to copy words, sentences, and stories written for them. Have students copy language experience stories, names and addresses of friends and relatives, and lists of words they have learned to read.

Write their reactions to stories, poems, and other materials you read to them, then have students copy their own words. Writing the stories, paragraphs, and words they are learning to read will reinforce students' developing reading skills.

As soon as students are able and willing, give them many opportunities to write original sentences, paragraphs, and stories. They can begin with sentence completion exercises, then move on to longer writing tasks.

Correction and evaluation of students' original writing is a critical issue. You need to find a balance between encouraging them to express their ideas and helping them to strengthen the skills that will sharpen that expression. As students begin writing their own ideas rather than copying something written for them, encourage them to write first and revise and correct, or edit, it later. To develop good writing skills, students must first learn to put their thoughts on paper easily and confidently, then revise as necessary. As you review their writing, concentrate first on the question of meaning. Have students read over, or read aloud if they are willing, what they have written, checking to see if their written words accurately express their intended meaning. Then, gradually work on sentence structure and spelling, taking one error or problem area at a time.

Following are a few sample writing activities. The tutor resource manuals mentioned in the bibliography at the end of this chapter also contain many suggested writing activities.

SAMPLE WRITING ACTIVITIES _____

1. Have students complete sentences such as:

   When I was a child, I _____.

   I used to be _____, but now I am _____.

2. Have students write a few sentences to summarize or react to an article they have read.

3. After students read a letter to an advice columnist, have them write a response.

4. Have students write captions to cartoons.

5. Have students describe an experience that made them sad, happy, angry, etc.

6. Have students write an advertisement for a product they use frequently.

7. Have students describe a favorite TV show.

8. Have students write letters to friends, family members, or to you.

9. Encourage students to keep a journal or write about personal experiences such as the ways in which they got along without reading. (They may not want to share such a journal with you, but encourage them to keep one anyway. Writing encourages thinking, so the more students write, the more perceptive they are likely to become about their experiences. Consider keeping your own journal as well, describing your view of the tutoring experience. You can share this with your students to whatever extent you feel appropriate.)

10. For advanced new readers, have them read articles from the perspective of analyzing or evaluating both content and writing style. Teach them to ask questions such as:

    Does the author support his or her opinion with facts?

    For what audience is the author writing?

    What is the tone of the work?

What feelings does the passage evoke in the reader?

What is the author's stated and/or apparent purpose in writing this article? Did the author achieve his or her purpose?

What did you learn from this article?

How would you briefly summarize this article for someone who hasn't read it?

Encourage the students to ask these same questions of their own writing.

11. Have students write reviews of books they have read or movies they have seen.

12. Have students write their own editorials about topics of importance to them.

13. Whenever possible, involve students in supporting activities of the literacy program by writing letters to accompany grant applications or writing to government officials in support of legislation affecting literacy.

Charting a Path of Reading Development

The reading skills chart that follows lists specific skills that learners need to master as they progress through the four stages of literacy development (see Chapter 3). Use this chart to help identify your students' places along the reading continuum by noting what each student can already do and what each needs to learn to do.

Reading Skills Chart

LEARNING TO READ → READING TO LEARN

Beginning New Readers	Intermediate New Readers	Advanced New Readers	Mature Readers
Recognize and write manuscript letters	Read and write cursive letters	Hear and read words with three-letter consonant blends	Read widely in a variety of subject areas and formats
Recognize common everyday trade names, such as Coke and McDonald's, as well as the written names of people in their families, street names, and other common words	Hear the sounds of consonant blends and match the sounds with the letters	Distinguish and read words with regular and irregular vowel patterns	Recognize subtleties of language, argument, and style
Know by sight many frequently used words, such as *but, and, the, this, that, he, his, hers*	Hear the sounds of vowel combinations and match the sounds with the letters	Spell most words that can be read by sight	Criticize style and quality as well as content
Hear single consonant sounds at the beginning, middle, and end of words and match sound to letter	Read words of more than two syllables	Know the rules of syllabication and read multisyllable words	
Hear simple vowel patterns and match sounds to letters	Read simple paragraphs and stories of interest	Write letters, applications, and essays in response to a range of possible questions	
Distinguish rhymes by sound	Read stories written for new readers	Read many selections from newspapers and magazines	
Recognize similar and different sounds	Read sections of a newspaper, such as advice columns or short articles	Read nonfiction books, such as cookbooks and how-to manuals	
Read simple sentences, especially from their own language	Read simple charts, such as a weather map	Read selected novels and other popular literature within their reading ability	
Listen to a poem or short selection from literature and retell the story, or express a reaction and identify words or phrases to explain their reaction	Using a newspaper comic strip, put the separated pictures in correct order	Choose books to read for pleasure and for information	
Listen to instructions, then carry out those instructions	Listen to a poem, then describe its tone and message	Use helpful features of print, such as indexes, titles, subtitles, and glossaries	
Listen to the description of an event from a newspaper article, for example, then describe that event to someone else	Read simple poems		
Look at photographs or paintings and discuss the message or main idea and details, infer relationships within the picture, place the picture in a larger context, or discuss a reaction to the picture	Read and write brief letters to family and friends		
Read simple greeting cards and write brief messages	Read nonfiction books from the children's collection		
Read advertisements and flyers from local merchants	Read food labels and simple recipes		
Read selected parts of a newspaper, such as simple comics, weather information, TV schedule, and at least some headlines			
Read some children's books appropriate to readers of all ages or as part of a family literacy program			

Sources: Skills adapted from Herbert Kohl's *Reading, How to* (New York: E.P. Dutton & Co, 1973), 124, and Helen Lyman's *Reading and the Adult New Reader* (Chicago: American Library Assn., 1976), 18–19. Continuum from Edward V. Jones, *Reading Instruction for the Adult Illiterate* (Chicago: American Library Assn., 1981), 79.

Resources for Teaching Adults to Read

Barasovska, Joan. *Getting Started with Experience Stories.* Syracuse, N.Y.: New Readers Press, 1988.

By using actual language experience stories, the author suggests how tutors can integrate the language experience technique into their reading lessons.

_____. *I Wish I Could Write: Ideas for Inspiring New Writers.* Syracuse, N.Y.: New Readers Press, 1978.

In each section of this book the author presents a writing idea to help new readers and examples of student writing.

Bowren, Fay F., and Miles V. Zintz. *Teaching Reading in Adult Basic Education.* Dubuque, Iowa: Wm. C. Brown Co., 1977.

This comprehensive textbook on reading instruction for adults discusses the physical, sociological, and psychological factors affecting adult students. Included are detailed descriptions of the skills to be learned and the methods used to teach those skills, an extensive discussion of diagnostic and assessment measures available for use with adults, and a section on teaching English to speakers of other languages.

Brookfield, Stephen D. *Developing Critical Thinkers.* San Francisco: Jossey-Bass, 1987.

This book reviews the nature and importance of critical thinking and offers practical suggestions for classroom exercises that will help students improve their thinking skills. Though not focused on literacy students, the discussion and exercises have many applications for this population of learners.

Brown, Cynthia. *Literacy in 30 Hours: Paulo Friere's Process in North East Brazil.* London, Eng.: Writers and Readers Publishing Cooperative, 1975.

Friere's ideas and methods regarding adult literacy instruction have had a profound effect on literacy programs worldwide. Brown provides a clear synopsis of Friere's ideas, illustrated with good examples of his techniques applied to real situations.

Center for Literacy. *Basic Literacy: A Tutor Handbook of the Center for Literacy, Inc.* Philadelphia: Center for Literacy, 1984.

This excellent handbook emphasizes language experience and other student-centered approaches to teaching reading, although it incorporates aspects of more structured programs as well. It includes an overview of phonics, suggestions for teaching spelling and writing, a discussion of comprehension, suggested ways to use the newspaper in literacy classrooms, and copious helpful exercises to reinforce all skills.

Champlin, Connie, and Barbara Kennedy. *Books in Bloom: Creativity Through Children's Literature.* Omaha: Special Literature Press, 1982.

Throughout the book, Champlin and Kennedy demonstrate a literature-based curriculum for teaching reading. They introduce several works of children's literature, then show how to use each book to teach skills that foster critical thinking skills and creativity. Although the book is intended for elementary school teachers and librarians, the principles discussed herein can be applied to instructional programs for adults by using adult-level material.

Jones, Edward V. *Reading Instruction for the Adult Illiterate.* Chicago: American Library Assn., 1981.

Jones begins the book with a comprehensive overview of the scope of adult illiteracy and a profile of the adult illiterate in society and as a learner. In Part II, he offers a detailed, well presented, and sound program of reading instruction for adults, emphasizing methods that incorporate familiar language and meaningful contexts.

Kennedy, Katherine, and Stephanie Roeder. *Using Language Experience With Adults.* Syracuse, N.Y.: New Readers Press, 1975.

In this resource guide for literacy teachers, Kennedy and Roeder discuss dictation, transcription, directed writing, and free writing exercises based on language experience stories.

Kohl, Herbert. *Reading, How to.* New York: E. P. Dutton & Co., Inc., 1973.

Although Kohl writes primarily about teaching children to read, he presents an excellent discussion of the process of reading and of teaching reading. The author emphasizes a cooperative approach in which teacher and student work together to find appropriate methods and materials.

Lyman, Helen Huguenor. *Reading and the Adult New Reader.* Chicago: American Library Assn., 1976.

An experienced librarian, Lyman discusses books and reading in relation to the evolving needs of adult new readers, and encourages librarians to reach out to populations who are not traditional library users.

Newman, Anabel P. *Adult Basic Education: Reading.* Boston: Allyn & Bacon, Inc., 1980.

Newman's excellent textbook on teaching reading to adult basic education students contains particularly good chapters on diagnosing students' skills and interests and on comprehension. The author also discusses setting goals, planning instructional programs, and evaluating progress, including a detailed, instructive account of one student's progress.

Pope, Lillie. *Guidelines to Teaching Remedial Reading.* Brooklyn, N.Y.: Book-Lab, Inc., 1975.

Pope suggests numerous activities and provides useful word lists to help tutors teach basic word recognition skills.

Robson, Ed, Marsha DeVergilio, and Donna DeButts. *Litstart*. 2d ed. Rev. Syracuse, N.Y.: New Readers Press, 1990.

In this basic literacy manual for tutors readers will find profiles of three literacy students and suggestions for various teaching strategies for each student.

Rosenthal, Nadine. *Teach Someone to Read: A Step-By-Step Guide for Literacy Tutors*. Belmont, Calif.: Fearon Education, 1987.

An excellent manual for tutors, the book presents a complete outline for an instructional program that is student centered and built on reading from a meaningful context. It contains a useful section describing informal, easy, and appropriate tests for both phonics and comprehension that can help tutors decide what specific skills need to be taught. It also discusses spelling and writing.

Rossman, Mark H., Elizabeth C. Fisk, and Janet E. Roehl. *Teaching and Learning Basic Skills: A Guide for Adult Basic Education and Developmental Education Programs*. New York: Teachers College Press, 1984.

The authors discuss the physiological and psychological nature of the adult learner in Adult Basic Education and developmental classes, as well as appropriate methods for teaching adult students. They also include particularly good sections on asking questions and simplifying materials.

Shaughnessy, Mina P. *Errors and Expectations*. New York: Oxford University Press, 1977.

Written by a teacher of writing and basic composition at the City University of New York, this book has become a classic discussion of the teaching of writing at all levels. Shaughnessy's understanding of the writing process and of students' writing problems, as well as the many suggested exercises, will help literacy tutors develop a sound writing program for their students.

Smith, Frank. *Reading without Nonsense*. New York: Teachers College Press, 1978.

Smith presents a highly readable book about the nature of reading and how it should be taught. He argues strongly for teaching methods that emphasize the importance of meaning over word recognition skills.

Soifer, Rena, et al. *The Complete Theory-to-Practice Handbook of Adult Literacy: Curriculum Design and Teaching Approaches*. New York: Teachers College Press, 1990.

Along with a good explanation of the whole-language approach to teaching reading, the authors provide several illustrative lesson plans. Chapters on computers and adult literacy, staff selection, and program management further round out the information.

Part Three

A LIBRARY-BASED
READING
PROGRAM

Language Experience Lessons in the Library

> Why are we reading, if not in hope of beauty laid bare, life
> heightened and its deepest mystery probed?[1]
>
> Annie Dillard

The language experience approach to teaching reading is used in many adult literacy programs and in some Adult Basic Education classes. As described in Chapter 3, this method uses the student's own language as its fundamental reading text.

Using language experience stories is a particularly good way to introduce the reading process to beginning level literacy students. Reading familiar words and speech patterns increases their chances for success in the crucial early lessons, and seeing their own words and ideas captured in print gives students a genuine sense of accomplishment, of having contributed something very important to their reading lessons. Such advantages have added impact if one student's language experience stories are shared with other students.

Eventually, however, all students need to explore the world beyond their own experience and to read the words and ideas of others. You can help students begin that exploration by building language experience lessons on a variety of books found in any public library. The process is the same: The tutor records what the student says in their conversation and then helps the student learn to read his or her own words in their written form. However, the starting point is different: Instead of speaking from personal experience, the student discusses what he or she sees or feels in response to pictures in library books that student and tutor examine together. Tutors can begin the discussion by asking students to describe what they see in as much detail as possible, then lead students to a more thoughtful examination of the pictures by asking them to imagine the feelings of the people pictured, to connect the pictures to events or circumstances in their own lives, or to express opinions about a particular picture or about the larger social issues suggested by the picture. Such discussions can help students sharpen their powers of observation, look at familiar situations from different perspectives, and express opinions about ideas and issues important to their communities. They can also lead to personal revelations or elicit strong opinions from students, opinions which may differ substantially from those held by the tutor. Generally speaking, such discussions help new readers understand that ideas are powerful and that reading elicits a range of emotions and reactions. At the same time, tutors need to be sensitive to their students' feelings as well as their own, and maintain an atmosphere in which both student and tutor feel comfortable. Encourage your student to tell you when any discussions cause discomfort, and feel free to do the same.

The following sections illustrate the language experience process as it applies to various visual materials available in a library. Sample activities for specific books, photographs, or collections can be adapted for use with other similar materials. The titles of the particular books discussed in the following sections are not as important as the kinds of books described. To find similar books in your library, browse the art and photography collections. Be aware, too, that many of these books are quite large, so they may be found on the oversize shelves. Search under subject headings such as "photojournalism," or any specific subject you are interested in, followed by the designations "pictorial works" or "photography, artistic." Of course, your local librarian can help you identify numerous books that will inspire thoughtful and far-reaching language experience lessons with literacy students.

Photodocumentaries

Photodocumentaries present social issues in pictures as well as words. A good example is Betty Medsger's *Women at Work: A Photodocumentary.* In more than 100 black-and-white photographs, Medsger shows women at work in jobs ranging from the traditional to the unusual. Women working as nurses, weavers, midwives, truck drivers, stock brokers, and surgeons are pictured, and many offer statements describing their jobs and their feelings about their work.

Photodocumentaries such as *Women at Work* illuminate the issues and events of our time with compelling pictures and a minimum of text. Browse through such works with students, describing the book informally and stopping to comment on pictures either you or your students find intriguing. Read the captions and as much additional text as you feel is necessary. Have students choose a picture to discuss, then use or adapt the following activities to sharpen students' observation or broaden their examination of the issue. Write the students' comments, then ask them to read their own words.

SAMPLE LANGUAGE EXPERIENCE LESSON
USING A PHOTODOCUMENTARY _____

Following are some suggestions that might lead to thoughtful comments in response to *Women at Work*. Similar approaches can be used with other books.

1. Ask students to describe the picture in detail: What are people doing? What are they wearing? How are they relating to other people? What other objects are included in the picture?

2. Ask: How do the people pictured feel about what they are doing? What can you tell from looking at the picture? What can you tell from any statements made?

3. Have students describe a job they have had. Ask: Was it traditional or unusual? Did you like it? What talents of yours did you use? Would you recommend it to others? If you could have your dream job, what would it be?

4. Ask: Do you think some jobs should be held only by men or only by women? Which jobs and why?

5. Discuss how students think they would feel in a job that is usually held by a person of the opposite sex, such as being a female truck driver or a male nurse.

6. Discuss how students think society changes when women work in nontraditional jobs. What do they think are the benefits? The disadvantages?

Photojournalism

Collections of photojournalism are another kind of book that can lead to wide-ranging discussions and thoughtful language experience stories. Such books document the events of our time in striking and memorable images, offering new readers the opportunity to recall their memories of a particular time or event or become acquainted with these events for the first time. Collections of photojournalism contain many different kinds of photographs that can evoke a range of responses. John Loengard's *Life Classic Photographs: A Personal Interpretation* is one example of a collection of photojournalism. For this book, Loengard chose more than 100 pictures he considers the best of what *Life* magazine offered, pictures described on the jacket cover as "the best of the best—photographs that astonish and amaze, delight and amuse, elicit compassion and alert us to history."

Good photographs capture our attention and remain in our mind's eye long after we've seen them in a book. These photographs, as Loengard says in the introduction to his book, "retain their power to surprise. Their depiction of a subject is telling and concise. They are rich in detail. They are apt, dramatic, and simple."[2] In fact, good photographs have the qualities of good writing. Helping students learn to "read" good photographs will help them develop the critical perspective necessary to read good writing later in their literacy development.

SAMPLE PHOTOJOURNALISM ACTIVITIES _____

1. For pictures that recall important events of history, ask questions similar to the following: If you were alive at the time, describe your memories of this event or time. How old were you? Where were you? What were you wearing or doing? How did you feel about the event at the time? Do you look on this event differently now? If this event is unfamiliar to you, what have you learned about it from the picture? Does it alter your previous understanding of the time or place involved?

2. For pictures that suggest a particular mood, ask questions similar to the following: What is the mood in this picture? What about the picture creates this mood? How does the mood of the picture affect you? Might it affect you differently at different times of the day, seasons of the year, or periods in your life?

3. For pictures that show famous people in unfamiliar circumstances, discuss what the picture tells students about the person pictured that they didn't know before.

4. For pictures that are striking because they are particularly graphic (such as a picture of a dramatic rescue) or because they point to some disturbing truth (such as a picture of a homeless person sleeping on the steps of the New York Stock Exchange), ask: What about this picture is disturbing or memorable? Why do you think the photographer took this picture?

5. For photographs that are artistically intriguing because of the interplay of lines or shapes or shadows, discuss: What catches your eye first? How does your eye travel across the picture? How do the objects in the picture relate to each other? How would you explain the picture to someone who can't see it? Does it strike you as easy to understand, or is it puzzling?

The following language experience lessons are based on works of photojournalism. The photographs reproduced on pages 89–91 were taken from newspapers, not specific books, but they are similar to photographs you will find in collections of photojournalism at the library. Sample questions for each photograph were designed to help students look beyond the surface of the picture and glean some additional meaning. Record your student's responses and help the student read them to you.

SAMPLE LANGUAGE EXPERIENCE LESSONS
USING PHOTOJOURNALISM

Painter's Web

Have students look at the picture of the painters on the power line tower. Then ask the following questions:

1. What first attracts your eye in this picture? How does your eye move about this picture? What directs your eye's movement?

2. If you saw this picture but did not know the workers were painting the tower, what would you imagine they were doing?

3. When you look at the center of the picture, beyond the tower, what do you see? What do you imagine?

Rebuilding

Tell students that to members of the Mennonite sect, hats are very important. Explain that this is one picture in a series and that the man in the picture chose to retrieve his hats before leaving his burning house. Then ask the following questions about the photograph:

1. What do you think of the man's choice?

2. If your house were burning, what handful of things would you retrieve?

Frozen Moment

Tell students that the picture shows a man waiting for a ride home in −10° weather, but the way the photographer shot this picture creates a layer of meaning that would not occur to most people passing the scene on the street. Then develop the following discussion:

1. Imagine you are describing this picture to someone who can't see it. Describe it in as much detail as possible to give the other person the sense of what it feels like and what it looks like.

[Lesson continued on p. 92]

Painter's Web, by Bill Garlow

Rebuilding, by Jim Witmer

Frozen Moment, by Allan Detrich

2. What does looking at this picture make you think about? What do you think the person pictured is thinking about?

3. There is a glass window between you, the viewer, and the person pictured. How does this window affect your view of the person?

4. When we encounter surfaces covered with ice, snow, or even dirt, we are often moved to write on those surfaces. Why? What would you be inclined to write?

Photography Collections

Collections of photographs of various kinds also offer numerous opportunities for students to "read" pictures and react to them. Some photography collections revolve around a theme, such as nature or city life. Others contain many pictures of one particular object. A good example of the latter is Val Clery's *Windows*. In this book, some 155 photographs of different windows are interspersed with quotations from poetry and literature discussing both the function and the metaphorical meaning of windows.

A collection such as *Windows* that pictures numerous examples of one kind of familiar object—an object we easily take for granted—can inspire the reader/viewer to look more closely at those objects. The windows in Clery's pictures are interesting for themselves—their design, their beauty, their place in a larger structure—and they are also interesting metaphorically, as the windows through which we view the world. They inspire memories of places we've known as children, homes we've lived in, windows through which we've looked at the real world as well as our own imaginary one.

**SAMPLE LANGUAGE EXPERIENCE LESSON
USING A BOOK OF PHOTOGRAPHS**

Following are some suggestions that might lead to thoughtful comments in response to *Windows*. Similar approaches can be used with other books.

1. Ask students to choose a picture of a window they like. Have them describe it in as much detail as possible, trying to create a "word picture" accurate enough for someone not looking at the picture to imagine the window in his or her mind.

2. Choose two pictures of windows to compare and contrast. Ask: How are the windows alike? How are they different? How is their difference in function reflected in their difference in design? How do they relate to their respective surroundings?

3. Have students think about their own environment: home, workplace, classroom, neighborhood. Then ask them to choose a window they are familiar with and describe it in detail. Discuss: How does the window's form match its function? How does the window reflect the style of the time in which it was built? Why do some buildings have huge windows and others none at all?

Not all photographs are representational or easily identifiable. In *Mountains of the Mind: A Fantastic Journey into Reality* by Andreas Feininger, for example, photographs of commonplace objects such as fish, shells, driftwood, and rocks are positioned, illuminated, and sometimes magnified to display the artistic impact of shapes, lines, contours, surfaces, and contrasts. The resulting pictures are arresting, but not immediately familiar.

Such photographs offer the possibility of discussion and writing activites that can stretch the imagination of new readers. As Feininger says of his work, "People who can see the wonder in a tree, who can extrapolate from a tree to a forest, who can look at a single tree and realize the cosmic implications of all plants—such people have scaled one of the mountains of the mind."[3]

SAMPLE ABSTRACT PHOTOGRAPH ACTIVITIES

Abstract photographs can be puzzling. To help your students look beyond the surface of such photographs, discuss points such as the following:

1. Discuss the most prominent features of the photograph.

2. Ask students how they would describe the picture to someone who can't see it.

3. Ask: What does this picture make you think of? Do you think the artist is conveying a certain message? What is that message? How does the picture make you feel? Why?

4. Have students look carefully at a picture without looking at its title. Ask them to guess what is pictured or what idea is expressed.

5. Ask students to describe some object to you without telling you what it is, then you guess what it is.

Painting Collections

Collections of works of art—paintings and drawings—offer many possibilities for discussion and language experience stories just as books of photography do. In the library are numerous books containing the works of artists from various countries, cultures, and eras. Some paintings will be representational and fairly easy to identify; others will be abstract and unfamiliar, at least at first. Students will have vastly different reactions to these paintings. Show them a variety and encourage them to express their opinions about the paintings and to discuss differences among the paintings.

Collections of works of art and photography present images that may be beautiful, unusual, nostalgic, or disturbing. New readers can respond to these images by describing what they see, by exploring memories the pictures recall, by describing feelings or images the pictures elicit, or by imagining what message the artist had in mind. These discussions can be the basis for language experience lessons, and they can also lead to writing and critical thinking skill activities. For example, looking at a photograph or reprint of a painting, students can identify specific details, infer relationships among various people, describe the mood conveyed, or imagine the larger context of a picture. Advanced students can write their own answers to probing questions you present; beginners can dictate their responses for you to record. The paragraphs that result from such an exercise will undoubtedly be more sophisticated and complex than the simple descriptions of personal events students produced earlier in their instructional programs.

The more you look at a picture or photograph—one that has the depth of a real work of art—the more you see beneath the surface. If your students develop the habit of doing this, they can extend their powers of perception, stretch their imaginations, and exercise their critical thinking. Honing these skills by looking at pictures—works of art—is a first step toward applying these skills to the process of reading.

Resources for Language Experience Lessons

Books such as the ones suggested in the following list can be used in many ways. They present ideas and images that can spark lively discussions among literacy students and lead to thoughtful language experience lessons. They offer numerous opportunities for building vocabulary with students of English as a foreign language. If used with classes, individual students will react differently to the images and ideas suggested, providing rich opportunities for discussion among the students themselves. Any public library will have many books similar to the ones suggested below. Librarians should consider adding some books such as these to the new readers' collection. Tutors in literacy programs might consider having some of these "coffee table" books around in the reception area or student lounge or any place where students are likely to gather. Although the books may be expensive when purchased new, they are often available in used book stores. In addition, if at all feasible, have local painters, photographers, and other artists come to the literacy program to display and talk about their work.

Abe, K., comp. *Jazz Giants: A Visual Retrospective.* New York: Billboard Publications, 1986.

    The photographs in this collection take you behind the scenes with some of the most famous names in the history of jazz. A short, but informative, introduction by jazz writer Nat Hentoff helps the reader put the pictures in historical perspective.

Bellows, George. *The Paintings of George Bellows.* Text by Mahonri Sharp Young. New York: Watson-Guptill Publications, 1973.

    Bellows was a member of "the ashcan school," a group of painters who found inspiration in the streets, at construction sites, and from the sports events of ordinary people in early twentieth century

America. His paintings are realistic, and yet they suggest many questions about the quality of the life depicted.

Capa, Robert. *Children of War, Children of Peace*. Edited by Cornell Capa and Robert Whelan. Boston: Little, Brown & Co., 1991.

Known as the preeminent photographer of war, Robert Capa also took hundreds of pictures of children, some in war-ravaged situations, others in moments of playfulness and peace. This haunting and beautiful collection of photographs spanning more than 20 years and several continents constitutes an extraordinary statement of hope.

Clery, Val. *Windows*. New York: Viking Press, 1978.

Clery's collection of 155 photographs of different kinds of windows includes numerous quotations from poetry and literature that discuss both the function and the metaphorical meaning of windows. An introductory essay tells of the historical development of windows, describes some different kinds, and offers reflections on the artistic and utilitarian uses of windows throughout the ages and across several cultures.

Collett, Ritter. *The Cincinnati Reds: A Pictorial History of Professional Baseball's Oldest Team*. Virginia Beach, Va.: The Jordan Powers Corporation, 1976.

Both black-and-white and color photographs chronicle the history of the Reds from the nineteenth century to the days of "The Big Red Machine."

Conner, Patrick. *People at Work*. Looking at Art. New York: Atheneum, 1982.

This is one of a series of books that reproduces works of art related by a theme. Each picture is accompanied by a brief description and some probing questions that help the viewer look more closely and perhaps see more than was noticed at first glance—an interesting approach that is well done.

Daniel, Pete, and Raymond Smock. *A Talent for Detail: The Photographs of Miss Francis Benjamin Johnston, 1889–1910*. New York: Harmony Books, 1974.

The first part of the book is a photographic biography of Miss Johnston, a pioneer both as photographer and professional woman. The second half is a collection of Johnston's photographs, which offer a fascinating view of life in the United States at the turn of the century.

Doane, James. *America: An Aerial View*. New York: Crescent Books, 1978.

Each state is represented, in alphabetical order, by four or five color photographs and a brief text describing the state's major features. The aerial views present an unusual perspective of familiar sights.

Edey, Maitland. *Great Photographic Essays from* Life. Boston: New York Graphic Society, Little, Brown & Co., 1975.

The collection of more than twenty photographic essays covers topics outside the realm of "news," such as life in a Montana boom town or the anxiety of a young boy meeting his adoptive parents. Each essay includes several black-and-white photos and a few paragraphs explaining the events. Collectively, they offer a "slice of life" view of mid-twentieth century America.

Evans, Walker. *Walker Evans.* Introduction by John Szarkowski. New York: Museum of Modern Art, 1971.

Walker Evans's photographs of people struggling through the Great Depression are an essential part of our historical archives. Some of those photographs are included here along with other works that document life in twentieth century America.

Feininger, Andreas. *The Mountains of the Mind: A Fantastic Journey Into Reality.* New York: The Viking Press, 1977.

This collection is of unusual photographs of nature. Photographs of objects such as fish, shells, driftwood, and rocks are positioned, illuminated, and sometimes magnified to display the artistic impact of shapes, lines, contours, and contrasts.

Frank, Elizabeth. *Pollock.* Modern Masters Series. New York: Abbeville Press, 1983.

The book presents the work of abstract expressionist Jackson Pollock. A discussion of Pollock's influences, development as a painter, and methods of working help illuminate the artist's work.

Gore, Art. *Images of Yesterday.* Palo Alto, Calif.: American West Publishing Co., 1975.

In his introduction to this collection of photographs, Gore asks the viewer to "refresh your own perspective on the beauty of the world, to look at the whole apple before you bite into it." His simple descriptions of the photos make this a particularly appealing and informative work.

Higgins, Chester. *A Photographic Essay on the Black Man in America.* Text by Orde Coombs. Garden City, N.Y.: Anchor Books, 1974.

A brief text introduces each of four sections of photographs of black men arranged by age. The photographer and writer team have also produced *Black Woman: A Photographic Essay.*

Iooss, Walter. *Baseball.* Text by Roger Angell. New York: Harry N. Abrams, Inc., 1984.

Just as baseball itself moves back and forth from high drama to routine plays, the color photographs in this book capture individual baseball players in moments of dramatic tension as well as in more light-hearted times on and off the field. Angell's essay offers insight into the success of certain players.

Jordan, June. *Who Look At Me*. New York: Thomas Y. Crowell, 1969.

Jordan has written a poem to accompany twenty-seven paintings of African-Americans from the days of slavery through the twentieth century. The powerful rhythmic poem could well stand alone, and the paintings on their own tell a haunting tale of resilience, love, and triumph. Together, poem and paintings weave a story line back and forth, drawing strength and insight from each other. The result is a brilliant tapestry.

Kaufman, Kenneth. *Of Trees, Leaves, and Ponds: Studies in Photo-Impressionism*. New York: E. P. Dutton, 1981.

This collection of evocative photographs of nature is accompanied by short excerpts from poetry.

Kertész, André. *On Reading*. New York: Penguin Books, 1982.

The photographs show people reading in moments and settings of all kinds, from elegant reading rooms to subways and rooftops.

Lanker, Brian. *I Dream a World: Portraits of Black Women Who Changed America*. New York: Stewart, Tabori, & Chang, 1988.

Stunning photographs of seventy-five black women, mostly from the worlds of politics and the arts, are accompanied by segments of interviews in which each of the women talks about her struggles, triumphs, and hopes for the future.

Lauber, Patricia. *Seeing Earth from Space*. New York: Orchard Books, 1990.

Photographs and illustrations from NASA show us the earth as seen from space—a perspective that alters our understanding of our physical world and gives us clues to our evolutionary past and uncertain environmental future.

Loengard, John. *Life Classic Photographs: A Personal Interpretation*. Boston: Little, Brown & Co., 1988.

Loengard has chosen more than 100 pictures he considers the best of what *Life* magazine offered. A brief description of the pictured event accompanies each photograph.

Melvin, Betsy, and Tom Melvin. *Robert Frost Country*. Garden City, N.Y.: Doubleday Inc., 1977.

Color photographs of New England scenes at various seasons are accompanied by excerpts from Frost's poetry.

Medsger, Betty. *Women at Work: A Photodocumentary*. New York: Sheed and Ward, Inc., 1975.

More than 100 black-and-white photographs present women engaged in jobs ranging from the traditional to the unusual. Several of the women offer statements describing their jobs and their feelings about them.

Menashe, Abraham. *The Face of Prayer.* New York: Alfred A. Knopf, 1983.

Menashe shows people from all over the world and of many faiths in prayer.

Meyerowitz, Joel. *A Summer's Day.* New York: Times Books, 1985.

Summer can be a time of fullness, reverie, and a seeming suspension of time itself. Meyerowitz's lovely color photographs follow a summer's day from dawn until twilight.

Michelson, Maureen R. *Women and Work: Photographs and Personal Writings.* Pasadena, Calif.: NewSage Press, 1986.

Michelson's collection of photographs shows women at work in occupations ranging from the traditional to the highly unusual. Each woman pictured also explains her feelings about her job.

Monk, Lorraine. *Photographs That Changed the World.* New York: Doubleday, 1989.

A photograph from 1826, one of the earliest on record, is included in this collection along with a photo of Abraham Lincoln, the flag raising at Iwo Jima, and the earthrise as seen by the astronauts aboard *Apollo 8.*

Owens, Bill. *Working (I Do It for the Money).* New York: Simon & Schuster, 1977.

From the crew on the missile pad at Cape Canaveral to the donut maker in New York City, this collection covers an intriguing spectrum of occupations. Comments from the workers pictured add an entertaining and personal touch.

Pippin, Horace. *Horace Pippin.* With an essay by Romare Bearden. Washington, D.C.: The Phillips Collection, 1977.

Having lost the use of his arm in World War I, Pippin nevertheless taught himself to paint. His first works were memories from the war, then scenes from the lives of black Americans, moving in later years to more universal subjects. His paintings are called primitive or folk-like, yet they possess a power that reflects the strength of will necessary to overcome many adversities as well as the clarity of perspective such adversity can bring. This is a simple book, one picture per page with a minimum of text, but it speaks volumes.

Ritter, Lawrence S. *The Babe: A Life in Pictures.* Picture research by Mark Rucker. New York: Ticknor & Fields, 1988.

The text in this picture biography, written by one who knows and enjoys the subject, is engaging and informative. But the illustrations tell an equally detailed and captivating story. Using photographs, newsclippings, old posters, baseball cards, and other memorabilia of one of baseball's greatest stars, the book presents the complex life of Babe Ruth with humor, honesty, and compassion.

Robeson, Susan. *The Whole World in His Hands: A Pictorial Biography of Paul Robeson*. Secaucus, N.J.: Citadel Press, 1981.

Written and compiled by his granddaughter, this book tells the extraordinary life story of Paul Robeson, grandson of a slave, athlete, scholar, actor, singer, and internationally renowned civil rights leader. Some of Paul Robeson's own words are interspersed with Susan Robeson's commentary.

Rockwell, Norman. *102 Favorite Paintings*. Introduction by Christopher Finch. New York: Crown Publishers, Inc., 1977.

A collection of many of the best known of Rockwell's works, the book presents one illustration per page. Each illustration is accompanied by a description of the work and its origins.

Smolan, Rick, and David Cohen, eds. *A Day in the Life of America*. New York: Collins Publishers, 1986.

Two hundred photographers were asked to take pictures anywhere in the United States during the 24 hours of May 2, 1986. The photos capture the diversity of land, people, and lifestyle in the United States. Most pictures are in color, a few are black-and-white; all are annotated.

Steichen, Edward. *The Family of Man*. Prologue by Carl Sandburg. New York: MACO Magazine Corp. for Museum of Modern Art, 1955.

The more than 500 photographs in this collection, taken in the middle of the twentieth century, come from 68 countries around the world. Arranged thematically around brief but thoughtful quotations, they give us some historical perspective on life in areas so different from, and yet so much like, our own.

Vincent Van Gogh. Commentary by Richard Shone. New York: St. Martin's Press, 1978.

Forty color plates, presented one to a page with a brief but informative commentary, offer a good introduction to the works of one of the world's most famous artists. The publisher has produced other volumes on the works of other well-known artists.

Westwater, James. *Ohio*. Text by Richard McCutcheon. Portland, Oreg.: Graphic Arts Center Publishing Co., 1982.

There are many collections of photographs from one state or region of the country. This is a particularly good one, including photographs of the natural, industrial, cultural, and historical life of Ohio.

Wyeth, Andrew. *The Art of Andrew Wyeth*. Commentary by Wanda M. Corn. Boston: New York Graphics Society, Little, Brown & Co., 1973.

Painted in spare and muted earth tones, Andrew Wyeth's paintings depict the rocks, soil, water, animals, farms, buildings, and people of his rural Pennsylvania. The incredible detail and the beauty lurking just below the surface of these pictures draw the viewer in, delight the eye, and awaken the imagination. An ordinary windowsill will never look quite the same again.

Wyeth, Jamie. *Jamie Wyeth*. Boston: Houghton Mifflin Co., 1980.

Jamie Wyeth's paintings are realistic images of people, nature, and common objects, but their simplicity is deceptive. Looking at these paintings, the viewer lingers and finds a depth and beauty not apparent at first glance.

6

Information Reading Lessons in the Library

> Books are the carriers of civilization. Without books,
> history is silent, literature dumb, science crippled,
> thought and speculation at a standstill.[1]
>
> Barbara Tuchman

Students come to literacy programs with many information needs. They need to be able to learn new tasks on the job, fix a leaky pipe at home, or understand the restrictions of their unemployment benefits. They also desire to learn about events in history that they missed in school or to study in greater depth about a sport or a hobby they are interested in.

The information reading technique, as described in Chapter 3, helps new readers obtain the information they want or need. This technique allows students to make the leap from reading their own words produced in language experience stories to reading the words of others. By applying the information reading technique to books from the general collection of any public library, you can introduce your students to a world of knowledge and information previously unavailable to them. There are four variations of this teaching method that can be particularly helpful to literacy students:

1. *Reading and Rewriting Text.* This technique involves having tutors read to students from books or other reading materials containing information the students need. Tutors and students discuss the information, then students explain what they have learned in their own words. Tutors record the students' explanations, just as they did with language experience stories. Students then read their own version of the information.
2. *Listening for Details in Text Read by a Tutor.* The tutor reads to the students, then asks them to recall specific details.
3. *Silent Reading for Information.* The tutor finds books and other materials within the students' reading levels that contain information important to them. Tutors can present questions and have students read to find the answers, or tutors can have students read and then respond, either orally or in writing, to questions about what was read.
4. *Reading Charts, Graphs, and Diagrams.* Students are asked to find information from graphics of various kinds.

Reading materials brought from home or the workplace are good source materials for information reading lessons. So are numerous books in the collection of any public library. The following sample lessons describe each of the variations of this teaching technique as applied to specific books from the library.

Reading and Rewriting Text

With your student, find books that contain information he needs to know. Read the book to your student, a section or paragraph at a time. Discuss the information with the student, then write down his understanding of what he heard. Use the student's own language as much as possible, making sure his explanation of the information is accurate. Then help your student read his words exactly as you've written them, just as you did with language experience stories. After he learns to read this material, develop exercises to help him practice both word recognition and comprehension skills.

In the following examples based on lessons from commonly available library books, a paragraph or two from the book is followed by the student's rewritten version. Sample questions designed to help students understand the information follow the revised text.

SAMPLE INFORMATION READING LESSON
FOR BEGINNING NEW READERS

Rewriting Text

The following question and answer excerpt is from the section on yeast breads in *Betty Crocker's Kitchen Secrets:*

Original Text

Question: What are the ingredients in yeast breads and what do they do?

Answer: Flour (mostly all-purpose enriched), which contains gluten, is the structure builder. When flour is mixed with liquid and kneaded or beaten, the proteins in it form gluten, which stretches like elastic, trapping bubbles of gas formed by the yeast to give bread its cellular structure. Because special-flavor flours (rye, whole wheat) develop fewer gluten strands, they most often are used in combination with all-purpose flour.[2]

Rewritten Version

The flour builds the structure of the bread. Flour and some liquid are mixed to make a dough. When the dough is kneaded, the proteins in the flour form gluten. The gluten stretches and traps gas bubbles from the yeast. Rye and whole-wheat flour have less gluten, so they are used together with all-purpose flour.

Sample Questions

1. What part of the flour forms gluten?

2. What forms bubbles of gas?

3. What do you think would happen if you used all whole-wheat flour to make a loaf of bread?

A book such as *Sports Illustrated Basketball* by Neil Isaacs and Dick Motta is useful for practicing the most basic of the thinking skills described in Chapter 4—understanding the facts and information presented. Questions that require students to describe a particular move in correct sequence, list the advantages of a particular play, or match penalties to particular infractions of the rules all test students' ability to understand the information provided in the text.

SAMPLE INFORMATION READING LESSON
FOR INTERMEDIATE NEW READERS

Rewriting Text

The following example presents two paragraphs from *Sports Illustrated Basketball* describing the jump shot. The excerpt was preceded in the text by a description of the set shot.

Original Text

The jump shot should be no different from a set shot. Merely raise the platform from which the shot is launched with increased flexion of the knees and the jump. By platform we mean simply the level from which the shot is launched; the platform for a set shot is the floor, for a jump shot the level achieved by the jump. The platform should be adjustable; the farther the shot the more power you need, and so the higher the platform. Sometimes you need to raise the platform to get the shot off over taller defenders. The ball should be released at the precise instant that you establish the platform.

Think of yourself as in a cylinder. Jump straight up in the cylinder, establish the platform, and shoot the ball up and out with the same form as for the set shot. Your body should sway neither right nor left. You should neither lean forward nor fall back. The feet should return to the floor right where they left. You should finish the shot just as you started it, smoothly and on balance, ready to move either way to follow for a rebound or pick up your defensive assignment.[3]

Rewritten Version

The jump shot is like the set shot. The only difference is you raise the platform, or the level, from which you shoot by jumping. The farther the shot, the higher you need to jump, although sometimes you need to jump high just to get the ball over tall defenders. You release the ball when you reach the platform, that is, the highest point of your jump.

Jump straight up. When you reach the top of the jump, shoot the ball up and out, just as you do for a set shot. Don't let your body sway right or left, backward or forward. Try to land right where you started your jump. Try to land smoothly and on balance so you are ready for the next move.

Sample Questions

1. In what order do you perform the moves for a jump shot?

2. How would you describe a good jump shot?

3. Under what circumstances would you choose a jump shot over a set shot?

Listening for Details in Text Read by a Tutor

Listening attentively to a text read by someone else is an important skill. It strengthens concentration while giving students practice in selecting important information, a skill they will need to apply to everything they read. This is a particularly good method to use with books that are beyond a student's reading level but about a subject with which the student is familiar.

The excerpt in the following sample lesson tells a fairly complicated story, using phrases and terminology specific to baseball. For students who are familiar with the terminology and the rules of the game, it is a good exercise in listening attentively to note specific details and remember the sequence of events. To be mature readers, students will need to read such informative material, so listening exercises such as this are good preliminary practice. The sample questions require the student to gather and retain pertinent information.

——————— **SAMPLE INFORMATION READING LESSON** ———————

Listening for Details

Read the following paragraph from Richard Whittingham's *The White Sox: A Pictorial History* aloud to your student.

Early Wynn—the premier Sox pitcher that year who had already won 20 games—took the mound for the Sox. He got the lead in the third when Luis Aparicio slashed a double to right, scoring Bubba Phillips. Billy Goodman then followed suit with another double to right to send Aparicio across the plate. Jimmy Piersall, the Indians' center fielder, drove in a run for Cleveland, but Al Smith got it back for the Sox in the 6th inning with a home run. Moments later Jim Rivera followed with another. The Indians got another run and came into the bottom of the ninth inning trailing 4–2. Early Wynn had sat down in the 7th, relieved by Bob Shaw. And now in the 9th Shaw was in trouble. The Indians had loaded the bases with only one out. Lopez went to his bullpen for reliable Gerry Staley, who pitched in 67 games that year. The workhorse Staley, however, would only have to throw one pitch that night. First baseman Vic Power swung at it and hit a hard grounder to Aparicio who grabbed it, raced to second for the force and fired to Kluczewski to complete the double play.[4]

Sample Questions

1. Who was the starting pitcher for the White Sox?

2. What had he already accomplished by the date of this game?

3. Which team scored first? How many runs did they score?

4. Which player scored the first run?

5. What was the score after Jim Rivera's home run?

6. In what inning did Early Wynn leave the game?

7. What White Sox pitcher pitched the last inning?

8. What was the last play of the game?

Silent Reading for Information

Almost all reading by mature readers is done silently. New readers need to practice reading silently right from the start. Arrange for your student to read silently for some time during each lesson, even if she reads only a brief language experience story that she initially read aloud.

In the children's section of any library, you will find many nonfiction books with useful and important information presented in a format that is appealing to adults. Some tutors and librarians automatically dismiss books from the children's collection when searching for materials for adult new readers; but doing so actually deprives new readers of a rich source of good reading material.

While there are certainly many children's books that would be inappropriate for adults, there are also many books in the children's department that could appropriately be shelved in the adult section. This is particularly true of works of nonfiction. Many good books written for children are informative and well researched, and they don't gloss over potentially controversial subjects. These books use the terminology appropriate to the subject, with definitions, and they include numerous illustrations, mostly photographs, that enhance their appeal as well as their content. Good books for children are written in an engaging, straightforward language that doesn't identify children as the intended audience.

Such crossover books can be both appealing and helpful to adult new readers. They provide an entry into the nonfiction literature for intermediate and advanced new readers interested in learning about history, science, geography, biography, and other areas of knowledge previously closed to adult new readers. They also provide good exercise for students in gleaning the details of a text by reading silently. Ask your local librarian to help you find examples of good nonfiction titles from the children's collection that will appeal to adults.

If you use books from the children's collection with adult new readers, make sure your students are comfortable with the specific books you choose. Talk to them about the many possible books that may appeal to them, and browse through several you select ahead of time. Once you have chosen a book that is acceptable and interesting to your adult students, have them read a section of the book silently, then write answers to questions you provide. Writing answers rather than just talking about the book forces students to think more about how best to make their point, so give students as much opportunity to respond to questions in writing as possible.

**SAMPLE INFORMATION READING LESSON
FOR INTERMEDIATE NEW READERS**_____

Silent Reading

Have students read the following excerpt from G.C. Skipper's *D-Day* silently, then answer the questions, or present the questions before the students read, then ask them to find the answers in the text.

> The Allied invasion—one of the greatest feats of organization, supply, and raw courage in the history of warfare—posed many unique problems. The solutions to these problems were just as unique.
>
> For example, there were no usable harbors, so the Allied armies brought their own gigantic, ten-story-high concrete artificial harbors code named "Mulberries." These were floated across the channel and sunk, along with a fleet of over-aged ships, to form breakwaters.
>
> The Allied forces also had to confront the problem of fueling thousands of vehicles for the world's most modern, highly mechanized army. They found the answer in something called PLUTO (Pipe Line Under the Ocean). Eventually, a total of twenty underwater rubber pipelines were laid across the channel to supply the invasion.[5]

Sample Questions

1. What were "mulberries"?

2. Why were mulberries needed?

3. How were mulberries used?

4. How did the Allies supply the fuel for their equipment?

5. Why do you think the Allies spent so much time and effort planning this invasion?

**SAMPLE INFORMATION READING LESSON
FOR ADVANCED NEW READERS**_____

Silent Reading

Have students read the following excerpt from Jack Rummel's biography, *Langston Hughes,* then answer the questions.

Hughes had spent a lot of his time during his first year in New York at the Harlem branch of the New York Public Library. One of the persons he met there was [Countee] Cullen, an up-and-coming poet. The two men got along well and traded poems with one another for appraisal and criticism.

Cullen and Hughes approached their poetry in different ways. Cullen was interested in poetry that demanded exact syllable counts and certain sounds to complete a rhyme scheme. Hughes, on the other hand, preferred to write in free verse. Like Cullen, he carefully chose his language so it would fit the subject and emotion of his poems, but his poetry was not so formal in style. Not only did their poetic styles differ, but the two poets held differing views about the relationship between their race and their poetry. Hughes could not separate his interest in blacks from his desire to write poetry. He wrote about black people, black music, and black experiences while using black American speech rhymes and slang. Cullen considered himself to be a poet first and foremost, a poet who just happened to be black, so he did not center his poetry on his blackness. Instead, Cullen tended to write in a private voice about personal matters.[6]

Sample Questions

1. Where did Hughes and Cullen meet? How did they help each other?

2. In what two ways did the poetry of Langston Hughes differ from the poetry of Countee Cullen?

Follow up by reading poems by Hughes and by Cullen to your students. Ask them to compare the poems in light of the discussion in this biography.

Reading for Information from Graphic Sources

Yet another way to apply the information reading technique to books and resources found in the public library requires students to gather information from printed sources of all kinds, including charts, diagrams, maps, illustrations, and other graphic presentations of information. There are numerous reference sources in the library that provide information in graphic formats. Almanacs, atlases, and statistical compendiums of various kinds plus weather maps, TV listings, and sports summaries found in virtually every newspaper are just some examples. Such resources offer new readers important information in formats they need to learn to use and, thus, are useful resources for the information reading technique.

SAMPLE INFORMATION READING LESSON
FOR BEGINNING NEW READERS

Using Graphic Sources

Betty Crocker's Kitchen Secrets, the book used in the first sample lesson in this chapter, presents some of its information in chart form. Following is a typical chart listing common types of legumes.[7]

Common Types of Legumes

Type	Color	Size and Shape	Use
1. Black beans	black	small, oval	baked, soups, stews
2. Black-eyed peas	white with a black spot	small, oval	casseroles
3. Garbanzo beans (chick peas)	brown	small, irregular	dips, casseroles, salads, soups, stews
4. Great Northern beans	white	medium, oval	baked, casseroles, chowder, soups, stews
5. Kidney beans	red	medium, oval	casseroles, chili, salads, soups
6. Lentils	brown or green	small, round disk	casseroles, salads, soups
7. Lima beans	white	large, small, flat	casseroles, soups
8. Navy beans	white	small, round	baked, soups
9. Pinto beans	pink speckled with brown	medium, oval	casseroles, soups
10. Red beans	red	small, round	casseroles, chili
11. Soybeans	tan	small, round	casseroles, salads
12. Split peas	green or yellow	small, round	soups

Introduce the chart by asking your students to look at the kinds of legumes mentioned and to choose one they know or like. Using the legume chosen as an example, show your students how to use the chart. Then check their understanding by asking questions such as the following.

Sample Questions

1. What color are Great Northern beans?

2. What kind of beans are generally used in chili?

3. What is the name of a bean that is white, large, and used in soups?

4. If you wanted to make a stew, what kinds of beans might you buy?

SAMPLE INFORMATION READING LESSON
FOR INTERMEDIATE NEW READERS

Using Graphic Sources

In the following chart from Bill James's *The Baseball Book 1990,* the author picks his all-time all-star team of players who are 41 years old. Have students look at the chart to answer the questions following it.[8]

AGE 41
ALL-TIME ALL-STAR TEAM

POS	Player, Season	G	AB	H	2B	3B	HR	Run	RBI	BB	SO	SB	Avg
C	Chief Zimmer, 1902	42	142	38	4	2	0	13	17	11		4	.268
1B	Pete Rose, 1982	162	634	172	25	4	3	80	54	66	32	8	.271
2B	Honus Wagner, 1915	156	566	155	32	17	6	68	78	39	64	22	.274
3B	Bert Campaneris, 1983	60	143	46	5	0	0	19	11	8	9	6	.322
SS	Luke Appling, 1948	129	497	156	16	2	0	63	47	94	35	10	.314
LF	Ted Williams, 1960	113	310	98	15	0	29	56	72	75	41	1	.316
CF	Ty Cobb, 1928	95	353	114	27	4	1	54	40	34	16	5	.323
RF	Stan Musial, 1962	135	433	143	18	1	19	57	82	64	46	3	.330

		G	IP	W	L	Pct.	SO	BB	ERA	ShO	Sv
RS	Cy Young, 1908	36	299	21	11	.656	150	37	1.26	3	2
LS	Warren Spahn, 1962	34	269	18	14	.563	118	55	3.04	0	0
3S	Ted Lyons, 1941	20	180	14	6	.700	50	26	2.10	0	0
4S	Pete Alexander, 1928	34	244	16	9	.640	59	37	3.36	1	2
5S	Rip Sewell, 1948	21	122	13	3	.813	36	37	3.47	0	0
RA	Hoyt Wilhelm, 1965	66	144	7	7	.500	106	32	1.81	0	20

Sample Questions

1. Who will play shortstop for this all-star team?

2. In what year was Ted Williams 41? What was his batting average that year?

3. Who played in the most games during his 41st year?

4. Who had the highest batting average?

5. The second part of the chart gives statistics for pitchers. Which pitcher won the most games?

6. According to these statistics, which player would you nominate as the most valuable 41-year-old? (Bill James's choice was Honus Wagner, but obviously opinions can vary. What matters is how well a student can support his choice by comparing statistics.)

Resources for Information Reading

The following list suggests but a small sample of the hundreds of books useful for information reading. Books marked with an asterisk (*) come from the children's collection but are appropriate for adult new readers. Since literacy students will read some of these books on their own, a suggested reading level is provided. Remember, though, that individual students can read over a range of reading levels depending on their interest, their knowledge of the subject, and the clarity and format of the writing. Ask your librarian to help you and your students build your own bibliographies, based on the needs and interests of the students.

*Adkins, Jan. *Toolchest.* New York: Walker & Co., 1973. [intermediate new reader]

With a distinctive style that is both whimsical and highly informative, Adkins describes a wide array of carpenter's tools. As in his other nonfiction books, Adkins has crafted a fine work with words and drawings.

*Ashabranner, Brent. *Always to Remember: The Story of the Vietnam Veterans Memorial.* Photographs by Jennifer Ashabranner. New York: Dodd, Mead & Co., 1988. [intermediate new reader]

This thoughtful and well-researched book discusses the building of the Vietnam Veterans Memorial in Washington, D.C. Ashabranner

profiles both the man who first proposed a memorial and worked
tirelessly to make it a reality and the young Asian-American woman
who designed it. Other chapters give brief accounts of the war and
the many controversies and problems encountered during the building of the monument. Beautiful photographs and statements from
some of the thousands of visitors tell of the memorial's emotional
impact.

*_____. *The New Americans: Changing Patterns in U.S. Immigra-
tion.* Photographs by Paul Conklin. New York: Dodd, Mead & Co.,
1983. [advanced new reader]

This study of immigration to the United States since 1965 focuses
on two groups, Asians and Latin Americans. It also briefly discusses
the history of immigration since the founding of the country. Several
case histories personalize this important issue.

*Asimov, Isaac. *How Did We Find out about Microwaves?* Illus. by
Erika Kors. New York: Walker & Co., 1989. [intermediate new reader]

One of a series of "How did we find out about" books, this book
describes the discovery of microwaves and explains their many uses
in science and everyday appliances. Asimov, a prolific and lively
writer, makes scientific facts fascinating to young and old alike.

*Ballard, Robert D. *Exploring the Titanic.* Illus. by Ken Marschall.
Toronto: Madison Press Books, 1988. [intermediate new reader]

Ballard is a marine geologist who discovered the wreck of the
Titanic in 1985. In the first half of the book he tells how the *Titanic*
was built and then sank on its maiden voyage. The second half tells
how it was found. This informative and fascinating book includes a
glossary and chronology.

Bethel, Dell. *Inside Baseball.* Rev. ed. Chicago: Contemporary Books,
Inc., 1980. [advanced new reader]

All aspects of the game of baseball are explained in clear, readable
text supplemented by numerous black-and-white photographs, drawings, and diagrams. Bethel includes chapters for each skill and posi-
tion. One chapter illustrates in words and diagrams numerous situations and corresponding strategies. (This publisher offers similar
books about other sports.)

Betty Crocker's Kitchen Secrets. New York: Random House, 1983.
[intermediate/advanced new reader]

Kitchen Secrets is not a recipe book, but rather a guide for
cooking all kinds of food. Information is organized according to food
category, such as pastry, seafood, vegetables, etc. Each section is
presented in a question-and-answer format. Questions are basic ones
all cooks ask; answers are easy to read and understand. The book
also presents information on cooking equipment, measuring, and

equivalencies. Some information is given in chart form, offering new readers a chance to develop the skill of obtaining information from charts.

*Brownmiller, Susan. *Shirley Chisholm.* Garden City, N.Y.: Doubleday & Co., 1971. [intermediate new reader]

A biography of the first black Congresswoman, this book tells Chisholm's story from her childhood in Barbados and Brooklyn through her political career. Written for young adults by a well-known author of adult books, it is highly readable and informative.

*Fradin, Dennis B. *New York in Words and Pictures.* Chicago: Childrens Press, 1981. [intermediate new reader]

One of a series on the states from this publisher, the book presents a brief but informative introduction to the history of New York State, including early Indian history, the growth of cities and industry, and sketches of some famous natives. It includes good color photographs on each page, with product maps and a historical chronology supporting the highly readable text.

*Freedman, Russell. *Buffalo Hunt.* New York: Holiday House, 1988. [intermediate new reader]

In this lovely book, text and illustrations combine to tell the fascinating story of the Great Plains Indians who hunted and revered the buffalo. The illustrations are reproductions of the works of painters who traveled throughout Indian country in the nineteenth century to record what they saw.

*_____. *Lincoln: A Photobiography.* New York: Clarion Books, 1987. [advanced new reader]

This wonderfully written biography discusses Lincoln's early life and influences as well as his later political career. Russell presents Lincoln as a thoughtful man whose opinions, especially about slavery, changed with time and experience. Numerous photographs as well as reproductions of posters, letters, and speeches enhance this portrait of a complex man who led his nation through turbulent times.

Hanley, Hope. *The Craft of Needlepoint.* New York: Chas. Scribner's Sons, 1977. [beginning–advanced new reader]

Books about crafts of all kinds are useful to new readers, and the clear, easy-to-read text and easy-to-follow diagrams make this book a particularly good example.

*Haskins, James. *Black Music in America: A History Through Its People.* New York: Thomas Y. Crowell, 1987. [advanced new reader]

From early slave songs through jazz, the blues, and soul, this book surveys the music of black Americans. Profiles of major figures personalize the story.

*Hughes, Langston. *Jazz*. 3d ed., updated and expanded by Sandford Brown. New York: Franklin Watts, 1982. [advanced new reader]

The roots of jazz—African rhythms, work songs, jubilees, and spirituals—along with the many forms jazz has taken—blues, bebop, and ragtime—are all described in lively, colorful prose. Photographs and illustrations of famous names and important events in the evolution of jazz add information and visual appeal. The book was revised and updated after Hughes's death, but it retains the rhythm and style of its original author.

Isaacs, Neil, and Dick Motta. *Sports Illustrated Basketball*. New York: Harper & Row, 1981. [advanced new reader]

This title is one of a series of books written about all major sports. Written for adults, it explains all the fundamentals of the game, suggests practice drills, and describes playmaking patterns. Also included is a chapter titled, "Basketball for the Spectator." Black-and-white photographs of college and professional players illustrate the text on almost every page. There are no diagrams or charts.

*Isaacson, Philip M. *Round Buildings, Square Buildings, and Buildings That Wiggle Like a Fish*. New York: Alfred A. Knopf, 1988. [intermediate new reader]

Who could resist such a title? And the contents will not disappoint. Using his own photographs, Isaacson takes the reader on a worldwide tour of beautiful buildings—some famous, some commonplace, some thousands of years old, some born of the modern age. Isaacson's descriptions of architectural styles and their effect on the people who live among these functional works of art tell a fascinating and enlightening story.

*Jacobs, William Jay. *Ellis Island: New Hope in a New Land*. New York: Chas. Scribner's Sons, 1990. [intermediate new reader]

Focusing on the year 1907, Jacobs describes the experiences of immigrants to America. Black-and-white photographs emphasize the human drama of this endlessly fascinating aspect of American history that touches all of us in some way.

*James, Bill. *The Baseball Book 1990*. New York: Villard Books, 1990. [intermediate/advanced new readers]

Providing more than just a review of the season just past, James interweaves numerous statistics and details into fascinating stories about the athletic achievements and human dramas that make baseball an enduring American passion.

*Jones, Hettie. *Big Star Fallin' Mama: Five Women in Black Music*. New York: The Viking Press, 1974. [advanced new reader]

Ma Rainey, Bessie Smith, Mahalia Jackson, Billie Holiday, and Aretha Franklin understood the blues as a way of life as well as a way of singing. This well-written book documents how their lives and careers reflected many of the social changes of their times.

*Lauber, Patricia. *Volcano: The Eruption and Healing of Mt. St. Helens.* New York: Bradbury Press, 1986. [intermediate new reader]

Wonderful photographs and good writing review the causes of the eruption of Mt. St. Helens in 1980, the destruction it wrought, and the process of healing and renewal that followed. Lauber has written other readable and well-researched books about science and the natural world.

*Macauley, David. *Underground.* Boston: Houghton Mifflin Co., 1976. [advanced new reader]

Under an imaginary intersection of a large city, Macauley exposes the foundations that support the tall buildings and the water, electrical, telephone, gas, and sewer systems that make modern life possible. This is a fascinating and creative look at an unknown but vital part of any city. (Other unique works from this author/illustrator include *Cathedral* and *Pyramid.*)

*Meltzer, Milton. *Black Americans: A History in Their Own Words.* New York: Thomas Y. Crowell, 1984. [advanced new reader]

Using letters, speeches, interviews, and other primary-source materials, Meltzer compiles the story of blacks in America from the first slaves in 1619 through the urban unrest of the 1980s. A brief preface to each piece sets the historical time and place and introduces the primary-source writers, some of whom are famous, some unknown. This is a lively and compelling history.

*Nabwire, Constance, and Bertha Vining Montgomery. *Cooking the African Way.* Minneapolis: Lerner Publications, 1988. [intermediate new reader]

This is one of a series of Easy Menu Ethnic Cookbooks, each of which offers introductory information on the country or region, a list of cooking terms and ingredients, and step-by-step directions for traditional dishes. Clearly laid out and well written, these cookbooks present the possibility of a joint exercise in reading and cooking.

National League Green Book—1987. New York: The National League of Professional Baseball Clubs, 1987. [intermediate/advanced new reader]

Books such as this, which is a compilation of statistics for the previous baseball season, appear each year. Included are team rosters (complete with phonetic pronunciation of names), information about each team's uniforms and ballparks, the season's record for every team, lists of statistics comparing the accomplishments of individuals and teams in numerous categories, and a review of the League Championship Series and World Series.

*Ride, Sally, with Susan Okie. *To Space and Back*. New York: Lothrop, Lee, & Shepard Books, 1986. [intermediate new reader]

Ride, the first American woman astronaut, talks of her trips on the space shuttle. Photographs of crew members at work and play are informative and amusing, while photographs of Earth from space inspire awe. The tone is factual, yet clearly touched by the wonder Ride obviously felt on such an extraordinary journey.

Ritter, Lawrence S., and Donald Honig. *The Image of Their Greatness: An Illustrated History of Baseball from 1900 to the Present*. New York: Crown Publishers, Inc., 1979. [advanced new reader]

Chapters cover each decade from 1900 through the 1970s. This big book has lots of information and was written by two of the best writers about baseball. The many black-and-white photographs tell a story all their own.

*Robbins, Ken. *Building a House*. New York: Four Winds Press, 1984. [intermediate new reader]

With black-and-white photographs and simple, clear text, Robbins describes the process of building a house from drawing the design to moving in.

*Roberts, Maurice. *Cesar Chavez and La Causa*. Chicago: Childrens Press, 1986. [intermediate new reader]

This book is one of a series called "picture-story biographies." It reviews the life of Chavez, concentrating on his work as a leader of the farm workers' union and a promoter of nonviolent protest.

*Rummel, Jack. *Langston Hughes,* Black Americans of Achievement series. New York: Chelsea House Publishers, 1988. [advanced new reader]

The poet Langston Hughes was a major literary figure in the Harlem Renaissance of the first half of the twentieth century. Some of Hughes's poems tap the rhythm and emotions of urban life, often reflecting the musical style of the blues, while others exult in the natural world. Some clearly depict the black experience, others are wide ranging in subject and express a universal human longing. His poetry is rich in meaning and rhythm yet very accessible to new readers. This biography concentrates on the varied experiences of Hughes's adult life that influenced his poetry. Though classed as juvenile literature, this book and the other titles in the series are highly appropriate for adult readers.

*Skipper, G. C. *D-Day,* World at War series. Chicago: Childrens Press, 1982. [intermediate new reader]

One of a series of books about World War II, each of which discusses a particular aspect of that war, this book describes the Allied attack on the beaches of Normandy, begun on D-Day, June 6, 1944. It explains the extraordinary planning that preceded the attack and presents many details of the difficult and bloody battles that followed. The text is very informative, but also clear, authoritative, and highly readable. Numerous black-and-white photographs provide additional information and visual reinforcement.

*Warren, James A. *Portrait of a Tragedy: America and the Vietnam War.* New York: Lothrop, Lee & Shepard Books, 1980. [advanced new reader]

Warren presents a well researched, balanced, and clearly written account of the Vietnam War. He discusses the historical origins of the conflict and the social upheaval it caused at home, as well as the major events of the war itself. Intended for young adults, the tone and level of information make the book particularly appropriate for adult new readers as well.

Whittingham, Richard. *The White Sox: A Pictorial History.* Chicago: Contemporary Books, Inc., 1981. [advanced new reader]

A history of the Chicago White Sox in the twentieth century, this book offers a good balance of photographs and text, as well as a number of simple but readable charts and graphs. The book discusses major players, particular seasons, and world series games. (Books such as this one have been written for most major sports teams.)

7

Using Poetry with Adult New Readers

A complete poem is one where an emotion has found its thought, and the thought has found the words.[1]

Robert Frost

Adult new readers have a lot of catching up to do. Children who easily learn to read have been immersed in a world of language from infancy. Adults talk to them frequently. Parents or older siblings read to them from literature ranging from nursery rhymes to complex stories. The language that children hear is far more complex than the language they speak, yet they understand most of what they hear. This language-rich environment motivates children to read and enables them to do so with relative ease.

We cannot duplicate such an environment for adult literacy students. We can, however, expose students to as much good language as time and circumstances permit. Doing so may make the difference for the students between learning to read well enough to get by and being inspired to read from an ever-increasing range of choices.

Poetry uses the sounds, rhythms, and rich variety of language to express its meaning. Many poems written for adults also happen to be short and to speak directly to the reader. Using language that is relatively simple but precise, these poems tell stories, create images, and express feelings that engage adult readers. Literacy students, even beginning level readers, can read many poems. They can also understand and react to poems read to them. By listening to poetry, reading it, and writing poems of their own, adult literacy students can begin to experience good language well used, an experience all good readers and writers have at some point in their lives.

What Poetry Offers

The sound of language is a powerful force in our lives. Just think of nursery rhymes, for example. Children memorize phrases and rhymes almost without effort. Adults can often recall favorite phrases from their own childhood. Rhyme and rhythm please us and attract our attention to the words, even when we know the meaning is nonsensical. Who can ever forget "one, two, buckle my shoe" or ignore the inevitable delight that "patty cake, patty cake" elicits from a two-year-old?

The current popularity of rap music also demonstrates this power of language. Teenage rap singers, many of whom might be considered functionally illiterate in their classrooms, can command an audience of street kids with their recitations of long rhythmic verses. Like the epic poets of ancient civilizations, rap musicians use the rhythm of the rap and the thread of the story to carry them from one verse to the next.

Good poets use the compelling sound of language to do more than tell a story. Read aloud the poem that follows, and listen to how Maya Angelou uses rhyme and rhythm to make us feel the pain and the triumph of Willie.

Willie

Maya Angelou[2]

Willie was a man without fame
Hardly anybody knew his name.
Crippled and limping, always walking lame,
He said, "I keep on movin'
Movin' just the same."

Solitude was the climate in his head
Emptiness was the partner in his bed,
Pain echoed in the steps of his tread,
He said, "I keep on followin'
Where the leaders led."

I may cry and I will die,
But my spirit is the soul of every spring,
Watch for me and you will see
That I'm present in the songs that children sing.

People called him "Uncle," "Boy," and "Hey,"
Said, "You can't live through this another day."
Then, they waited to hear what he would say.
He said, "I'm living
In the games that children play.

"You may enter my sleep, people my dreams,
Threaten my early morning's ease,
But I keep comin' followin' laughin' cryin',
Sure as a summer breeze.

"Wait for me, watch for me.
My spirit is the surge of open seas.
Look for me, ask for me,
I'm the rustle in the autumn leaves.

"When the sun rises
I am the time.
When the children sing
I am the Rhyme."

Poetry also gives words to thoughts we can't articulate for ourselves. As Bill Moyers said in the introduction to his PBS television series on poetry, when we hear a poem that engages us, we say, "I know that, and didn't even know I knew it."[3]

Too many of us have been taught to read poetry as if we were solving a puzzle: What is the hidden meaning? What is the author really saying here? When that meaning is not apparent, we become discouraged and convinced that we just don't understand poetry. Or perhaps our introduction to poetry in school was filled with exercises about identifying metaphors and explaining symbolism, with no encouragement to simply listen to the poem and let the words affect our senses, our feelings, our imagination.

Poetry needn't be obscure or difficult. In fact, poems that describe commonplace events in simple yet original ways are among the most compelling. Using the language of kitchens and babies and the company of women, Lucille Clifton tries "to render big ideas in a simple way."[4] Read aloud the poem that follows, and listen to how Clifton uses images of everyday life to describe her relationship to each of her four daughters.

4 daughters
Lucille Clifton[5]

> i am the sieve she strains from
> little by little
> everyday.
>
> i am the rind
> she is discarding.
>
> i am the riddle
> she is trying to answer.
>
> something is moving
> in the water.
> she is the hook.
> i am the line.

Good poetry uses words selectively and precisely. Frequent reading of good poetry will give students an intuitive feel for the power of words. As students try to write their own poems, they will become more aware of and careful about the words they use. Their vocabularies and their understanding of words will grow because they are intently using language.

Poetry also deals with feelings, sometimes very strong feelings. Reading poetry can help us understand our own feelings as we recognize them in others. Writing poetry can help us confront our frustration, sorrow, anger, pride, love, and joy and use those feelings to create something tangible, perhaps even beautiful.

Writing poetry offers another advantage to adult literacy students. While some poetry adheres to strict conventions of meter and form, much contemporary poetry imposes no particular rules. Conveying meaning or feeling is the task of the poet, who can use words in any way he or she chooses to accomplish this task. In this free verse, rules of grammar and punctuation are stretched and bent to enhance the poet's message. Writing poetry in free verse provides students an opportunity to express ideas or tell stories without worrying about the conventions of correct writing. Not that those conventions are unimportant, but it's helpful for new writers to be able to concentrate on what they want to say without worrying about punctuation or grammar.

Poetry can awaken adult new readers to both the power and the beauty of language. It will give voice to ideas and feelings they recognize but cannot express. Poetry can nurture what Kenneth Koch calls "the imaginative intelligence."[6] It teaches students that through language they can communicate across time and distance with people they would otherwise never have the chance to know. Poetry will help adult new readers to understand themselves and others in deeper ways. This is one of the powers of language that excites good readers and brings them to read book after book. This is the kind of language we want to give our adult literacy students as they learn to read.

How to Teach Poetry

The thought of teaching poetry is a daunting one for a literacy teacher. Very few of us are familiar with poetry. For too many of us, the poetry we learned in school was either intimidating or not worth taking seriously. We did not learn to love poetry simply for its own sake.

For all the reasons cited in the previous section, however, poetry is worth teaching to new readers. But first, literacy tutors themselves need to become more familiar with poetry. The following sections present some suggestions for achieving this goal.

Do Some Background Reading

Literacy tutors should do some background reading about poetry and about teaching poetry. There are numerous books to choose from. An excellent example is Jack Collum's *Moving Windows: Evaluating the Poetry Children Write.* The fact that this book discusses children's poetry is really not important. What is important is the process. Collum presents some of the best poetry he has collected over his years of teaching, then offers his poet's perspective on what makes them good. As you read the poems and Collum's comments, you develop a feel for what works in a poem, for what makes it memorable or striking. This book teaches by example, not by explication. Collum doesn't tell you how to evaluate poetry. He just does it, and in observing the process you see a master poet and teacher at work, gaining a rare insight into the poet's mind as well as valuable experience to bring to your own teaching.

Kenneth Koch is another teacher and poet whose books will inspire you as they help you understand poetry. Koch has taught poetry to children, high school and college students, and nursing home residents, many of whom had little formal education. In each case he inspired reluctant students to read poetry, to write expressive poems of their own, and to enjoy the process. Koch's method is straightforward. He reads poems to his classes, talks in specific detail about why he likes the poems, generates discussions about the poems, then asks students to write their own poems, using those read as a kind of jumping-off point. As you read his accounts of his classroom experiences, you gain an understanding of what poetry is all about, as well as numerous practical suggestions to help you and your students enjoy reading and writing poetry.

These and other helpful books are listed in the resources at the end of this chapter.

Read Poetry Yourself

Read as much poetry as you can, which is the best way to become familiar with it. Browse through some of the anthologies recommended at the end of this chapter, or ask for suggestions from your librarian. Read in a relaxed way, out loud if at all possible. Don't get hung up looking for meaning. Just listen to the sounds and rhythms, and let the words affect your feelings.

When I first started thinking of poetry as reading material for new readers, I was not very familiar with the genre myself. I had a friend who was fond of quoting verses from the Irish poet William Butler Yeats, so I picked up a volume of Yeats's poems.

While some of the poems were obscure to me, many were haunt-
ingly beautiful. I found myself going back to read those poems
again and again, even memorizing some of them. I didn't always
understand them, but it didn't matter. I just loved the way the
words were put together. Although I didn't use any of those particular poems with my students, they were teaching me what
poetry was about.

Then I started reading from the works of Langston Hughes,
Robert Frost, Lucille Clifton, and a few others whose names I'd
heard. I began browsing the poetry shelves of the children's
section in the public library looking for poems that would be
suitable for adults. I found wonderful poems, many of which are
included in the anthologies listed at the end of this chapter. It was
very much a process of discovery. As I read the poems, certain
words or phrases or rhythms stayed with me and popped into my
mind days and weeks afterward. This is how I began to develop a
sense of what I really liked, and it was the poems I liked that I
decided to share with new readers. Following are a few examples
of short poems that I particularly like, and why:

Winter Moon
Langston Hughes [7]

How thin and sharp is the moon tonight!
How thin and sharp and ghostly white
Is the slim curved crook of the moon tonight!

I like the phrase "slim curved crook of the moon tonight!" It is
so simple, and yet in its simplicity it creates an exact picture of
a winter moon.

Dust of Snow
Robert Frost [8]

The way a crow
Shook down on me
The dust of snow
From a hemlock tree

Has given my heart
A change of mood
And saved some part
Of a day I had rued.

In this poem, Frost describes an experience we've all had, but he uses an image that is at once so apt yet so unexpected that it is arresting.

Young Woman at a Window
William Carlos Williams[9]

She sits with
tears on

her cheek
her cheek on

her hand
the child

in her lap
his nose

pressed
to the glass

This poem imprinted a picture on my mind as clear as a photograph or painting. Williams uses so few words, yet we see the woman and child clearly, and even have some sense of their feelings. It is an exquisite word picture.

By reading lots of poetry, you too will gain a sense of what poetry is about and of what you like. Then you can share those poems with your adult literacy students.

Read Poetry to Your Students

We all know that children love to be read to. It is part of a total immersion in language through which they learn to speak and ultimately to read and write. Adults like to be read to also, new readers and experienced readers alike. Poetry is meant to be read aloud. Reading poetry to your students encourages them to listen to language, a skill that will help them learn to read as surely as it helps children learn to speak.

Begin with poems you like. Don't restrict your selections to poems with words or ideas you are sure they will understand— you will miss too many good poems. Have you ever read the same book to a six-year-old and a three-year-old? Each one understands something about the story, although not necessarily the same thing. Good poems, like good stories, convey meaning on many different levels.

After you've read a poem, discuss it informally with your students. Ask if they liked the poem or not, and why. A response such as, "It just sounds nice," is acceptable. We often react to a work of art without being able to explain why. Try to draw out their responses by offering your own. Tell them why you chose the poem or why you like it. Be specific. Indicate particular words or phrases that you like. Describe the feelings or memories it inspires. By detailing your reactions, you are also telling the students what to look for in a poem, and helping them develop a feel for poetry. Such discussions can give students a much better understanding of poetry than formal lessons describing rhyme, meter, theme, or any other textbook element of poetry.

If the meaning is obvious to students, discuss it. But don't insist that they understand the meaning. Help students to relax and feel free enough to listen and enjoy, not to be anxious about picking out a word or meaning they will later be questioned about.

Eventually, the students' reactions will guide your choice of poems to read. As students express interest in a particular author, subject, or type of poem, search for poems you think they will enjoy. Again, don't be intimidated by length or sophistication of language when choosing poems to read to students. They understand complex language spoken to them, even if they cannot read equivalent language. Reference sources, such as *Granger's Index to Poetry* or *Index to Poetry for Children and Young People,* list poems by author and by subject. Or choose poems from the anthologies listed at the end of this chapter. Consulting these sources will lead you to many books of poetry to examine yourself and share with your students.

As soon as possible, encourage your students to read the poems, too. With beginning level students, start by reading a simple poem, such as Hughes's "Winter Moon," then have them read along with you, using the assisted reading technique, discussed in Chapter 3, if necessary. Encourage students to read on their own as soon as they are able. Ask students at higher skill levels to choose poems to read aloud to you, or set a time for you to read favorite poems to each other. Remember that poetry is as much an oral art form as a written one, so reading aloud is important to taking the full measure of the poem.

With beginning new readers, use the language experience technique, described in Chapter 3, to elicit responses. Have students dictate a reaction to the poem or describe an event the poem recalls. Write their comments, read them aloud, then help the students learn to read their own words. Ask more able students to write their own comments about a poem.

If you are working with a class, teachers Florence Howe and Barbara Danish suggest that you ask several students to read the same poem; then discuss the poem with the class after each reading. Each student will read differently, and the difference in emphasis or phrasing may evoke different responses or indicate alternate meanings. This practice helps students understand, in an intuitive way, that poems do not necessarily have one universally accepted meaning, but rather poems can have many different interpretations.[10]

Reading poems leads to many useful language lessons. Be cautious, though, about using the poems too mechanically. Don't just pick out obvious elements, such as rhyming words or words beginning with the same consonant. Any kind of writing offers opportunities for those exercises, but poetry is special. Talk about those elements of a poem that make it striking or funny or beautiful. Ask students to read phrases they like. Have students describe the pictures a poem creates in their minds or the feelings it elicits. Ask them if they agree with what the poet says. Suggest that students imagine what the poet was thinking or what his life was like or what he would be like if they met him today. Discuss the background of the poet or the historical events that figure in the poem. Questions such as these engage the students' minds and lead them to understand that reading has to do with meaning and ideas and the sound of language, not just with the mastery of skills.

Stretch students' understanding of the poems you read by finding information about the historical events or particular eras mentioned in poems of interest to them. Both the adult and children's collections of any public library will contain relevant material. Choose what is suitable and acceptable to your students.

If students are attracted to a particular poet, find some biographical information about that person. Many biographies have been written about famous poets such as Robert Frost or Langston Hughes. Some biographies will be found in the children's collection, though still suitable for adults. Information about lesser-known poets can be found in the library in resources such as *Contemporary Authors, Contemporary Poets,* or *Something about the Author.* Once you've found some information, read it to your students, then discuss how the poet's life may be reflected in his or her poetry.

Writing Poetry with Literacy Students

Not many people read poetry; even fewer write it. Is it realistic to think that adult literacy students can write poetry? That tutors who never thought of themselves as poets can teach them how? Absolutely!

First, consider the general principles that will help you teach students how to write poetry:

1. Have students write poems in the class or tutoring session, not at home, and read the poems aloud within the same class session to maintain interest and excitement.

2. Encourage students to write in their own words, their own voice, not in a language they may think of as poetic. As one elderly woman in poet Marc Kaminsky's class described her own poetry, "The wording is just the way I felt it. It's natural talk."[11]

3. Teach by example, not explanation. Students don't need textbook definitions of metaphors, similes, and other poetic elements to understand and appreciate many poems. As they become more proficient readers and writers, however, an understanding of the techniques of good writing will deepen their appreciation for poetry and improve their own writing. Help students discover the prevalent use of metaphor, for example, by having them read or listen to many poems containing metaphors, then asking them to pick out and discuss the comparisons used in those poems.

4. Give students concrete examples before asking them to write their own poems. For example, if you ask students to

describe a parent using specific details, give them some examples:

> I started to watch baseball games with my father when I was nine. Sometimes he gave me a sip of his beer.

> My grandmother used to answer the letters to Santa Claus that the neighborhood children wrote.

5. Write poems yourself. It will not be easy at first, but you will learn so much more from the process if you plunge in and do whatever you ask the students to do. Let them know that you are not an expert, that you have misgivings about your skill or about expressing your own thoughts. Share your successes and failures and any insights you gain from the experience.

6. When evaluating poems, offer positive comments, not corrections. All teaching requires a balance between encouraging students' efforts and helping them to improve those efforts. This is a particularly sensitive issue when the work in question is a form of creative, personal expression, such as a poem.

    Comment on what is good or what you like about the poem. Be specific. Praise poetic elements you hear in their words: precise details, vivid descriptions, appealing rhythms, unexpected twists of meaning, deep feelings, new ways to say something. By your comments and suggestions, you will teach them, without saying so directly, that these are the elements that catch a reader's attention and make a poem memorable. Then read the poem again so the students can hear it in light of your comments.

Following are some specific writing exercises to use with students. Try others that you devise as well, or, as students become more comfortable, ask them to suggest exercises.

SAMPLE POETRY ACTIVITIES

1. Write collaborative poems. Suggest a theme for the class, such as memories from childhood. Ask students to recall particular memories. As they respond, press them for specifics, such as the color of a room or the name of a street. Try to record at least one

memory from each student. The resulting poem will be a kind of montage of memories. Read the poem as a whole to the class.[12]

A collaborative poem is a good way of introducing students to the idea of writing. Since it is a group effort, no one feels too pressed, but everyone can share in the accomplishment. Adult Basic Education teachers can do this with their classes. Tutors working with one student can use a modified version in which you and the student each contribute alternating memories.

2. Suggest both a subject and a form. For example:

Write everything you can say about a color, putting the name of the color in every line.[13]

Write a poem in which every line begins with the same phrase, for example, "I remember..."[14]

Write a poem in which every line contains a contrast, for example:
I used to be..., but now...
I seem to be..., but really I am...
I wish..., but really...[15]

Giving students both subjects and forms in the early stages of their writing is particularly helpful because it provides them with good, evocative subjects, relieving them of the burden of finding their own, and it gives them a sense of what Koch calls the "slight arbitrariness of poetry," such as putting a color in each line.[16]

3. Suggest poems that describe specific things. Poet Richard Wilbur says of his own work that he likes to write about seemingly mundane things from a slightly different point of view or to describe something so accurately that you really get close to its essence.[17] Bring some objects to class—flowers, food, a piece of clothing, a work of art, anything you find interesting. Discuss Wilbur's goals for his poetry, then ask students to try to meet one of those goals by writing about the object on display. Encourage them to observe closely, to look at, touch, or smell the object as appropriate.

4. Suggest poems that recall memories of a specific time or event, such as the first jobs students ever had or the first time they ever drove a car. Remind them to give specific details, and not to talk in generalities.

5. Use music to spur imaginative poems. Play a piece of music that you like. Instrumental music is better than songs for this purpose.

Ask the students to close their eyes, listen closely, then write about what they see or feel.[18]

6. Use poetry ideas suggested by poems you like. Choose to read aloud poems that suggest a particular theme or follow a similar form. Then ask your students to write poems inspired by the ones you've read to them.

The sample lessons that follow suggest poetry ideas. Each lesson contains three to five poems reflecting aspects of an idea, followed by some discussion questions and suggested writing activities. The format for each lesson is the same:

Read the poems to your students.
Discuss the poems, asking questions similar to those suggested.
Introduce and explain the writing activity based on the poems.

Each lesson centers about a theme that the poems suggest in one way or another. As students talk about the poems, remember that there are no correct answers to the questions, nor are there single interpretations of the poems. Any response is a valid one, although it is instructive to probe your students a little—as far as they will let you—and ask them to support their reactions. Sometimes in such a discussion new ideas appear, or an initial response deepens into a perspective that was not apparent at first.

SAMPLE POETRY LESSON ON THE THEME OF FAMILY

The following five poems have to do with the general theme of family. In the first three, a parent is speaking to or about a child. In the second two, the poets recall their parents.

Because
Nikki Giovanni [19]

i wrote a poem
for you because
you are
my little boy

i wrote a poem
for you because
you are
my darling daughter

and in this poem
i sang a song
that says
as time goes on
i am you
and you are me
and that's how life
goes on

Discussion Questions

1. How would you describe the rhythm in this poem? What words or phrases give it rhythm? How do the rhythm and the meaning support each other?

2. How do you see your own children in yourself? Yourself in your children?

Response

Bob Kaufman[20]

for Eileen

Sleep, little one, sleep for me,
Sleep the deep sleep of love.
You are loved, awake or dreaming,
You are loved.

Dancing winds will sing for you,
Ancient gods will pray for you,
A poor lost poet will love you,
As stars appear
In the dark
Skies.

Discussion Questions

1. What particular lines or phrases do you like in this poem? Why do you like them?

2. Why do you think the poet calls this poem "Response"?

3. Who is the "poor lost poet"?

4. What repeating phrases give rhythm to the poem?

The Party
Reed Whittemore[21]

They served tea in the sandpile, together with
Mudpies baked on the sidewalk.
After tea
The youngest said that he had had a good
   dinner,
The oldest dressed for a dance,
And they sallied forth together with watering pots
To moisten a rusted fire truck on account of it
Might rain.

I watched them from my study,
Thought of my part in these contributions to world
Gaiety, and resolved
That the very least acknowledgment I could make
Would be to join them;
             so we
All took our watering pots (filled with pies)
And poured tea on our dog. Then I kissed the
   children
And told them that when they grew up we
   would have
Real tea parties.
"That did be fun!" the youngest shouted, and
   ate pies
With wild surmise.

Discussion Questions

1. How do you picture this scene in your mind? How old are the children? Are they boys or girls? What are they wearing? What words and phrases helped create this mental picture?

2. How would you describe the tone or voice of the poet?

3. What do you think the poet means by the last line, "With wild surmise"?

Writing Activities

Ask students to write a poem about their own children or about any child who is important to them. If they want to write a poem that describes a scene or event, remind students to include specific facts and details, such as the color of a dress or the flavor of cake that was baked, to help a reader get a clear mental picture of the event they are describing. If they plan to write a poem like "Response" or "Because," in which they imagine themselves talking to a child, encourage students to say something to the child, then allow their imaginations to carry that thought wherever it will go (as Kaufman does when he tells the child to sleep, then begins talking about the dancing winds and ancient gods and poor poets who will watch over her).

"Good Night, Willie Lee,
I'll See You in the Morning"
Alice Walker [22]

Looking down into my father's
dead face
for the last time
my mother said without
tears, without smiles
without regrets
but with *civility*
"Good night, Willie Lee, I'll see you
in the morning."
And it was then I knew that the healing
of all our wounds
is forgiveness
that permits a promise
of our return
at the end.

Discussion Questions

1. Upon hearing the title of this poem, what did you expect it to be about? Did your feelings and expectations change as you listened to the poem? How? Where in the poem did those changes occur?

2. "Good Night, Willie Lee, I'll See You in the Morning" is both the title and the central line of this poem. Try reading the poem through, leaving out the phrase Willie Lee. How does that change the rhythm and feel of the poem?

Those Winter Sundays
Robert Hayden[23]

Sundays too my father got up early
and put his clothes on in the blueblack cold,
then with cracked hands that ached
from labor in the weekday weather made
banked fires blaze. No one ever thanked him.

I'd wake and hear the cold splintering, breaking.
When the rooms were warm, he'd call,
and slowly I would rise and dress,
fearing the chronic angers of that house,

Speaking indifferently to him,
who had driven out the cold
and polished my good shoes as well.
What did I know, what did I know
of love's austere and lonely offices?

Discussion Questions

1. What are some things we know about this father? What specific words and phrases describe him?

2. Picture the house this boy and his father lived in. What does it look like? What words or phrases in the poem help you create this picture?

3. What does the poet know about his father's life now that he didn't understand as a boy?

Writing Activities

Ask students to write a poem based on a memory of one of their parents, a grandparent, or anyone who was special to them in their youth. Suggest that they be as specific as possible, using remembered bits of conversation or phrases often repeated, as Alice Walker does. Alternatively, encourage students to concentrate on one or two images, like Robert Hayden's father heating the house on cold mornings. Tell them not to actually describe the person but to try to give a sense of what the person was like by providing just a few descriptive details.

SAMPLE POETRY LESSON TO TELL STORIES OR CREATE WORD PICTURES

Some poems tell a story. Others create vivid word pictures. William Carlos Williams was a master at writing both kinds of poems. Following are three of his poems that illustrate that point.

This Is Just to Say
William Carlos Williams[24]

I have eaten
the plums
that were in
the icebox

and which
you were probably
saving
for breakfast

Forgive me
they were delicious
so sweet
and so cold

Discussion Questions

1. How do you think the poet feels about what he has done? Is he sorry? Would he do it again?

2. How would you react if you opened the refrigerator and saw the space where the plums should have been? Would this "note" alter your reaction?

Complete Destruction
William Carlos Williams[25]

It was an icy day.
We buried the cat,
then took her box
and set match to it

in the back yard.
Those fleas that escaped
earth and fire
died by the cold.

Discussion Questions

1. We all know we are going to die. Yet this poem startles us to attention and makes us think about this fact as if we didn't already know it all too well. How does Williams use words and set them up to make us think anew about a well-known fact?

2. Read "Complete Destruction" and "This Is Just to Say" aloud. How would you compare the tone of these two poems? What particular words or phrases do you think account for the difference in tones?

The Great Figure
William Carlos Williams[26]

Among the rain
and lights
I saw the figure 5
in gold
on a red
firetruck
moving
tense
unheeded
to gong clangs
siren howls
and wheels rumbling
through the dark city.

Discussion Questions

1. What feelings does this poem evoke? What specific words or phrases create those feelings?

2. How does the firetruck look in your mind's eye?

3. Why do you think the poet chose to put so few words—sometimes only one—on each line?

Writing Activities

1. Ask students to write a poem in which they tell a story, either something they did or something they observed. Reread Williams's two poems "This Is Just to Say" and "Complete Destruction" to them. Point out that although the poems are short, the poet chooses words with such care that a few simple words carry the story perfectly.

2. Students may choose to write a poem more like "The Great Figure," in which they create a word picture by describing some object or scene as precisely and vividly as they can. Again, encourage them to choose their words very carefully.

SAMPLE POETRY LESSON ON THE THEME OF LOVE

Following are three love poems. Love is one of those themes that is very difficult to write about because we tend to be too general or abstract, to say grand things. In two of these examples, the poets use ordinary objects to create vivid images of the love they feel. In the third, a simple conversation reveals the poet's feelings.

Juke Box Love Song
Langston Hughes[27]

> I could take the Harlem night
> and wrap around you,
> Take the neon lights and make a crown,
> Take the Lenox Avenue buses,
> Taxis, subways,
> And for your love song tone their rumble down.
> Take Harlem's heartbeat,
> Make a drumbeat,
> Put it on a record, let it whirl,
> And while we listen to it play,
> Dance with you till day—
> Dance with you, my sweet brown Harlem girl.

Discussion Questions

1. How would you describe the rhythm of this poem? What gives it this rhythm?

2. What particular words or images strike you? Why?

Scaffolding
Seamus Heaney[28]

> Masons, when they start upon a building,
> Are careful to test out the scaffolding;
>
> Make sure that planks won't slip at busy points,
> Secure all ladders, tighten bolted joints.

And yet all this comes down when the job's done
Showing off walls of sure and solid stone.

So if, my dear, there sometimes seem to be
Old bridges breaking between you and me

Never fear. We may let the scaffolds fall
Confident that we have built our wall.

Discussion Questions

1. What words would you use to describe the love this poet speaks of?

2. What connection do you see between the words that describe the poet's love and the words that describe the building?

He Said:
Alice Walker[29]

He said: I want you to be happy.
He said: I love you so.
Then he was gone.
For two days I was happy.
For two days, he loved me so.
After that, I was on my own.

Discussion Questions

1. How does the tone change in the last line of this poem?

2. What clues do you have to the poet's feelings about this situation?

Writing Activities

Suggest that students write a poem about love. Explain that they may choose to describe their feelings by using very concrete images, the way Hughes and Heaney do. Alternatively, they may want to write about a specific experience—the first person they loved, for example, or a love gone wrong. In either case, encourage students to be as specific as possible. For example, if students plan to write about a specific person, ask them to tell enough so that readers can picture the person or sense something about his or her personality. If students plan to describe a feeling, ask them to use words that will make the reader feel the same way the writer does.

Resources for Poetry Collections

Poetry and adult new readers belong together. The following re-sources offer simple, well-written poems appropriate for adults. Some of the books contain the works of one poet; others are collections of poems from several different writers. Many of the anthologies listed will be available at your public library. Those titles marked with an asterisk (*) may be found in the children's section of the library, although in many cases copies of the same title appear in adult collections. The illustrations, poems, and general appearance of all the books listed are suit-able for new readers. The range of poems contained within these anthologies is great. Some are very short; others may be as long as two pages. Some are very easy and can be read by beginning level students; others are more difficult and suitable for interme-diate or advanced new readers, or for tutors to read aloud to students.

At first, select poems that you like to read to your students, then follow their interests and tastes as you bring more poetry into your lessons. Let your students know that you are learning about poetry as well and that you are learning together. You will soon be teaching each other. Can you imagine a better way to enhance a student's self-esteem?

*Adoff, Arnold. *All the Colors of the Race: Poems*. Illus. by John Steptoe. New York: Lothrop, Lee & Shepard Books, 1982.

Written in the voice of a teenage girl who is the child of a black mother and a white father, these poems speak simply and directly about conflicting feelings of racial and individual identification. Adoff has written several other books of poetry that are also suitable for adults.

*_____, comp. *My Black Me: A Beginning Book of Black Poetry*. New York: E. P. Dutton, 1984.

Adoff is a prolific anthologizer as well as a respected poet in his own right. The poems in this collection present an excellent intro-duction to the work of many African-American poets. Other anthol-ogies compiled by Adoff include *Black Out Loud* (1970) and *Cele-brations* (1977), which is a much longer collection.

Angelou, Maya. *And Still I Rise*. New York: Random House, 1978.

Using vivid imagery and language that virtually sings, Maya An-gelou speaks of the joys and the pains of being black, being female, and being alive to the extraordinary possibilities of life. Other collections of her poetry include *I Shall Not Be Moved* (1990), *Just Give Me a Cool Drink of Water 'Fore I Diiie* (1971), and *Oh Pray My Wings Are Gonna Fit Me Well* (1975).

Bruchac, Joseph, ed. *The Light From Another Country: Poetry From American Prisons.* Greenfield Center, N.Y.: The Greenfield Review Press, 1984.

> Many of these poems have been published previously in various literary magazines. Each writer's work is introduced by a personal statement in which the writers talk about their lives, the experience of writing within the walls of a prison, and the sources of their inspiration. The poems range from easy to difficult and cover the gamut of emotions.

Clifton, Lucille. *Good Woman: Poems and a Memoir 1969–1980.* Brockport, N.Y.: BOA Editions, Ltd., 1987.

> With stunning insight and a masterful control of the language of everyday life, Clifton writes from her experience as daughter, wife, mother, grandmother, and black woman in America. This volume also contains a short memoir of her family. Clifton has published many other volumes of poetry, including *Next: New Poems* (1987) and *An Ordinary Woman* (1974).

Cole, William, comp. *Eight Lines and Under.* New York: The Macmillan Co., 1971.

> Writing short, incisive poems can be difficult, but the short poems in this collection hit the mark. The same editor has also produced *Poetry Brief.*

Evans, Mari. *Nightstar.* Los Angeles: Center for Afro-American Studies, University of California, 1981.

> In simple, direct language, Evans writes of her experiences as a black woman.

*Frost, Robert. *You Come, Too.* New York: Holt, Rinehart & Winston, 1959.

> Although intended for children, this collection of some of the easier works of one of the twentieth century's most prolific and best-known poets is highly suitable for adults.

Giovanni, Nikki. *Those Who Ride the Night Winds.* New York: William Morrow & Co., 1983.

> These poems about people who tried to change things are highly accessible to new readers. Other collections of Giovanni's work include *Cotton Candy on a Rainy Day* (1978) and *The Men and the Women* (1973).

*Hopkins, Lee Bennett, comp. *A Song in Stone: City Poems.* Photographs by Anna Held Audette. New York: Thomas Y. Crowell, 1982.

The vitality of city life comes sharply into focus in this brief collection of twenty poems, matched with photographs that are themselves evocative works of art. A simple but lovely book.

*_____. *On Our Way: Poems of Pride and Love.* New York: Alfred A. Knopf, 1974.

Each poem in this lovely collection is accompanied by a striking black-and-white photograph that helps elucidate and extend the poem. Although the introduction indicates that it is a book intended for children, nothing about its very appealing format and simple but thought-provoking poems would deter adult readers.

*Hughes, Langston. *Don't You Turn Back.* Selected by Lee Bennett Hopkins. Woodcuts by Ann Grifalconi. New York: Alfred A. Knopf, 1978.

A good representative collection of the poems of this prolific African-American poet.

_____. *The Dream Keeper.* New York: Alfred A. Knopf, 1937.

An excellent collection of poems, some lyrical, some thought-provoking, some blues-like, some speaking of the black experience, some universal in theme, and all enhanced by the simple beauty of the black-and-white woodcuts.

_____. *The Panther and the Lash.* New York: Alfred A. Knopf, 1987.

These powerful poems derive from Hughes's experiences as a black man in America, growing up in segregation and participating in the burgeoning civil rights movement.

*Jones, Hettie, comp. *The Trees Stand Shining: Poetry of the North American Indians.* Paintings by Robert Andrew Parker. New York: Dial Press, 1971.

The poems are actually traditional songs gathered from various tribes. The paintings have a folklike quality that complements the poems beautifully.

*Larrick, Nancy, comp. *Crazy to Be Alive in Such a Strange World.* New York: M. Evans & Co., 1977.

Larrick is a prolific and skillful anthologizer. This selection of poems reveals fascinating variety among the people with whom we share this life. Both the poems and the accompanying photographs are appropriate for adult new readers.

*_____. *On City Streets.* New York: Bantam Books, 1968.

Selected with the assistance of schoolchildren in New York City, these poems speak in the varied voices of city life. Most of the poems were originally written for adults, and the black-and-white photographs accompanying the poems add to the book's appeal to an adult new reader audience.

*_____. *Room for Me and a Mountain Lion.* New York: M. Evans & Co., 1974.

Larrick has gathered poems about living in or finding inspiration from open spaces. As with *On City Streets,* the poems were selected with the help of schoolchildren, but the poems and photographs are highly appropriate for adults.

*Livingston, Myra Cohn, comp. *A Tune Beyond Us.* New York: Harcourt, Brace & World, 1968.

Livingston is another anthologizer whose many wonderful collections are geared to children but often work with adult new readers. In this book she has gathered some excellent poems, including some translated from languages other than English.

*Moore, Lilian, comp. *Go with the Poem.* New York: McGraw-Hill Book Co., 1979.

Contemporary in spirit, this collection, aimed at "middle graders" according to the jacket description, offers a good range of subjects, styles, and levels of difficulty. Both content and appearance are appropriate for adult new readers.

*_____. *I Thought I Heard the City.* New York: Atheneum, 1969.

In this collection of her own work, Moore has written very simple poems that speak about bridges and pigeons and rooftops and other common sights that define city life.

*_____, and Judith Thurman, comps. *To See the World Afresh.* New York: Atheneum, 1974.

Believing that the need "to see the world afresh" is an urgent one in today's society, the compilers have chosen works that help us look at the ordinary and familiar in new ways. This well-chosen and thought-provoking collection is highly suitable for adult new readers.

*Morrison, Lillian. *Sidewalk Racer and Other Poems of Sports and Motion.* New York: Lothrop, Lee & Shepard, 1977.

For sports enthusiasts, whether doers or spectators, this collection offers amusing comments—some wry, some lighthearted—on sports activities of all kinds.

Niatum, Duane, comp. *Carriers of the Dream Wheel: Contemporary Native American Poetry.* New York: Harper & Row, 1975.

The beauty and poignancy of the Native American experience is captured in the interplay of the illustrations and the poetry of sixteen poets. This title is the fifth in a series of such works published by Harper & Row.

*Plotz, Helen, comp. *The Gift Outright.* New York: Greenwillow Books, 1977.

The poems in this collection describe America as an idea and a dream. Some poems focus on individuals, both the famous and the unknown, others reflect on historical events, while others offer personal responses to America. The collection is well suited to adults.

*_____, comp. *Poems of Emily Dickinson*. Drawings by Robert Kipniss. New York: Thomas Y. Crowell, 1964.

    The choice of poems and the simple appealing artwork make this collection of Dickinson particularly suitable for adult students.

Sandburg, Carl. *Honey and Salt*. New York: Harcourt Brace Jovanovich, 1953.

    This Sandburg collection includes some difficult poems, but in a number of memorable short poems Sandburg muses about love and the meaning of life.

*_____. *Rainbows Are Made*. Selected by Lee Bennett Hopkins. San Diego: Harcourt Brace Jovanovich, 1982.

    Much of Sandburg's poetry evokes the prairies and growing cities of midcentury middle America, but it does so without sentimentality and often with the sting of wit and social protest. This is an excellent selection of Sandburg's poems, well suited to adults.

Smith, William Jay, comp. *A Green Place*. New York: Delacorte Press, 1982.

    This substantial collection of modern poetry, frequently used in college classes, contains many simple but good poems within reach of adult new readers.

Walker, Alice. *Good Night, Willie Lee, I'll See You in the Morning*. New York: The Dial Press, 1979.

    Walker speaks in a strong clear voice of her experiences as a woman and an African American. Other collections of her poems include *Horses Make a Landscape Look More Beautiful* and *Revolutionary Petunias*.

*Worth, Valerie. *Small Poems*. Pictures by Nancy Babbitt. New York: Farrar, Straus, 1972.

    Worth gives us simple but perceptive poems drawn mostly from nature. Similar books are *More Small Poems* and *Still More Small Poems*.

Resources for Teaching Poetry

Bernhardt, William F. *Granger's Index to Poetry*. 9th ed. New York: Columbia University Press, 1990.

    This reference indexes thousands of poems by subject and helps readers locate specific poems in anthologies that will be generally available in most public libraries.

Collum, Jack. *Moving Windows: Evaluating the Poetry Children Write*. New York: Teachers and Writers Collaborative, 1985.

Drawing on his many years of experience teaching poetry to children, Collum offers numerous examples of children's poetry as well as comments on what makes particular poems work. As we read, we observe a master poet and teacher at work and learn more about poetry than textbooks can possibly explain.

Hopkins, Lee Bennett. *Pass the Poetry, Please.* Rev. ed. New York: Harper & Row, 1987.

Bennett, who has compiled many poetry anthologies, offers suggestions for bringing poetry to young people that can be adapted to working with adult new readers.

Kaminsky, Marc. *What's Inside You It Shines Out of You.* New York: Horizon Press, 1974.

The author writes of his experiences conducting a poetry class among senior citizens in New York City. Many of his students were immigrants and lacked formal education, but Kaminsky believed that reading good poetry to them would help them express their own feelings and ideas more clearly. His enthusiasm for poetry and for reading of all kinds is inspiring, and his practical suggestions of activities to help students appreciate and create poetry will be very useful to adult literacy tutors.

Kazemek, Francis, and Pat Rigg. "Four Poets: Modern Poetry in the Adult Literacy Classroom." *Journal of Reading* 30 (Dec. 1986): 218–225.

The authors discuss how the poetry of Lucille Clifton, Langston Hughes, Carl Sandburg, and William Carlos Williams can help adult literacy students use language creatively.

Koch, Kenneth. *I Never Told Anybody: Teaching Poetry in a Nursing Home.* New York: Random House, 1977.

Koch, who is a poet himself, describes how he taught poetry to a group of nursing home residents. The author's faith in the power of poetry was affirmed by the moving and heartfelt poems that many of his students wrote. All his books offer numerous insights into poetry as well as practical suggestions for teaching students not accustomed to reading and writing poetry.

_____. *Rose, Where Did You Get That Red? Teaching Great Poetry to Children.* New York: Random House, 1973.

Believing that teaching children only simple, childish poems means giving them "nothing to understand they have not already understood," Koch set out to stretch his young students' minds by teaching them great poetry, mostly written for adults. The power and complexity of the poetry generated by the students in return affirmed his belief. Many of the techniques described can be used with adult new readers.

_____. *Wishes, Lies and Dreams: Teaching Children to Write Poetry.* New York: Random House, 1970.

   Koch outlines his methods for teaching children to write poetry. The comments he offers on the poems the children write provide insights into what poetry is all about.

_____, and Kate Farrell. *Sleeping on the Wing: An Anthology of Modern Poetry with Essays on Reading and Writing.* New York: Random House, 1981.

   The authors present several works of some important modern poets, along with some facts and comments about each poet's life to help the reader better understand the poetry. Writing in a style that is friendly and informal, Koch and Farrell guide the reader to a recognition that poetry is both wonderful and accessible to all who are willing to approach it with an open ear and a willing heart.

Vinson, James, and D. L. Kirkpatrick, eds. *Contemporary Poets.* 4th ed. New York: St. Martin's Press, 1985.

   This book contains brief biographies of living poets and a list of their published works.

Weibel, Marguerite Crowley. *The Library Literacy Connection.* Columbus, Ohio: The Department of Education and the State Library of Ohio, 1984.

   This work introduces the idea of using simple poetry written for adults with beginning level literacy students.

8

The Uses of Literature

> ... the terrible isolation of the nonreader, his life without meaning or substance because he cannot comprehend the world in which he lives.[1] John D. MacDonald

The first literacy student I ever met came to our literacy program because of the television miniseries, "Roots." She had been so moved by the story of many generations of slaves and their descendents traced into the twentieth century that she wanted to read the book for herself.

Alex Haley's best-selling book, on which the television series was based, tells two stories. One is the story of Haley's ancestors; the other is an account of how he learned that story. Haley recalls his grandmother telling stories about her ancestors, including one Kunta Kinte, who was captured by slave hunters when he left his West African village to look for wood to make a drum. Growing up, Haley longed to know more about the people his grandmother spoke of. When he finally got a chance to travel to Africa, the names and the few African words he remembered from his grandmother's stories helped him follow a trail that eventually led to a small village in Gambia. There he met the village historian who recited from memory the long history of the village's ancestors, including the story of one Kunta Kinte who disappeared from the village while out looking for wood to make a drum. That fragment of a story made the connection that enabled Haley to trace the path of Kunta Kinte and his descendants, all the way to the grandmother he had known.[2] By telling his own story, Haley inspired our literacy student, and many other readers and viewers, to embark on a similar quest for their family stories.

Human beings crave stories. We want to hear the stories of our ancestors to learn where we've come from. We want to tell our own stories to share the events and feelings of our lives. Stories of people living in different places and in different times offer us some escape from the routine of everyday life and help us understand more about ourselves than our own immediate circumstances can teach us.

The literature of any culture tells these stories. Whether the stories are real or imaginative, they reveal some truth about the lives of the people who inhabit that culture. Stories help us to understand ourselves and our neighbors, to know our past and to imagine our future. All of us, including adult new readers, need access to the treasure of human experience contained in literature.

The Oral Tradition

For centuries, literature has passed from one generation to the next through the oral tradition, that is, through spoken language and long memory. In the ancient world, Homer and others recited long and complex tales that entertained their listeners and acquainted them with the history and legends of their ancestors. These storytellers skillfully used rhyme, meter, repetitive verses, and developing plot to help them remember the stories they told. They held positions of respect in their communities, because they were the repositories of communal history. Only many years later were these ancient stories written down as *The Iliad* and *The Odyssey* and other classic stories that remain central to Western culture.

The oral tradition remains alive and vital, even in our contemporary society. One of the most telling examples of this oral tradition lies in the story of the magazine *Foxfire*. In the 1960s,

Eliot Wigginton, a teacher in Rabun County, Georgia, sent his high school students to interview folks who had lived in that rural region all their lives. The stories, songs, recipes, and folklore the students collected were printed in a literary magazine called *Foxfire*. Wigginton hoped this exercise would inspire his reluctant students to take more interest in their own learning. He succeeded beyond his wildest dreams. Collecting the stories of their community and writing them in *Foxfire* made the tasks of education meaningful and exciting to these students. But *Foxfire* affected more than the students who created it. The magazine became the pride of the whole community, captured the attention of folklorists at the Library of Congress, and drew acclaim from writers and educators the world over. It continues to be published, and it still proclaims the treasure of stories held by a people considered disadvantaged by sociologists and illiterate by educators.[3]

Roots, The Iliad, The Odyssey, and *Foxfire* are examples of stories, poems, and folklore that were preserved and passed down through an oral tradition and only written as literature years after their original telling. One of our ultimate goals in literacy education is to enable adult new readers to read the heritage of our culture contained in its literature. When students begin literacy instruction they cannot read well enough to do this, so we need to find ways to introduce them to the world of literature while they are learning the skills that will eventually enable them to read on their own. Applying some of the lessons learned from cultures that rely on an oral tradition is one way to introduce new readers to the power and the importance of literature.

Our literacy students have stories to tell—stories about their own lives and about the communities they live in. These stories, as poet William Carlos Williams said, are "what we all carry with us on this trip we take, and we owe it to each other to respect our stories and learn from them."[4] By inviting new readers to tell their own stories, we invite them into the world of literature.

With beginning new readers, we can start with the language experience technique, a method of teaching reading that invites adult literacy students to tell stories about their experiences, their families, their feelings, hopes, and dreams. Initially, students read only their own stories. But we can expand this technique by having students share their stories with other students and perhaps with the community at large.

Many libraries and literacy programs have developed means to collect and share the stories of their students. Some programs, for example, bind their students' stories together in a book to be shared by all students or to be sold to other literacy programs. An excellent example is the series *New Writers' Voices,* anthologies of stories written by new readers and published by the Literacy Volunteers of New York City. This series is listed in the bibliography at the end of this chapter.

Other programs have embarked on ambitious oral history projects, reaching out beyond the literacy program into the culture of the wider community. The Columbus Metropolitan Library sponsored such a project, known as "Blackberry Patch." The Blackberry Patch was a poor but vibrant neighborhood in Columbus, Ohio, in the 1920s and 1930s. Although the neighborhood no longer exists as it did then, many of its residents still live nearby. Library personnel requested information from former residents and others who remembered stories about the Blackberry Patch. On several occasions, librarians invited these folks to gather at the library to tell their stories and sing their songs to an audience. Later, many of these stories were collected in a book titled *Beyond Poindexter Village: The Blackberry Patch.* Following is an example of one of those stories:

The Rag Man

When the "rag man" called out "Iron, rags, glass," the people knew that they could exchange things for money. For days, they would carry buckets around the neighborhood. They would put any rags, any iron scraps, any large pieces of glass into their buckets. When the "Rag Man" came, they would empty their buckets into his cart. Then he would give them money—dimes, quarters, some pennies. This man was in the business of recycling many years ago.[5]

Sharing their own stories and those of others in their community through language experience and oral history projects such as Blackberry Patch is a wonderful initiation for new readers into the world of literature, the world of storytelling. But literacy students will eventually want to read stories that take them beyond their own experiences. To grow in their literacy, new readers need to enter other worlds, to read about lives and cultures different from their own. They also need, as they expand their language capabilities, to be exposed to the broader vocabulary, varying sentence structures, and different writing styles found in good literature.

The Written Word

Public libraries house a treasury of literature to share with adult literacy students. There are stories, poems, collections of letters, newpaper columns, and numerous other materials that tutors can read aloud to students in classes or in one-on-one tutoring sessions. There are numerous crossover books that may be classed as children's literature, young adult literature, or high interest/easy reading books, although they are highly suitable for adults. And there is literature written at varied reading levels that will be accessible to more advanced students reading independently. In these days of heightened awareness of the problems of illiteracy, there is also literature written specifically for adult new readers (see Chapter 10). The present chapter, however, emphasizes books and resources not commonly recommended for adult literacy students.

Literature to Read Aloud to Literacy Students

As stated earlier, it is not too late for adult new readers to listen to good literature read aloud and to glean from that reading some understanding of the uses of language, just as children do. Familiarity with the sounds of written language and the ability to imagine a scene or a character, understand relationships, follow sequences, draw conclusions, and make predictions are enhanced through listening to a story read aloud. Students will need these skills when they read stories to themselves, and the practice gained through listening to stories will help advance students toward independent reading.

Collections of short stories, newspaper columns, interviews, letters, or speeches offer numerous read-aloud possibilities. These pieces are short enough to be read in one or two class sessions, and their brevity may entice reluctant readers to read independently some of the pieces they enjoyed listening to.

Following is a sample from a fascinating book of interviews collected during the Depression by writers working for the Federal Writers' Project. The book, called *First-Person America*, is a kind of oral history of life in the United States just before World War II. This piece was written by May Swenson, from an interview with a young man employed at Macy's department store in New York City:

> There's a supervisor to each floor, who's generally snooping around hoping to catch you loafing on the job. Mostly the workers call them "supers"; when I was there, we called them "snoopers." One super we had was a tough guy. He had a voice like a dog's bark and he was proud of the way he could lash speed out of the boys picking stock. One Christmas, we all chipped in and bought him a horse whip, one of those old-fashioned ones. He must have caught on to the idea O.K. because he came back after the holidays with a pretty sour face, and gave us tougher treatment than before.[6]

Studs Terkel is a master interviewer who has created several books from the words of ordinary people. By letting the workers tell their own stories in his book *Working*, Terkel presents a vivid and insightful picture of Americans at work. Following is an excerpt from an interview with a sanitation worker:

> In this particular neighborhood, the kids are a little snotty. They're let run a little too loose. They're not held down the way they should. It's getting a little wild around here. I live in the neighborhood and you have to put up with it. They'll yell while you're riding from one alley to another, "Garbage picker!" The little ones usually give you a highball, seem to enjoy it, and you wave back at 'em. When they get a little bigger, they're liable to call you most anything on the truck. (Laughs.) They're just too stupid to realize the necessity of the job.[7]

Reading sections or excerpts from longer works of literature will acquaint new readers with the works of good writers that they may eventually seek out for independent reading. Collections of such excerpts, specifically chosen for new readers, are published in the series *Writers' Voices*. These attractive paperback volumes are published by the Literacy Volunteers of New York City. (See the Resources for Tutors and Librarians at the end of this chapter for additional information about obtaining this series.)

When choosing books to read to your students, don't worry about reading level. Choose stories that reflect students' interests as well as works that will challenge their thinking, even if at first glance the books seem difficult. Marc Kaminsky demonstrates this point tellingly in his book, *What's Inside You It Shines Out of You.* He tells of his experience conducting a poetry class with senior citizens. Most of Kaminsky's students were immigrants with little experience with school or formal learning. He read to them from Loren Eiseley's *The Immense Journey,* a book which discusses the origins of life and which is found on many college reading lists. Kaminsky read a passage describing the emergence of fish from the familiar environment of water into the totally different environment of land. The fish struggled, but ultimately survived and thus expanded the possibilities of life. Such a reading may sound esoteric and inappropriate for this audience, but it led to discussions of faith and open-mindedness, of Genesis vs. Darwin, and of the difficulty and the importance of being an immigrant (looking at the fish as "immigrant") as so many of the group participants were. Although the book was well beyond the group's reading level, it was not beyond their level of understanding. Kaminsky believed that good literature had the power to captivate his audience, and the spirited discussion and inspired poetry that followed the reading proved him right.[8]

Initially, you will choose most of the books, short stories, magazine articles, or sections of books that you read to your students. Encourage them to express their opinions about the readings. Offer your own views as well. When students feel comfortable discussing the readings and recognize that their opinions matter, they will voice their opinions more freely. Eventually, they will suggest topics or even specific books they wish to hear.

Regardless of who chooses the books, it is wise to read them yourself before you read them aloud. Knowing the mood and style of a piece of writing, as well as specific details to come, will make your oral reading smoother and more pleasing to the audience. It will also help you avoid potentially embarrassing situations. Good literature is not bland. Some books describe circumstances or use language not acceptable to everyone. Choose books that you and your listeners will be comfortable with.

Crossover Books

Numerous works of literature fall into the category of crossover books. These are books that may be found, variously, in the adult collection, the young adult collection, collections of high interest/easy reading books, and sometimes in the children's collection. In many instances, multiple copies of one title will be shelved in several locations within a library because of the book's broad appeal. All of the crossover books, however, by virtue of their subject matter, writing style, depth of information, overall appearance, even size, are appropriate for adults. One example is a book classified as children's literature called *The Black Americans: A History in Their Own Words,* by Milton Meltzer. It is a collection of the words of black people—some famous but many unknown—reflecting life from the days of slavery through the urban problems of the early 1980s. One section is an excerpt from the autobiography *Narrative of the Life of Frederick Douglass.* It begins like this:

> Very soon after I went to live with Mr. and Mrs. Auld, she very kindly commenced to teach me the A, B, C. After I had learned this, she assisted me in learning to spell words of three or four letters. Just at this point of my progress, Mr. Auld found out what was going on, and at once forbade Mrs. Auld to instruct me further, telling her, among other things, that it was unlawful, as well as unsafe, to teach a slave to read.[9]

James Baldwin's *If Beale Street Could Talk* is a title recommended in many "high/low" lists, yet I found it in the undergraduate library of a major university. It is an extraordinary love story told in the voice of a pregnant teenage girl. The language is simple, and yet it conveys the hopes and fears and yearnings of two young people who are so much the products of their environment and yet so much like all of us. In this brief excerpt, Tish describes a visit with her boyfriend, who is in jail:

> He's in jail. So where we were, I was sitting on a bench in front of a board, and he was sitting on a bench in front of a board. And we were facing each other through a wall of glass between us. You can't hear anything through this glass, and so you both have a little telephone. You have to talk through that. I don't know why people

always look down when they talk through a telephone, but they always do. You have to remember to look up at the person you're talking to.

I always remember now, because he's in jail and I love his eyes and every time I see him I'm afraid I'll never see him again. So I pick up the phone as soon as I get there and I just hold it and I keep looking at him.

So, when I said, "—Alonzo—?" he looked down and then he looked up and he smiled and he held the phone and he waited.

I hope that nobody has ever had to look at anybody they love through glass.[10]

Literature to Foster Independent Reading

As literacy students move through the intermediate and advanced levels and beyond, they become increasingly able to read on their own. This is a crucial time in their literacy development, a time when they know *how* to read but are not necessarily frequent or enthusiastic readers. It is a time when many students have mastered the basic skills of reading but have not yet incorporated reading into the routine of their everyday lives. At this stage, literacy students need to be convinced of the power of literature by reading books that offer an escape from the boredom of a routine job or allow a vicarious experience of conflicts that, even though they are not real, are so much like the conflicts they feel themselves. They need to discover books that amuse and entertain, books that teach and inspire.

Librarians are particularly important to new readers at this turning point in students' literacy development. In their traditional role as readers' advisors, librarians connect a diverse population of readers with appropriate books. Librarians are uniquely able to perform this task because they know the books in their collections. Of course, librarians have not read every book, but it is their job to know about books, to read book reviews and consult bibliographies, and to think about the books in their libraries in terms of the readers who read them. Furthermore, since libraries keep books long after they have faded from popular or commercial memory, librarians can suggest books no longer in print and often forgotten in our culture's eager embrace of the new. Using these skills, librarians can play the pivotal role in bringing adult literacy students—poised on the verge of becoming real readers—together with a vast collection of literature.

Connecting new readers with books is a particularly important role for librarians to play with students who are no longer in a literacy program. Students who have reached the level of advanced new reader have moved beyond one-to-one tutoring sessions, perhaps to high school equivalency classes or community college programs. Many former literacy students will not be in any formal education programs at all. But if they continue to come to the library and see the librarians as their reader-advisors, they will continue to read and to increase the depth of their literacy.

Any library's collection contains works of literature accessible to literacy students who are reading independently. Some now-classic works of adult fiction, such as Ernest Hemingway's *The Old Man and the Sea* or John Steinbeck's *Of Mice and Men,* are powerful stories written for adults in a style and language that are accessible to advanced new readers. Many libraries actually have multiple copies of these titles, shelving one with adult fiction, another in a young adult collection, and perhaps a third in a section designated "high interest/low reading level" books.

New readers who have reached the stage of advanced new reader or beyond are ready to experience one of the great joys of reading: placing yourself in the hands of a skillful writer who vividly creates another world, stealing you away from the ordinary for however long a time you will allow. As adult new readers gain skill and confidence, they will become more comfortable with higher level books and with language that is laced with images and metaphors. This high level skill grows over time and through a great deal of reading. Not all literacy students will reach this point, but for those who do, the library will have many books to lead them on their journey to mature literacy. New readers may not consciously recognize all the intricate uses of language in the more difficult books they read, at least not at first, but they will be engrossed by a good story, well told.

In the two examples that follow, the scenes, the writers, and the stories they tell are very different. However, as they begin their stories, each writer draws a compelling scene that captivates readers and leads them eagerly into an unknown but enticing world.

In her memoir *All God's Children Need Traveling Shoes*, Maya Angelou recalls the years she lived in Africa, thinking that there she would find home. The opening paragraph sets the scene for the whole book: Africa, an air of mystery, the excitement of adventure, and the uncertainty of the traveler.

> The breezes of the West African night were intimate and shy, licking the hair, sweeping through cotton dresses with unseemly intimacy, then disappearing into the utter blackness. Daylight was equally insistent, but much more bold and thoughtless. It dazzled, muddling the sight. It forced through my closed eyelids, bringing me up and out of a borrowed bed and into brand new streets.[11]

Pete Hamill's novel *The Gift* describes a Christmas when a young man returns home after his first months away in the Navy. It is a story of family and neighborhood, of love lost and greater love found, and of a young man's coming of age. As he stands at the tollbooth of the Jersey Turnpike waiting for a bus, the young sailor recalls an earlier Christmas.

> It began somewhere else, in some other year, in a place thick with steam. I was sure of that. I slept on a couch in an aunt's house in Bay Ridge, eight years old, and it was the first time I had ever seen a radiator. The steam sprayed itself upon the windows in the deep winter night, and when I awoke, I thought it was the snow come at last, the White Christmas that Bing Crosby had promised, or the Christmas of horse-drawn sleighs, trees with serrated bark, children with heavy wool mufflers bundled against the cold, and all the fine-drawn English faces I had seen in the dank-smelling bound volumes of the *St. Nicholas* magazine in the public library on Ninth Street. But mine was no greeting-card Christmas, and there was no snow; only steam, forced from the radiator, glazing the window of that strange house, like the breath of an old and very fat man. Standing on the Jersey Turnpike, I remembered that Christmas, my mother gone to the hospital, and no word from my father, no touch of his rough beard, his slick black hair, his hoarse voice.[12]

All good teaching requires a balancing act. We want our students to read good books. But we are facilitators in this process, not censors or critics. We want to root learning experiences in the immediate needs and interests of the students, but we also have a responsibility to expose them to ideas and perspectives beyond their current experience and to books that are well written and provide models for the many uses of language. Ultimately, the choice is always the reader's, but if, as librarians and tutors, we have done our job well, then we will have prepared a bountiful environment and given the students sufficient skill to make their choice from a rich collection of possibilities.

In an essay in the *New York Times* Pete Hamill vividly describes how the public library opened up a world of possibilities to him as a boy growing up amid the poverty and angers of postwar Brooklyn. Out on the street, Hamill says, he consumed the popular culture of his day: comic books, radio and movie serials, and the kind of boys' books not found in the library. He was "swept away by the primary colors of melodrama." But in the library he began to glimpse a different world. He says, "The library took that instinct for the lurid and refined it." In the library Hamill discovered adventurers and revolutionaries, poetry and the varied uses of language, exotic places he longed to visit, and books that were themselves beautiful works of art. "I went to the library in search of entertainment," says Hamill, "and discovered the world." [13]

Adult literacy students need to become acquainted with good literature. Read aloud to students at every class or tutoring session, even if only for brief periods. Invite a local librarian to talk about works of literature from the library's general collection that will appeal to literacy students reading independently. Invite students to participate in book discussions, to write reviews of books, or to prepare lists of good titles to share with other libraries and literacy programs. There are literally hundreds of possibilities for you and your students to discover in the library.

Resources of Literature for Adult Literacy Students

The following bibliography suggests works of literature suitable for adult new readers. Some of the titles are particularly good for reading aloud; others are within reach of intermediate and advanced new readers reading independently. I've suggested several older books to give you some idea of what is available but no longer popular. Several titles may be shelved in special collections such as those for young adults or for reluctant readers. Ask your librarian about any other potential sources of reading material for adults available in your local library.

Angelou, Maya. *All God's Children Need Traveling Shoes.* New York: Random House, 1986. [advanced new reader]
This volume of Angelou's autobiography presents a picture of Africa in the 1960s as seen through the eyes of a keen and intelligent observer. A story about a black American woman's search for home and for identity, it is also the universal story of each individual's attempt to understand his or her unique place in the world. Other volumes in Angelou's autobiography are: *I Know Why the Caged Bird Sings* (1970), *Gather Together in My Name* (1974), *Singin' and Swingin' and Gettin' Merry Like Christmas* (1976), and *The Heart of a Woman* (1981).

_____. *Conversations with Maya Angelou.* Ed. by Jeffrey M. Elliot. Jackson, Miss.: University Press of Mississippi, 1989. [advanced new reader]
Maya Angelou, a writer of enormous and varied talent, is an inspiration to many. This collection of newspaper columns and interviews is arranged chronologically from 1971 to 1987. It gives readers some insight into the events and influences that shaped this woman who grew up poor and black in the segregated American South to become an artist acclaimed around the world for the exquisite beauty and humanity of her work.

Aurandt, Paul. *Paul Harvey's "The Rest of the Story."* Garden City, N.Y.: Doubleday & Co., Inc., 1977. [intermediate new reader]
This collection of broadcaster Paul Harvey's radio shows can help win literacy students to the practice of listening to stories. Each brief piece tells a little-known part of the story of someone famous, living or dead, but doesn't reveal the name of the person until the end. Once listeners get the pattern, they will also enjoy trying to figure out who the subject is. Subsequent editions also have been published.

Baldwin, James. *Go Tell It on the Mountain.* New York: Grosset & Dunlap, 1952. [intermediate new reader]
Focusing on three generations of a family, Baldwin paints a vivid portrait of one Sunday in the life of the congregation of a fundamentalist church in Harlem.

_____. *If Beale Street Could Talk.* New York: New American Library, 1974. [advanced new reader]
Tish, pregnant and 19, and Fonny, 22 and in jail, discuss their problems and their dreams in this extraordinary love story.

Banks, Ann, ed. *First Person America*. New York: Alfred A. Knopf, 1980. [intermediate/advanced new reader]

Gathered by writers working for the Federal Writers' Project during the Depression, these oral histories give brief accounts of the lives of pioneers, miners, meat packers, factory workers, and other laborers. The short pieces are good for reading aloud and for sparking a discussion about the conditions of working people at that time in our history.

Bradbury, Ray. *The Illustrated Man*. Garden City, N.Y.: Doubleday & Co., Inc., 1951. [advanced new reader]

This is a collection of eighteen science fiction short stories inspired by the numerous tattoos covering the body of "the illustrated man."

Breslin, Jimmy. *The World According to Breslin*. New York: Ticknor & Fields, 1984. [advanced new reader]

In his newspaper columns for *The New York Daily News,* Breslin writes about the street kid or the celebrity in a way that connects to all of us. His narrative is straightforward and carries the force of truth, humor, and compassion.

Collier, James Lincoln, and Christopher Collier. *My Brother Sam Is Dead*. New York: Scholastic Inc., 1975. [advanced new reader]

Set during the American Revolution, this novel tells the story of a family divided by differing loyalties. Like all good historical fiction, it helps us see the complexity and feel the human anguish of a war most of us know only as an important but impersonal event in our nation's history.

Craven, Margaret. *I Heard the Owl Call My Name*. Toronto: Clark, Irwin, & Co., Ltd., 1967. [advanced new reader]

A young minister with two years to live is sent to work among the Indians of the Canadian Northwest. He shares the pain of a dying Indian culture and learns not to fear his own death.

Frank, Anne. *Anne Frank: The Diary of a Young Girl*. Trans. B. M. Mooyaart. Garden City, N.Y.: Doubleday & Co., Inc., 1967. [advanced new reader]

This is the translated diary of a young Dutch girl who lived in hiding from the Nazis for two years during World War II. Frank's adolescent yearnings and her indomitable spirit have captured the minds and hearts of readers for several decades.

Fulghum, Robert. *All I Really Need to Know I Learned in Kindergarten*. New York: Villard Books, 1988. [intermediate/advanced new reader]

Fulghum has the gift of seeing the little twists and quirks that turn seemingly mundane circumstances into a good story. The brief observations offered here are funny and wise, written by a man who obviously cares about the people and places around him.

Gaines, Ernest J. *Autobiography of Miss Jane Pittman*. New York: Bantam Books, 1971. [intermediate new reader]

Written in the guise of tape-recorded recollections of a 110-year-old black woman, this story, the basis of a popular TV show, is one of endurance and of dignity. It personalizes history from the days of slavery to the civil rights movement of the 1960s.

Georgia Writers' Project. *Drums and Shadows*. Athens, Ga.: The University of Georgia Press, 1986. [advanced new reader]

Compiled during the Depression by the Georgia Writers' Project, this unusual book is a collection of photographs and oral histories of the people, many descended from slaves, who lived in the coastal regions of Georgia.

Greene, Bob. *American Beat*. New York: Atheneum, 1983. [advanced new reader]

Greene is a syndicated columnist whose work appears in many newspapers and magazines. A few of the people described in these short selections are famous, but most are ordinary folks whom Greene has discovered in an unusual moment, such as the ladies' room attendant in a fancy night club who sings her heart out after the club is empty or the girl who held a party to celebrate a wedding that didn't happen. These are good stories to read aloud and to inspire literacy students to write about people they have known. *Cheeseburgers* is a similar collection by the same author.

Hamill, Pete. *The Gift*. New York: Random House, 1973. [advanced new reader]

Written from the perspective of twenty years after the fact, this brief novel recalls the Christmas when a seventeen-year-old sailor returned home to Brooklyn after his first months in the Navy. Amid Irish saloons, old songs, and the friends of his old gang, he loses his girl but finds his father. In an almost cinematic re-creation of a particular time and place, Hamill expresses the yearnings for identity, understanding, and love that we all feel throughout our lives.

————. *The Invisible City: A New York Sketchbook*. New York: Random House, 1980. [intermediate/advanced new reader]

Being neither journalism nor short stories, the sketches were written quickly against newspaper deadlines. They highlight brief personal moments in the lives of ordinary people—moments of loss and loneliness, of joy and triumph.

Hemingway, Ernest. *The Nick Adams Stories*. New York: Chas. Scribner's Sons, 1978. [intermediate new reader]

This collection arranges chronologically stories that were originally published separately. The stories explore many themes of
growing up as they follow Nick from boyhood to manhood. The
prose is simple, but rich.

_____. *The Old Man and the Sea.* New York: Chas. Scribner's Sons,
1952. [intermediate new reader]

This short novel, which tells the story of a Cuban fisherman who
kills and then loses a giant marlin, has become a classic of American
literature.

Hentoff, Nat. *Jazz Country.* New York: Harper & Row, 1965. [advanced
new reader]

When a white teenage boy tries to break into the black world of
jazz, he learns a lot about himself and about the world beyond his
own environment.

Hoffman, Nancy, and Florence Howe, comps. *Women Working: An
Anthology of Stories and Poems.* Old Westbury, N.Y.: The Feminist
Press, 1979. [beginning–advanced new reader]

This collection includes some poems brief enough for beginning
level new readers, as well as longer stories and personal statements
that provide good material for reading aloud or reading independently. The topic centers around women and work of all kinds—work
that is uplifting and transforming, and work that is oppressive. It is a
very thought-provoking book.

Lipkin, Catherine, and Virginia Solotaroff, eds. *Words on the Page,
the World in Your Hands.* New York: Harper & Row, 1990. [inter-
mediate/advanced new reader]

This wonderful three-volume anthology of poetry and prose written by established authors such as Garrison Keillor, Nikki Giovanni,
and E. L. Doctorow was compiled specifically for adult literacy students. An accompanying teacher's manual includes discussion questions and lesson plans.

Meltzer, Milton. *The Black Americans: A History in Their Own
Words.* New York: Harper & Row, 1984. [advanced new reader]

Using letters, diaries, and other primary source materials, Meltzer
has created a powerful statement on the history of blacks in America
from the days of slavery to the urban distress of modern society.

_____. *Underground Man.* Scarsdale, N.Y.: Bradbury Press, 1972.
[advanced new reader]

Using actual letters, court records, and broadsides from the time,
Meltzer tells the story of a runaway slave who crosses back into slave
territory to save others.

Ravitch, Diane. *The American Reader: Words That Moved a Nation.*
New York: HarperCollins Publisher, 1990. [intermediate/advanced
new reader]

In this lively and informative collection of documents, speeches, poems, songs, and illustrations, we find the well-known words of famous Americans such as Jefferson and Lincoln, as well as the writings of ordinary people whose names we may not remember but whose words and actions altered the flow of history. Chosen for their readability and for their historical significance, these selections review American history and literature from our earliest settlers to the 1980s. Many entries are short and can easily be read aloud, offering adult literacy students, eager to catch up on the information they missed in school, a chance to learn about and discuss people, events, and issues essential to our national identity.

Schulman, L. M., sel. *The Random House Book of Sports Stories.* Illus. by Thos. B. Allen. New York: Random House, 1990. [advanced new reader]

The stories in this collection cover several sports including baseball, basketball, and tennis, and are written by the likes of James Thurber, Roger Angell, and Jack London. Many of the stories are good for reading aloud.

Spielberg, Steven. *Close Encounters of the Third Kind.* New York: Dell, 1977. [advanced new reader]

This science fiction story describes an attempt to communicate with extraterrestrial beings through the medium of music. Spielberg also wrote and directed the popular movie of the same name.

Steinbeck, John. *Of Mice and Men.* New York: Bantam Books, 1965. [intermediate new reader]

Loneliness and friendship among homeless men is a topic as timely today as it was when this story was first published more than fifty years ago. Several other Steinbeck stories are also simply but beautifully written and have become American classics. They include: *The Red Pony, The Pearl,* and *Tortilla Flat.*

Terkel, Studs. *Working.* New York: Pantheon Books, 1974. [intermediate new reader]

In this collection of interviews ordinary people talk about what they do all day and how they feel about what they do. Entries are short, but each contributes to an overall sense of working America more descriptive than any statistical or sociological study. Terkel has compiled other collections of interviews including *Hard Times,* about the Depression, and *"The Good War"* about World War II.

Wigginton, Eliot, ed. *Foxfire 9.* Garden City, New York: Anchor Press, Doubleday & Co., Inc., 1986. [intermediate/advanced new reader]

Like the eight volumes that came before it, this volume is a collection of stories, recipes, photographs, and rural folklore from the hills of Georgia that were first published in *Foxfire* magazine. The stories are fascinating in themselves, but they also serve as a model for the kind of oral history that many adult new readers may collect from their own neighbors and relatives.

Resources for Developing Literature Collections

The following books provide information about using works of literature with adult literacy students.

LiBretto, Ellen V., comp. and ed. *High/Low Handbook: Encouraging Literacy in the 1990s.* New York: R. R. Bowker, 1990.
   Although this book is intended for teachers, librarians, and others working with reluctant teenage readers, the discussions on evaluating and selecting books can also be helpful to anyone working with adult new readers. The well-annotated bibliography of books for reluctant readers contains many potential crossover titles that may be suitable for some adult literacy students.

Literacy Volunteers of New York City. 121 Ave. of the Americas, New York, NY 10013.
   This adult literacy program publishes two series: *Writers' Voices,* a series of slim, attractive paperbacks containing selections from the works of writers such as Tom Wolfe, Ann Tyler, Ray Bradbury, and Alex Haley, and *New Writers' Voices,* a collection of the works of literacy students. Write to the above address for a catalog and ordering information.

National Council of Teachers of English. Committee to Revise High Interest-Easy Reading. *High Interest Easy Reading.* 5th ed. Urbana, Ill.: NCTE, 1988.
   This bibliography lists more than 400 books recommended for reluctant readers in junior and senior high school. The list contains many crossover titles that may appeal to adults. The annotations are informative, and the categorizations by easily understood terms, such as war experiences, ethnic experiences, and technology, are particularly helpful.

Ryder, Randall J., et al. *Easy Reading: Book Series and Periodicals for Less Able Readers.* 2d ed. Newark, Del.: International Reading Association, 1989.
   This is a bibliography of book series written for reluctant middle and high school students and adult literacy students. The introductory chapter discusses questions of readability and interest level.

Using the Children's Collection

I read [to my children] because *my* father had read to *me*.
And because he'd read to me, when my time came I knew
intuitively there is a torch that is supposed to be passed
from one generation to the next. And through countless
nights of reading I began to realize that when enough of
the torchbearers—parents and teachers—stop passing the
torches, a culture begins to die.[1]

Jim Trelease

I had tutored adult literacy students for several years before I
thought of using selected materials from the children's department of the library. I had assumed, as many tutors do, that books
from the children's collection were simply not appropriate for
adult new readers. Once I began examining the possibilities,
however, I discovered that many children's books are not just for
children.

The collection of children's literature in any public library
offers a rich resource to be mined for adult new readers. There
are books that offer appealing illustrations, interesting stories,
and informative text, some of which are appropriate for readers
of all ages and some of which can be used with literacy students
participating in a family literacy program.

Using books from the children's collection with adult new
readers obviously requires tutors and librarians to be sensitive
to the feelings and circumstances of the students. Tutors can
show students a range of books they have preselected from the

children's collection, then talk about the books with the students and ask them to choose any they wish to read. If the students are receptive, the tutor can offer to find other appropriate books. Some students may want to select books together with their tutors, although, at least initially, many students may prefer not to go into the children's department of the library.

The following discussion centers around children's books for readers of all ages and books to use in a family literacy program.

Children's Books for Readers of All Ages

Many works of children's literature, by virtue of their artistic and literary quality, appeal to readers of all ages. Some are picture books that combine beautiful illustrations with good descriptive writing to tell their stories with vivid words and images. Others are collections of poems that, in many cases, were originally written for adults but happen to be simple enough for children to enjoy. (Several were suggested in Chapter 7.) Some children's books recall history or explain natural or scientific concepts in clear, simple language, language not obviously directed to children as its intended audience. (Several were suggested in Chapter 6.) Still others are biographies of popular entertainers or easy-to-read adventure stories meant to appeal to reluctant readers. In recent years, a resurgence of interest in children's literature as an art form as well as the efforts of publishers seeking to attract reluctant readers have greatly increased the number of well-written children's books that will appeal to readers of all ages. A list of suggested titles of children's books for readers of all ages appears in the resources at the end of this chapter.

Children's Literature for Family Literacy

One of the most encouraging developments in literacy education in recent years is the increasing emphasis placed on family literacy programs. Recognizing that children are less likely to learn to read if they grow up in a household where adults do not read for themselves or to the children, family literacy programs teach adult new readers, who also happen to be parents, grandparents, or adults attached to children in some way, to learn to read books they can then read to the children in their lives.

As C. S. Lewis, who wrote for both children and adults, once said, "I am almost inclined to set it up as a canon that a children's story which is enjoyed only by children is a bad children's story."[2] In fact, many books written for children are beautiful works of art—of language and of illustration—that appeal as much to the adult who reads them aloud as to the child who listens. Quality children's literature, like all good literature, operates on multiple levels. Children may enjoy a book on the surface level, as a good story, but adults see beyond the surface and appreciate such things as historical references, the ambiguous meaning of certain words, an ironic or witty line, or the rhythm and appeal of language well used. Children's books of quality are written to be shared by adults, who appreciate their beauty, and children, who eagerly enter the imaginative world that stories create.

Let's look at a few "classics" from the children's shelf to see what makes them powerful books and perennial favorites with children and adults alike.

Children's literature is not bland. It deals with powerful and complex emotions. It uses art to elicit a range of reactions, from nostalgia to fear. The large looming ogres who cavort with Max, the naughty boy in Maurice Sendak's *Where the Wild Things Are,* are startling—even frightening. But they also strike a familiar chord with all children who have experienced the conflicting emotions of growing independence. The reassuring conclusion brings relief to young listeners, even as it makes them eager to turn back to the beginning and visit the "Wild Things" once again.[3]

The language in good children's literature is usually simple and spare but never simplistic or condescending. It fits the situation. In Robert McCloskey's *Make Way for Ducklings,* Michael, the policeman, "raised one hand to stop the traffic, and then beckoned with the other, the way policemen do."[4] *Beckoned* is not an easy word for beginning readers, but the text is accompanied by an illustration of Michael beckoning to the ducks that is both charming and completely illustrative of this unusual word (for children). No other word would fit the story so well.

Children's literature also exploits the sounds of language and the interaction of descriptive writing with appealing artwork. In *Mr. Gumpy's Motor Car,* by John Burningham, two children and several animal friends go for a ride on a spring day. When the car gets stuck in the mud, the passengers reluctantly get out to push. "They pushed and shoved and heaved and strained and gasped and slipped and slithered and squelched."[5] These are clearly difficult and unfamiliar words for early readers, but the illustrations leave no doubt about their meaning and the barrage of verbs underscores the climax and moral of the story, adding just the right touch of humor. Simpler words would diminish the story's impact.

Reading books together, children and adults share more than a story. They share a physical warmth and closeness, and, however briefly, they enter a different world together. They "share a frame of reference," as Dorothy Butler says in her book, *Babies Need Books.* Because of this shared experience, "incidents in everyday life constantly remind one or the other—or both simultaneously—of a situation, a character, an action, from a jointly enjoyed book, with all the generation of warmth and well-being that is attendant upon such sharing."[6] Reading aloud to children helps establish a pattern of discussion and communication between adult and child, a pattern that may lead to discussions of real-life problems as well as those found in books.

Reading aloud to children is also fundamental to the development of literacy in the young. Children who are read to early and frequently are more likely to become good readers themselves. If adult new readers cannot read to their children, they miss that opportunity for closeness that reading together can bring, and they also endanger the literacy development of their children.

A desire to read to their children brings many adults into a literacy program. Family literacy programs capitalize on this desire by helping new readers read books they can subsequently read to their children. The number of family literacy programs has increased significantly in recent years. Services offered in such programs will vary from site to site, but, in general, they offer some combination of tutoring for adults, advice on how to stimulate a child's interest in reading, and numerous opportunities for adults and young children to come together for story hours and related activities.

Family literacy programs vary in setting also. The public library is obviously a wonderful place to accommodate a family literacy program, and several libraries have done so. One example is the family literacy program of the Napa City–County Library of Napa, California. As part of its family literacy program, this library has produced a manual for tutors and students. One section of the manual offers information on the stages of child development and suggests many activities for parents who want to encourage the intellectual growth of their children. Another section, directed at tutors, suggests activities to help literacy students encourage reading in their children. A third section provides numerous activities to reinforce the skills both literacy students and their children are learning. This library-based family literacy program has also prepared bibliographies recommending titles of children's literature useful in family literacy programs.[7]

Not all family literacy programs are in libraries, although they all take advantage of the resources offered by the library. The Family Reading Project of Chester, Vermont, for example, sponsored by the Vermont Council on the Humanities, engages parents and other interested adults in discussions of children's literature. The goal of this project is to encourage adults to read to children and to talk with them about what they read. A theme is chosen for each series of discussions. Three books at three different reading levels are suggested. In the discussions, a local scholar relates the theme to the three books in an interactive discussion with participants who are recruited from the general public as well as through the Vermont Adult Basic Education program, so discussion groups include a mix of new readers and persons already literate.[8]

Adult new readers who participate in a family literacy program learn to share books with children and enjoy the physical and emotional closeness that such sharing can bring. As literacy students improve their own reading skill, they provide a model for learning and reading that can help their own children break out of the cycle of illiteracy. The wealth of children's literature available at any public library will support family literacy programs. The resources section at the end of this chapter lists many titles useful for family literacy programs.

Resources of Children's Literature for Readers of All Ages

Librarians might consider purchasing an additional copy of books such as the following to shelve with a new readers' collection.

Ancona, George. *The American Family Farm: A Photo Essay by George Ancona.* Text by Joan Anderson. San Diego: Harcourt Brace Jovanovich Publishers, 1989. [intermediate/advanced new reader]

This pictorial essay on the American family farm focuses on three families living on three types of farms: a dairy farm in Massachusetts, a chicken farm in Georgia, and a hog farm in Iowa. Large black-and-white photographs and an engaging narrative pay realistic tribute to the farming life.

Angelou, Maya. *Now Sheba Sings the Song.* Illus. by Tom Feelings. New York: E. P. Dutton/Dial Books, 1987. [intermediate new reader]

In this intensely sensuous poem, Angelou celebrates the power, beauty, and spirit of black women. Feelings's sepia-toned drawings match the poem beautifully.

Baylor, Byrd. *The Way to Start a Day.* Illus. by Peter Parnall. New York: Chas. Scribner's Sons, 1978. [beginning new reader]

With poetic text and vivid illustrations, the author and illustrator combine to describe how people from many cultures celebrate the sunrise. The rituals all reflect an attitude that sees human beings living in rhythm with nature's patterns. Other works by this author and illustrator will also appeal to many adults.

————. *When Clay Sings.* Illus. by Tom Bahti. New York: Chas. Scribner's Sons, 1972. [intermediate new reader]

In this unusual book Baylor tells the story of American Indian children who find pieces of pottery from generations past and imagine the lives of the people who made and used them. The colors, designs, and motifs are common to pottery of southwestern peoples. The text suggests a belief in the interdependence of people and nature.

Baynes, Pauline, illus. *Noah and the Ark.* New York: Henry Holt & Co., 1988. (Text from the Revised Standard Version of the Bible) [beginning/intermediate new reader]

Many adult new readers are familiar with the Bible; some even know stories and verses by heart. Books such as this one provide the opportunity for new readers to read in print words they have known and loved for years. Baynes's lovely illustrations accompany the standard Biblical text, with no additional text. Middle level students can read the text on their own, or tutors can read the text to beginning students interested in biblical stories.

Berger, Melvin. *Disease Detectives*. New York: Thomas Y. Crowell, 1978. [advanced new reader]

Berger tells the story of the search for the cause of Legionnaires' disease. He discusses the work of various scientists and physicians involved and describes the role of the Centers for Disease Control in Atlanta. The book is informative as well as suspenseful. Although the appropriate medical or scientific terminology is used, all terms are always explained clearly. Black-and-white photographs of scientists at work provide additional information and add to the appeal of the book.

Bryan, Ashley, sel. and ed. *Walk Together, Children*. New York: Atheneum, 1982. [beginning/intermediate new reader]

This collection of the words and music for several American spirituals, accompanied by lovely woodcuts, is a wonderful book for any students who know or enjoy these beautiful songs. A second volume, titled *I'm Going to Sing,* is also available.

Carlisle, Norman, and Madelyn Carlisle. *Bridges*. Chicago: Childrens Press, 1982. [beginning new reader]

One of the New True Book series, this book explains the history of bridges and describes all the major types. As with other books in this series, it is clearly and simply written, is illustrated with good color photographs, and includes a glossary and index.

Coucher, Helen. *Antarctica*. New York: Farrar, Straus & Giroux, 1990. [beginning new reader]

In the strange and beautiful land of Antarctica, penguins and seals raise their young. But danger lurks everywhere, especially from the intrusion of humans. With beautiful illustrations depicting the simple text, Coucher makes a powerful statement about the interdependence of all creatures.

Fleishman, Paul. *Rondo in C*. Illus. by Janet Wentworth. New York: Harper & Row, Publishers, 1988. [beginning new reader]

As a young piano student plays Beethoven's "Rondo in C," each member of the audience is stirred by a different memory.

Foreman, Michael. *War Boy: A Country Childhood*. New York: Arcade Publishing, 1989. [intermediate new reader]

Foreman, who grew up in England during World War II, draws his own illustrations to accompany his memories of a bomb coming through his roof, of the tragedies and triumphs among his small-town neighbors, of the great excitement among the boys and young ladies when the "Yanks" came to town, and of the "war games" he and his friends delighted in playing, even after a terrifying night in the air raid shelter. Although classed as children's literature, the funny, touching, and sometimes irreverent stories in this rather long book will easily appeal to adults.

Greenfield, Eloise. *Daydreamers.* Illus. by Tom Feelings. New York: Dial Press, 1981. [beginning new reader]

This book is one poem about daydreamers—children caught in a still moment of thoughtfulness. Tom Feelings's muted drawings convey the mood of contemplation and childlike hope perfectly. Children may well enjoy this book, but adults will really appreciate the beautiful mingling of art and language that expresses a yearning only adults can feel when looking at children.

Hamilton, Virginia. *The Bells of Christmas.* Illus. by Lambert Davis. San Diego: Harcourt Brace Jovanovich Publishers, 1989. [intermediate new reader]

A black family, living along the National Road in Ohio in 1890, gathers to celebrate Christmas in the tradition of the times. (Hamilton has written numerous books for children and young adults, many of which will be suitable for adults.)

Harvey, Brett. *Immigrant Girl: Becky of Eldridge Street.* Illus. by Deborah Kogan Ray. New York: Holiday House, 1987. [intermediate new reader]

The time is 1910. The situation is that of a young Jewish girl seeking refuge on the Lower East Side of New York City from the persecutions in Russia. But the crowded living conditions, adjustment to a new language, taunts of other children, labor troubles, and dependence of the family on each other are circumstances as common to present-day immigrants as they were to earlier generations.

Horwitz, Joshua. *Night Markets: Bringing Food to a City.* New York: Thomas Y. Crowell, 1984. [intermediate new reader]

Horwitz chronicles an unknown side of New York night life: the markets and workers that supply fresh food to stores and restaurants every day. Descriptive black-and-white photographs accompany a clearly written text set in large, easy-to-read type.

Huff, Barbara A. *Greening the City Streets: The Story of Community Gardens.* Photographs by Peter Ziebel. New York: Clarion Books, 1990. [intermediate new reader]

Huff tells the hopeful story of the many community gardens springing up in vacant lots in some of our most depressing urban areas. More than a story of growing food and pretty flowers, it is a story of courage and optimism, of people struggling to gain control of their environment and make productive and beautiful use of once-abandoned land.

Hutton, Warwick. *Jonah and the Great Fish*. New York: Atheneum, 1983. [intermediate new reader]

Watercolors add beauty and dramatic effect to this simple retelling of the biblical story of Jonah and the whale. (This author/illustrator has produced other illustrated versions of biblical tales.)

Isadora, Rachel. *Ben's Trumpet*. New York: Greenwillow Books, Inc., 1979. [beginning new reader]

With striking black-and-white illustrations reminiscent of the art deco period, Isadora tells the story of a young black boy who dreams of being a jazz trumpeter.

Langstaff, John, sel. and ed. *What a Morning! The Christmas Story in Black Spirituals*. Illus. by Ashley Bryan. New York: Margaret K. McElderry Books, 1987. [beginning new reader]

Biblical quotations declaring the birth of Jesus are matched with black spirituals proclaiming the same story. Brilliantly colored paintings illustrate each entry. This is a simple book; anyone who knows the stories of the Bible or who enjoys black spirituals will recognize the words in the limited text.

Lawrence, Jacob. *Harriet and the Promised Land*. Verses by Robert Kraus. New York: Windmill Books, Simon & Schuster, 1968. [beginning new reader]

In dramatic illustrations and simple verse, Lawrence and Kraus tell the story of Harriet Tubman, who led many slaves to freedom.

Lessac, Frané. *Caribbean Canvas*. New York: J. B. Lippincott, 1987. [beginning–advanced new reader]

This beautiful book is a collection of paintings by the Caribbean artist Frané Lessac. The paintings are bright with tropical colors and almost folklike in their portrayal of life on a small tropical island. Poems and proverbs from Caribbean writers accompany each painting. Some are hard to read because of the unique dialect, others are simple. This is a book that students can look at many times over, seeing different things each time. It could be an inspiration for language experience stories, writing exercises, or perhaps just a conversation about individual perspectives on beauty.

Locker, Thomas. *Family Farm*. New York: Dial Press, 1988. [intermediate new reader]

In this story, a threatened farm family finds a creative way to stay solvent for yet one more year. The luminous, museum-quality oil paintings that illustrate this very contemporary story remind us that the struggle to work the land is an old and noble one. Part of the proceeds of this book go to Farm Aid.

McGovern, Ann. *Black Is Beautiful*. Photographs by Hope Wurmfield. New York: Four Winds Press, 1969. [beginning new reader]

Photographs showing black objects from nature and black people engaged in everyday life cover a range of subjects and emotions. Brief poems refer indirectly to each picture, leaving plenty of room for the reader's own thoughts.

O'Kelley, Mattie Lou. *From the Hills of Georgia: An Autobiography in Paintings*. Boston: Little, Brown & Co., 1983. [intermediate new reader]

Each page presents a painting of folk artist Mattie Lou O'Kelley accompanied by a remembrance in the artist's words of the event on which the painting is based. Words and pictures together create a lyrical portrait of childhood in the hills of rural Georgia.

Patterson, Francine. *Koko's Kitten*. Photographs by Ronald H. Cohn. New York: Scholastic Inc., 1985. [intermediate new reader]

Patterson tells the intriguing and true story of a gorilla who learned to communicate with her keeper through sign language. The gorilla developed a deep attachment to a little kitten, and when the kitten was killed, the gorilla used sign language to express much grief and sadness.

Peet, Bill. *Bill Peet: An Autobiography*. Boston: Houghton Mifflin Co., 1989. [intermediate new reader]

In words and pictures, Peet tells about his early interest in drawing, his work for the Walt Disney studios, and his later career as writer and illustrator of children's books. This is a fascinating life story, told with humor and grace.

Pienkowski, Jan. *Easter*. Text from the King James Version of the Bible. New York: Alfred A. Knopf, 1989. [beginning–advanced new reader]

The illustrations in this book are silhouette figures on watercolor-wash backgrounds set within gilded borders, creating a dramatic and opulent effect. Pienkowski has also created a companion volume, *Christmas*.

Robbins, Ken. *Bridges*. New York: Dial Books, 1991. [intermediate new reader]

With beautiful, hand-tinted photographs and clear text, Robbins helps us see the beauty of form and function welded together in all kinds of bridges.

Rylant, Cynthia. *Soda Jerk*. Illus. by Peter Catalanotto. New York: Orchard Books, 1990. [intermediate/advanced new reader]

This book is a collection of rhythmic, unrhymed poems written in the voice of a teenage boy working at a small-town soda fountain. Everyone who comes into the store comes under the boy's scrutiny. He is a keen observer, sufficiently detached to see the small details

that make an individual unique while retaining the kindly accep-
tance of a still-hopeful adolescent.

Schroeder, Alan. *Ragtime Tumpie*. Illus. by Bernie Fuchs. Boston:
Little, Brown & Co., 1989. [intermediate new reader]

This fictional story is based on the life of Josephine Baker, who
grew up amid the poverty of St. Louis in the early 1900s and yearned
to build a life in the world of ragtime and jazz. The text and illustrations ring with the warmth and rhythm of their subject.

Segal, Lore. *The Book of Adam to Moses*. Illus. by Leonard Baskin.
New York: Alfred A. Knopf, 1987. [advanced new reader]

In this thoughtful translation of the first five books of the Bible,
the text is simplified somewhat to accommodate early readers, but a
sense of the beauty and precision of biblical language remains.

Siebert, Diane. *Heartland*. Illus. by Wendell Minor. New York: Thomas
Y. Crowell, 1989. [intermediate new reader]

Siebert's poem sings of the beauty, simplicity, and power of nature
as seen in the farming heartland of America. Minor's bright, realistic
paintings convey the clarity and cyclical nature of farming life. This
is an exquisite collaboration between writer and artist, who have also
produced *Mojave,* celebrating the vast California desert.

Sills, Leslie. *Inspirations: Stories About Women Artists*. Niles, Ill.:
Albert Whitman & Co., 1989. [intermediate new reader]

This book profiles four artists: Georgia O'Keeffe, Frida Kahlo, Alice Neel, and Faith Ringgold. The text briefly discusses each artist's
life, emphasizing the events and influences that affected her artistic
development. Representative pieces of each artist's work are reproduced in color.

Thurber, James. *The Last Flower*. New York: Harper & Row Publishers,
1939. [intermediate new reader]

Subtitled "A Parable in Pictures," this story, written just before the
outbreak of World War II, uses simple but telling words to warn of the
dangers of war and destruction and remind us of the fragility of life
on Earth.

Walker, Alice. *To Hell with Dying*. Illus. by Catherine Deeter. San
Diego: Harcourt Brace Jovanovich, 1988. [intermediate new reader]

Recalling a story from her childhood, Walker tells of Mr. Sweet, an
old man often on the verge of dying who could be revived by the
attention she and her brother gave him. A powerful story of the
passions, pain, and joy of life, it also reminds us of the gifts that the
old can give the young, and what the young can give back in return.
Beautiful illustrations, one per page, convey the story and its emotional depth very well.

Resources of Children's Literature for a Family Literacy Program

There are easily hundreds of books that can be used in a family literacy program. The titles suggested here as a sample are grouped according to general format or purpose of the books, in part to give tutors and students a sense of the range of types and topics available in this rich genre of literature.

First Books

Using few words, these books present objects and concepts drawn from the everyday life of babies and toddlers. Some are published on sturdy card stock. The bright colors and simple drawings or photographs are designed to appeal to children just learning to differentiate the sights and sounds of their environment.

Barton, Byron. *Machines at Work.* New York: Thomas Y. Crowell, 1987. [beginning new reader]

    Each page pictures a construction truck accompanied by a 3- or 4-word sentence explaining its function. The illustrations are large, bright, and simple. Barton has produced several good books for children.

Crews, Donald. *Light.* New York: Greenwillow Books, 1981. [beginning new reader]

    From sunset to sunrise, the city is never dark. Crews takes readers on a tour of the city to see all kinds of lights, one on each page, described by two or three words. Crews has produced other simple but beautiful books, including *Freight Train.*

Hoban, Tana. *Red, Blue, Yellow, Shoe.* New York: Greenwillow Books, 1986. [beginning new reader]

    This very simple book presents one object and one color on each page, in card stock format. Hoban, a master photographer, has published many simple books for children, all of which are a delight to the eye.

Krementz, Jill. *Jack Goes to the Beach.* New York: Random House, 1986. [beginning new reader]

    Bright photographs show a family at the beach, doing all the things families at the beach do. There is one sentence for each activity. *Lily Goes to the Playground* is a similar book by Krementz.

Mealtime. Look at Me series. New York: Dutton's Children's Books, 1991. [beginning new reader]

Produced on card stock, this book presents color photographs of toddlers in high chairs eating what toddlers eat and using all the equipment familiar to young families. Other titles in the series include *Playtime* and *Bathtime*.

Oxenbury, Helen. *Dressing*. New York: Simon & Schuster, 1981. [beginning new reader]

Oxenbury's baby, as cuddly as a teddy bear, is shown in this book putting on all the necessary items babies wear. There is only one word per page. Oxenbury has produced numerous "first books," all with her simply drawn baby that real children are quickly attracted to.

Rhymes and Repetition

This category includes nursery rhymes, stories built on the repetition of words and phrases, and lullabies and songs of all kinds. Rhymes delight children, and the good ones delight adult readers as well. Rhymes are an introduction to the music and the fun of language. Books that employ the repetition of certain phrases engage children in the enjoyable act of anticipating remembered words and offer great help to an uncertain new reader as well. Books that illustrate familiar songs have the added advantage of presenting in print words already known to many new readers.

Brett, Jan. *The Twelve Days of Christmas*. New York: Dodd, Mead & Co., 1986. [intermediate new reader]

This is one example of a nicely illustrated version of a popular song.

Emberley, Barbara, adapt. *Drummer Hoff*. Illus. by Ed Emberley. New York: Simon & Schuster, 1987. [beginning new reader]

With whimsical rhymes, each new soldier is introduced, the battle scene is prepared, and the recitation of responsibilities for the cannon is repeated. Finally, Drummer Hoff fires it off.

Go In and Out the Window: An Illustrated Song Book for Children. Music arr. and ed. by Dan Fox, commentary by Claude Marks. Illus. from the Metropolitan Museum of Art in New York City. New York: Henry Holt & Co., 1987. [intermediate new reader]

Each song, with accompanying musical notation, is matched with one or more paintings from the Metropolitan's collection. A brief text discusses the historical background of both the painting and the song. This is a beautiful book to browse through with children, and the songs are traditional ones that families have been singing for generations.

Michels, Barbara, and Bettye White, comps. *Apples on a Stick: The Folklore of Black Children.* Illus. by Jerry Pinkney. New York: Coward-McCann, Inc., 1983. [beginning/intermediate new reader]

Jump-rope rhymes, counting rhymes, and other examples of the playground verse of black children are collected in a book that will remind many adults of their childhood.

Prelutsky, Jack, sel. *Read Aloud Rhymes for the Very Young.* Illus. by Marc Brown. New York: Alfred A. Knopf, 1986. [beginning/intermediate new reader]

More than 200 nursery rhymes and short poems, some familiar and some not, are delightfully illustrated.

———. *Ride a Purple Pelican.* Illus. by Garth Williams. New York: Greenwillow Books, 1986. [intermediate new reader]

This is a book of contemporary nursery rhymes. The brightly colored, hilarious illustrations match the rollicking fun of these silly but rhythmically wonderful rhymes. Although some of the words are unusual, the language is clever, rhythmic, and a delight to read.

Sendak, Maurice. *Chicken Soup with Rice.* New York: Harper & Row Publishers, 1962. [beginning new reader]

For every month of the year, a silly but memorable rhyme celebrates the joys of chicken soup with rice. By the time they get to the rhyme for March, young listeners will be anticipating the refrain.

Shaw, Nancy. *Sheep in a Jeep.* Illus. by Margot Apple. Boston: Houghton Mifflin Co., 1986. [beginning new reader]

With sentences like "Sheep leap to push the jeep," this hilarious bit of absurdity will delight children and adults. The illustrations are as wacky as the story.

Spier, Peter. *The Star-Spangled Banner.* Garden City, N.Y.: Doubleday, 1973. [beginning–advanced new reader]

The words are those of our national anthem. The illustrations vividly portray the battle that inspired the song as well as scenes from American life up to modern times that inspire its singing. The book also includes a reproduction of the handwritten original, as well as a brief narrative setting the historical context for the song, making this a most informative and appealing work. The words of the song are difficult, but the first verse at least will be familiar to many new readers.

Wildsmith, Brian. *All Fall Down.* Oxford: Oxford University Press, 1983. [beginning new reader]

"I see a ball. I see a bird and a ball," and the list grows as each object is pictured beneath the previous one, ultimately balancing on the nose of a seal. The repetition aids the new reader, the growing list of items adds a note of suspense, and the inevitable collapse brings squeals of delight from young listeners.

Participation Books

Some children's books invite young readers to answer a question, find a hidden figure, anticipate an outcome, create a story for a wordless book, or otherwise participate in the literary activities suggested by the book. These books provide enjoyable practice of the language and prereading skills toddlers and preschoolers need to learn. Because they are easy to read, the books cast new readers in the role of teacher very quickly.

Ahlberg, Janet and Allan Ahlberg. *Each Peach Pear Plum.* New York: Scholastic Inc., 1978. [beginning new reader]
> On each page the reader spies a familiar figure from the world of fairy tales. Can the young listener find the figure, too?

_____. *The Jolly Postman.* Boston: Little, Brown & Co., 1986. [beginning new reader]
> Real little letters arrive in real little envelopes for real little fingers to open. This book delights the toddler set.

_____. *Peek-a-Boo.* New York: The Viking Press, 1981. [beginning new reader]
> On one page a simple rhyme asks what the baby sees, and the reader looks through a hole in the opposite page to find the answer. This is a cozy little book for toddlers and preschoolers.

Carle, Eric. *The Very Hungry Caterpillar.* New York: Philomel Books, 1979. [beginning new reader]
> As the little ones turn the pages, they watch the caterpillar eat his way through a succession of fruit and goodies, build his cocoon, then turn into a beautiful butterfly.

Hoban, Tana. *Where Is It?* New York: Macmillan Publishing Co., 1974. [beginning new reader]
> Fewer than 50 words tell this story of a rabbit searching for something unknown to the reader until the end of the story. Toddlers enjoy searching with the rabbit and guessing what it is he is looking for.

Spier, Peter. *Rain.* Garden City, N.Y.: Doubleday, 1982. [beginning new reader]
> This is a wordless book, as are many of Peter Spier's books for children. It follows the activities of two children on a rainy summer afternoon. Books such as this one provide opportunities for rich conversation between adults and children learning to speak.

Together, adult and child can discuss details in the pictures, relationships between characters, the sequence of events, and similarities and differences between the pictures and their own experiences.

Picture Books/Beginning Stories

Picture books combine a simple story with pictures that illustrate and often extend that story. The best of them are beautiful works of art in which text and illustrations complement and enhance each other.

Picture books are generally intended for children from toddler age through about third grade, but many will appeal to older children as well and to the adults who read them. Children's librarians are well acquainted with the picture books in their collections and can suggest suitable books for a range of ages and subjects. Each year awards are given to recognize the best of the genre, among them the Caldecott Medal, awarded by the American Library Association. A list of Caldecott winners, easily available from the children's librarian, would provide an excellent initial collection of picture books for a family literacy program.

Brown, Margaret Wise. *Goodnight Moon.* Illus. by Clement Hurd. New York: Harper & Row Publishers, 1947. [beginning new reader]
　　As the light gradually fades, a little rabbit says goodnight in rhyme to all the things in "the great green room." This is a classic bedtime book.
Burningham, John. *Mr. Gumpy's Outing.* New York: Henry Holt & Co., 1970. [beginning new reader]
　　The kind Mr. Gumpy takes two children and an assortment of animals for a boat ride. The inevitable dumping is delightful. *Mr. Gumpy's Motor Car* is a similar work from this author/illustrator.
Flournoy, Valerie. *The Patchwork Quilt.* Illus. by Jerry Pinkney. New York: Dial Books for Young Readers, 1985. [intermediate new reader]
　　A grandmother takes the time to explain quilting to her granddaughter. When the grandmother gets sick, the young girl tries to finish grandmother's "masterpiece."
Hall, Donald. *Ox-Cart Man.* Illus. by Barbara Cooney. New York: The Viking Press, 1979. [intermediate new reader]
　　A nineteenth century New England farmer and his family use or sell everything they raise, even their beloved ox. The illustrations match the quiet lyricism of the text and capture the integrity of a life lived in harmony with the cycles of nature.

Hendershot, Judith. *In Coal Country.* Illus. by Thomas B. Allen. New York: Alfred Knopf, 1987. [intermediate new reader]

Hendershot recalls her experience growing up in a coal-mining town in Appalachia. Life was hard, but children found fun anywhere. The setting is marked by physical labor and soot but also by love and family loyalty. The illustrations are subdued but convey a certain dogged optimism.

Johnson, Angela. *Tell Me a Story, Mama.* Illus. by David Soman. New York: Orchard Books, 1989. [beginning new reader]

A little girl asks her mother to tell a story from her childhood, but the child seems to know most of the stories already. Still, Mama is there to add words of confirmation and assurance in this tale of togetherness and the beginnings of separation.

Locker, Thomas. *Where the River Begins.* New York: Dial Books, 1984. [intermediate new reader]

With paintings reminiscent of the Hudson River School painters, this book tells the story of two boys and their grandfather who set off to find the source of the river that runs by their house. A story of an exciting adventure, it is also a story of death and enduring love made memorable by illustrations that are extraordinary works of art.

McCloskey, Robert. *Make Way for Ducklings.* New York: The Viking Press, 1941. [intermediate new reader]

Still a perennial favorite after fifty years, this reassuring book tells the story of a family of ducks who, after much searching, find a home in Boston's Public Garden.

Maestro, Betsy. *Taxi: A Book of City Words.* Illus. by Giulio Maestro. New York: Clarion Books, 1989. [beginning new reader]

As a yellow taxi travels through the city, it introduces the reader to a different city word on each page.

Pinkwater, Daniel. *Guys from Space.* New York: Macmillan Publishing Co., 1989. [beginning new reader]

This is a wry, funny book about visitors from space who appear in the backyard and take a little boy on a fantastic voyage, then bring him back in time for dinner. The language is particularly helpful to adult new readers because many words and phrases are repeated, although in humorous and enjoyable ways.

Pomerantz, Charlotte. *The Chalk Doll.* Illus. by Frané Lessac. New York: J. B. Lippincott, 1989. [intermediate new reader]

A mother tells her daughter stories about growing up on the island of Jamaica. She was too poor to own a "chalk doll," that is, one bought from the store, so she made her own rag doll. After listening to her mother's stories, the little girl decides she is lucky to have so many "chalk dolls," but she'd also like to have a rag doll. Wonderful illustrations by Caribbean artist Lessac match the story perfectly.

Ringgold, Faith. *Tar Beach.* New York: Crown Publishers, 1991. [intermediate new reader]

This unusual book had its origins in a story quilt that now hangs in the Guggenheim Museum in New York City. It is the story of a young girl and her family who seek relief from hot summer nights on the roof of their Harlem apartment. Up on the roof, the girl dreams of flying, and freedom, and righting the wrongs of real life.

Stevenson, James. *July.* New York: Greenwillow Books, 1990. [intermediate new reader]

In this third installment of a series of reminiscences of childhood summers in the 1930s, soft, almost child-like pastel drawings complement a story of children eager to grow beyond the constraints of their elders. Two earlier titles are *When I Was Nine* and *Higher on the Door.*

Concept Books

These books present a concept important to children in graphic and appealing images. Some books present physical concepts, such as the idea of bigger and smaller; others present language concepts, such as the idea of opposites; still others deal with feelings common to children, such as fear of strangers or the desire to do things independently.

Ahlberg, Janet, and Allan Ahlberg. *The Baby's Catalogue.* Boston: Little, Brown & Co., 1982. [beginning new reader]

With very few words, this book introduces the idea of categorization by grouping illustrations of items and situations familiar to babies and their older siblings.

Hoban, Tana. *More than One.* New York: Greenwillow Books, 1981. [beginning new reader]

Large, appealing black-and-white photographs illustrate words meaning more than one: pile, bunch, bundle, row, stack, flock, herd, group, crowd, team.

_____. *Push Pull Empty Full.* New York: Macmillan Co., 1972. [beginning new reader]

Facing pages have one word each, and they are opposites. Appealing black-and-white photographs graphically explain the words. Hoban has produced many excellent books explaining different concepts. The quality of the photography and layout of these books makes them particularly appropriate and easy for adult new readers.

Rogers, Fred. *The New Baby.* Photographs by Jim Judkins. New York: G. P. Putnam's Sons, 1985. [beginning new reader]

Mr. Rogers talks reassuringly to children about their feelings when a new baby arrives in the family. In several other books Mr. Rogers discusses other problems and events common to the lives of children.

Sis, Peter. *Beach Ball.* New York: Greenwillow Books, 1990. [beginning new reader]

As Mary runs after a beach ball the wind has blown away, the reader follows her through pages of A–Z alphabet words, numbers 1–10, opposites, shapes, and more. This amusing, instructive, and delightful book has very few words.

Alphabet Books

Numerous alphabet books teach the name, initial sound, and sequence of the letters of the alphabet.

Base, Graeme. *Animalia.* New York: Harry N. Abrams, Inc., 1986. [intermediate new reader]

The words used in this alphabet book are not easy, but they are great fun to say and hear, and the bizarre and stunning illustrations are not to be missed. Each page is filled with all kinds of hidden objects beginning with the letter on display. Every time an adult and child look at these pictures, they will find something missed in earlier viewings. It is a book to have fun with and to come back to again and again.

Bayer, Jane. *A My Name Is Alice.* Illus. by Steven Kellogg. New York: Dial Books, 1984. [beginning new reader]

A rhyme for every letter fits the pattern of "A my name is Alice," a popular bouncing-ball game. Rhymes are all slightly wacky, and the illustrations match them well. Reading the book is fun; making up rhymes of your own with little ones will be even better.

Isadora, Rachel. *City Seen from A to Z.* New York: Greenwillow Books, 1983. [beginning new reader]

In this "alphabet book for all ages," black-and-white drawings depict city scenes for each letter. With just one word per page, the book is easy to read, but the deceptively simple drawings have an unexpected emotional power that will cause adults and children to linger and discover a wealth of feelings and ideas lurking just beneath the surface.

Lobel, Arnold. *On Market Street.* Illus. by Anita Lobel. New York: Greenwillow Books, 1981. [beginning new reader]

On Market Street a little girl buys something for every letter of the alphabet. Whimsical drawings and a clever ending add to the pleasure.

Counting Books

Once children learn to count, they want to count everything in sight. Books that offer counting opportunities are numerous and highly imaginative. They also have very few words, making them easy books for beginning new readers to read to toddlers and preschool children.

Bang, Molly. *Ten, Nine, Eight.* New York: Greenwillow Books, 1983. [beginning new reader]
Warm and cozy pictures show a father helping his little girl get ready for bed by counting familiar objects, beginning with ten little toes and ending with one little girl.

Crews, Donald. *Ten Black Dots.* Rev. ed. New York: Greenwillow Books, 1986. [beginning new reader]
Black dots can be the eyes of a fox or the wheels of a train in these simple but imaginative drawings that help the reader count from one to ten.

Hamm, Diane Johnston. *How Many Feet in the Bed.* Illus. by Kate Salley Palmer. New York: Simon & Schuster, 1991. [beginning new reader]
Two by two, feet appear in the bed, but as the day progresses, each member of the family finds something to do, and the feet disappear. This is a warm-hearted counting book.

Hoban, Tana. *Count and See.* New York: Macmillan, 1972. [beginning new reader]
Black-and-white photographs of objects from everyday urban life illustrate the numbers. Each number is identified by an array of dots as well as by its numeral and name. This is a simple book, beautifully executed.

Pacovská, Květa. *One, Five, Many.* New York: Clarion Books, 1990. [beginning new reader]
Every page of this book invites the child to lift a flap or open a door and find a surprise as well as something to count. Bold colors and an ingenious sense of design make this an unforgettable counting book.

Wildsmith, Brian. *Brian Wildsmith's 1, 2, 3's.* New York: Franklin Watts, Inc., 1965. [beginning new reader]

Each number in this book is illustrated by imaginative, collage-like illustrations using bright colors and the basic shapes of rectangles, triangles, and circles.

Poetry

Using words selectively and well, poetry creates pleasing rhymes and rhythms, amuses us with a clever turn of phrase or unexpected insight, questions our conventional perspectives, or expresses our deepest thoughts—thoughts that we often cannot give words to ourselves. Reading poetry can spark discussions between adult reader and child listener over a wide range of issues. The rhyme, rhythm, repetition, and recurring images of poetry assist new readers even as they underscore the meaning and power of the message.

Baylor, Byrd. *Desert Voices*. Illus. by Peter Parnall. New York: Chas. Scribner's Sons, 1981. [intermediate new reader]
 The poet imagines herself as various animals describing their homes in the desert. The poems reflect a love and understanding of the natural environment, and the black-and-white drawings splashed with striking colors create intriguing images of the desert.

Ciardi, John. *Fast and Slow*. Illus. by Becky Gaver. Boston: Houghton Mifflin Co., 1975. [intermediate new reader]
 The title page tells us that these are "poems for advanced children and beginning parents." They are whimsical and wise, rhythmical and easy to read or listen to. Another collection of Ciardi's work, *You Read to Me, I'll Read to You,* presents poems to be read alternately by adults and children.

Frost, Robert. *Stopping by Woods on a Snowy Evening*. Illus. by Susan Jeffers. New York: E. P. Dutton, 1973. [intermediate new reader]
 This is an illustrated version of Frost's famous poem about a man stopping for a few moments "to watch his woods fill up with snow." Soft, crayon-like drawings complement the quiet mood of the words.

Greenfield, Eloise. *Nathaniel Talking*. Illus. by Jan Spivey Gilchrist. New York: Black Butterfly Children's Books, 1988. [intermediate new reader]
 In a rap song, nine-year-old Nathaniel B. Free talks about his "philosophy." Black and white illustrations convey the enthusiasm and poignancy of a young boy's view of the world.

Larrick, Nancy, comp. *When the Dark Comes Dancing*. Illus. by John Wallner. New York: Philomel Books, 1983. [intermediate new reader]
   This collection of bedtime poems and lullabies was compiled by a noted anthologizer of poetry for children.

Livingston, Myra Cohn. *Celebrations*. Illus. by Leonard Everett Fisher. New York: Holiday House, 1985. [beginning/intermediate new reader]
   This book offers a poem for every holiday with large colorful illustrations to set the mood. Livingston is a prolific writer and anthologizer of poetry for children.

Siebert, Diane. *Truck Song*. Illus. by Byron Barton. New York: Thomas Y. Crowell, 1983. [beginning/intermediate new reader]
   One long rhythmic poem follows a tractor trailer traveling across the country. Wonderfully simple but colorful illustrations reflect the changing landscapes and varying moods of the journey. *Train Song* is a similar work by this writer.

Silverstein, Shel. *A Light in the Attic*. New York: Harper & Row Publishers, 1981. [beginning/intermediate new reader]
   Silverstein understands the fears, the silliness, and the disarming truthfulness of children, and young readers and listeners take his poetry right to their hearts. Adults who follow the child's lead will be glad they did. *Where the Sidewalk Ends* is another collection of Silverstein's poetry that will please children and adults alike.

Folklore

Every culture has its traditional stories that are handed down from generation to generation. These folktales are an enduring source of pleasure to young children and to adults who can willingly "suspend their disbelief" and enter into a magical world that often presents some surprising lessons about what it means to be a human being. Whether based on traditional practices or tales of fantasy, these stories share ideas and experiences that have mattered to people for a long time.

Carrick, Carol. *Aladdin and the Wonderful Lamp*. Illus. by Donald Carrick. New York: Scholastic Inc., 1989. [intermediate new reader]
   The vivid retelling of a tale from the Arabian Nights (about the boy whose life and spirit are saved by a magic lamp) is illustrated with rich paintings inspired by the art of the Middle East.

Grifalconi, Ann. *The Village of Round and Square Houses*. Boston: Little, Brown & Co., 1986. [intermediate new reader]

Grifalconi presents the true story, beautifully told and illustrated, of a remote village in Central Africa where the men live in square houses and the women in round ones.

Kellogg, Steven. *Jack and the Beanstalk*. New York: Morrow Junior Books, 1991. [intermediate new reader]

This retelling of this well-known folktale is full of the energy and adventure that make Jack such an appealing character to young children. Kellogg has retained the flavor and much of the language of the original but adapted it sufficiently to make it readable to a modern audience.

Lewis, J. Patrick. *The Tsar and the Amazing Cow*. New York: Dial Books for Young Readers, 1988. [intermediate new reader]

In this old Russian folktale of resurrection and transformation, a cow's magic milk restores youth and happiness to her owners.

McDermott, Gerald. *Anansi the Spider*. New York: Holt, Rinehart and Winston, 1976. [beginning new reader]

This tale from the Ashanti people in the country of Ghana tells of Anansi who gets into trouble many times but is saved by the help of his sons. The simple text and striking, cutout-like illustrations combine to tell a riveting and beautiful story.

Perl, Lila. *Blue Monday and Friday the Thirteenth*. Illus. by Erika Weihs. New York: Clarion Books, 1986. [intermediate new reader]

This book presents a fascinating review of the myths and legends relating to each day of the week. It includes the names for the days in various languages.

Religion

Religious traditions and activities are important to the lives of many families. In fact, some adult literacy students are motivated to enroll in literacy classes because of their desire to read the Bible or other sacred books. Religious books for children illustrate familiar religious and biblical stories. Some books use text taken directly from the Bible, enabling adult readers to read words already familiar from their religious experiences. Other books adapt the language of sacred texts to a simpler form, making it more accessible to beginning readers. Still others discuss religious traditions.

Branley, Franklyn M. *The Christmas Sky*. Illus. by Stephen Fieser. New York: Thomas Y. Crowell, 1990. [intermediate new reader]

Recognizing that some Christians accept the Christmas story as a miracle while others look for explanations, this book presents a thought-provoking discussion of some of the possible, scientifically based explanations of the events surrounding Christ's birth. Lovely, subdued color illustrations enhance the text.

Fisher, Leonard Everett. *The Seven Days of Creation*. New York: Holiday House, 1981. [beginning new reader]

Beautiful acrylic paintings illustrate the biblical story of the seven days of the Creation.

Hutton, Warwick. *Moses in the Bulrushes*. New York: Margaret K. McElderry Books, 1985. [beginning new reader]

This simple retelling of the story of the birth of Moses is illustrated by lovely watercolors.

Pienkowski, Jan. *Christmas*. New York: Alfred A. Knopf, 1984. [beginning/intermediate new reader]

The words of this book are taken directly from the gospels of Luke and Matthew, King James Version. The striking illustrations employ silhouettes, brilliant colors, and ornamental gilding.

Nature and Science

Human beings are curious by nature. Children approach the world around them with wonder and an eagerness to learn. Adults also like to learn new things, but literacy students lack the skill to seek the information they need. Reading books that help explain the physical world in simple but accurate language enables adults and children to learn together. Many nonfiction books written for children are well-illustrated and authoritative sources of information for adults as well as for children.

Billings, Charlene W. *Fiber Optics: Bright New Way to Communicate*. New York: Dodd, Mead, 1986. [intermediate/advanced new reader]

A well-organized text and colorful photographs review the history, manufacture, operation, and future of optical fibers—a technology becoming increasingly important as a method of transmitting information.

Branley, Franklyn M. *Flash, Crash, Rumble, and Roll*. Rev. ed. Illus. by Barbara and Ed Emberly. New York: Thomas Y. Crowell, 1985. [beginning new reader]

This is one of the Let's Read and Find Out science series, a particularly well-written series of books on scientific topics for children. The text is clear, and the drawings, including several schematics, are very helpful. Branley has published several other titles of science-related books for children.

Cole, Joanna. *Cars and How They Go.* Illus. by Gail Gibbons. New York: Thomas Y. Crowell, 1983. [beginning new reader]

Bright colors and simple but detailed diagrams illustrate this informative description of the working parts of an automobile.

Gibbons, Gail. *Monarch Butterfly.* New York: Holiday House, 1989. [intermediate new reader]

In her usual clear and concise style, Gibbons details the life cycle of the butterfly, a story which fascinates children.

_____. *Tunnels.* New York: Holiday House, 1984. [beginning new reader]

With illustrations that are at once simple and detailed, Gibbons describes all kinds of tunnels built by humans and animals.

Jessel, Camilla. *The Joy of Birth.* New York: Hillside Books, 1982. [intermediate new reader]

With lovely photographs and direct, accurate, and sensitive language, this book describes a baby's growth from egg to newborn.

Geography, History, and Biography

Adult new readers come from many countries and backgrounds, and they have lived through important historical events. They want to know more about the community they live in, as well as the wider world around them. Many geography, history, and biography books written for children provide accurate information in a format that will appeal to adults. When new readers share these books with children, they can share their personal perspective on the topic discussed, or, if the subject is new to both, adults and children can learn new things together.

Bode, Janet. *New Kids on the Block: Oral Histories of Immigrant Teens.* New York: Franklin Watts, 1989. [intermediate new reader]

In their own words, teenage immigrants tell their experiences of being uprooted from their familiar surroundings to come to the strange and sometimes hostile world they encounter in the United States. They speak of fear and loss, of humiliation and adjustment, and of pride and hope.

Fisher, Leonard Everett. *Ellis Island: Gateway to the New World.* New York: Holiday House, 1986. [intermediate new reader]

Black-and-white photographs and drawings and a clearly written text document the history of immigration through Ellis Island and the port of New York City.

Fritz, Jean. *And Then What Happened Paul Revere?* Illus. by Margot Tomes. New York: Coward, McCann, & Geoghegan, Inc., 1973. [intermediate new reader]

In a whimsical but historically accurate account, Fritz tells the many fascinating but largely unknown details of Paul Revere's famous ride, as well as of other activities in his long and very busy life. Fritz has written many informative and highly entertaining historical books for children.

Provensen, Alice. *The Buck Stops Here.* New York: HarperCollins, 1990 [beginning/intermediate new reader]

Although this book contains very little text in sentence form, its creative format conveys an amazing amount of information about the history of the American presidency.

Stein, R. Conrad. *The Home Front.* World at War. Chicago: Childrens Press, 1986. [intermediate new reader]

Each book in this series focuses on a particular aspect of World War II. This one discusses many of the effects of the war on life in the United States, including massive recycling efforts, recruitment campaigns, and the internment of Japanese-Americans. Black-and-white photographs add to this book's appeal.

Stewart, Gail B. *China.* New York: Crestwood House, 1990. [intermediate new reader]

Stewart's brief history of China since 1949 focuses on the events leading up to the massacre of Tiananmen Square in 1989. It includes color photographs, a glossary, and a brief index.

Resources for Establishing Family Literacy Programs

The following books offer practical advice on using children's literature or on establishing family literacy programs. Many of the books suggested here include annotated bibliographies of titles for children or young adults. Librarians are likely to be very familiar with the resources mentioned here, literacy teachers somewhat less so. By working together, librarians, literacy teachers, and literacy students can use these resources to choose books from the children's collection of the library to advance the skills of adult new readers.

American Library Association. *Fact Sheets.* Chicago: ALA, 50 East Huron Street, Chicago, IL 60611.

These fact sheets on family literacy are produced in conjunction with the Bell Atlantic/ALA Family Literacy Project and are available free of charge from ALA. They offer many helpful hints on planning and implementing a family literacy program.

Butler, Dorothy. *Babies Need Books.* New York: Atheneum, 1982.

Butler describes the first five years of a child's life and recommends specific books to help both child and parent grow through each developmental stage. The author, a mother and grandmother many times over, sprinkles her book talks with humorous and insightful anecdotes from her rich personal experience. Although many additional titles have become available since 1982, most of the selections discussed herein are still in print or available at the library. Even without the book lists, however, Butler's impassioned encouragement of reading to children and her understanding of the parent-child relationship make this book an important addition to the family literacy library.

Cullinan, Bernice E. *Literature and the Child.* 2d ed. San Diego: Harcourt Brace Jovanovich, 1989.

Cullinan provides an excellent sourcebook on children's literature for a family literacy program. The book discusses in depth all genres of literature, giving numerous examples of each. Specific books are highlighted both for their intrinsic quality and for their value for children at particular developmental stages. Numerous profiles of many authors and illustrators will give tutors and librarians useful insight into an author's work that can greatly enhance the experience of sharing that author's books with children. Extensive bibliographies follow each chapter.

First Teachers: A Family Literacy Handbook for Parents, Policy-Makers, and Literacy Providers. Washington, D.C.: The Barbara Bush Foundation for Family Literacy, 1989.

This book describes ten family literacy programs operating in different settings around the country. Each entry reviews the background, procedures, and funding of a program as well as evidence of its success. The last section offers helpful advice to policy-makers and practitioners.

Hearne, Betsy Gould. *Choosing Books for Children: A Common Sense Guide.* Rev. ed. New York: Delacorte Press, 1990.

Hearne writes with a blend of enthusiasm, common sense, and a thorough knowledge of children's literature. She discusses books of different types and books for different age groups. Each chapter ends with a helpful annotated bibliography of books in the category discussed.

Lipson, Eden Ross. *The New York Times Parent's Guide to the Best Books for Children.* New York: Times Books, 1988.

This extensive annotated bibliography of more than 1,000 titles of children's books, both new and old, was written by the children's book editor for *The New York Times.* Lipson includes books appropriate for babies through young adult years. Particularly helpful are the indexes that list books by appropriate age level and by special subject.

McCracken, Robert A., and Marlene J. McCracken. *Stories, Songs, and Poetry to Teach Reading and Writing.* Chicago: American Library Assn., 1986.

This book presents a reading instruction program for children based on the use of language experience stories and children's literature, poetry, and songs. Although written for elementary teachers, the principles and many of the practices can be applied to teaching adult literacy students.

Trelease, Jim. *The New Read-Aloud Handbook.* New York: Penguin Books, 1989.

The first half of this book is an eloquent, impassioned plea to parents, teachers, and librarians to read aloud frequently to children of all ages. The second half presents a "treasury" of books suitable for reading aloud, organized by type of book and age level. Trelease's enthusiasm is infectious, and his knowledge of the world of children's literature is encyclopedic. This is an indispensable guide for a family literacy program.

*10*___

Special Collections
for New Readers

> I learned enough at the Boston Public Library last
> summer to transform me from a homeless ex-con and
> day-laborer into a full-time free-lance writer in less than
> a year.[1]   Michael Brennan

Up to this point, the discussion has centered around ways to help
adult literacy students use books from all sections of the library's
general collection. The objective has been to help tutors and
students feel at home everywhere in the library. Some books,
however, are written specifically for the adult new reader population. As publishers have recognized the needs of this audience,
they have produced an increasing quantity of books covering a
wide range of topics. Some books for new readers address various
life-coping skills, such as filling out job applications, managing
budgets, reading labels, and becoming a more discerning consumer. Other titles include fictional stories about adults dealing
with common problems and nonfiction works including biographies of popular sports and entertainment figures and accounts
of historical and contemporary events of general interest.

Special collections for new readers are common in public
libraries and often are the first point of contact with the library
for a literacy student. In order to attract and sustain its intended

audience, a new readers' collection should be large, including multiple copies of popular titles. It should be comprehensive, covering the many categories of books available, such as life-coping skill books, examples of student writing produced by other literacy programs, and a wide sampling of the available works of fiction and nonfiction. And the new readers' collection should be easy to find and attractively displayed.

The task of selecting books for the new readers' collection can best be accomplished by a selection committee consisting of librarians working closely with tutors and students representing the local literacy programs. To build a comprehensive collection, the selection committee can consult annotated bibliographies of books recommended for new readers, bibliographies that recommend high interest/easy reading books, promotional flyers from publishers, information from other literacy programs, and student recommendations. Some of these resources are listed at the end of this chapter.

Specific books for new readers are not discussed in this chapter, since they are covered in detail in the bibliographies mentioned. However, the following sections deal with several factors that any selection committee needs to consider when choosing books for a new readers' collection, including readability, criteria for selection, building a comprehensive collection, organization, and user evaluation of the materials.

Readability

Librarians and tutors typically consider the designated reading level when choosing books for new readers. Reading levels are determined by readability formulas that measure elements such as word length, sentence length, and average number of sentences, then assign a level of difficulty correlated with elementary school grade levels. Readability formulas can be helpful if used judiciously, but they have limitations as well.

First of all, choosing books based on reading level alone limits a student's choice of reading material. Too often, tutors and librarians assume that new readers can read only those books judged to be suitable for the grade level the student scored on a reading test, but this is often not the case. Students can read books written well above their tested reading levels if they are knowledgeable about a particular subject or interested in learning about it.

Readability formulas measure quantitative elements such as sentence length and word length. But they cannot measure the clarity of style, the persuasive power of the writing, the quality of the illustrations, the presence of rhyme and repetition that enhance readability, or the reader's interest in or background knowledge of the story or information. Readability formulas also measure adult materials against a scale developed for children, so they fail to account for the advantages in oral vocabulary and life experience that adults bring to the reading of a book. Finally, readability formulas have a margin of error at least one grade level above or below the level determined by the formula.[2]

Used with discretion and common sense, however, readability formulas can be helpful tools. Consider reading level along with the more subjective criteria discussed in the next section. Be flexible when applying readability formulas. For example, most formulas use sentence length and number of sentences as factors determining readability. But straightforward compound sentences can generally be read as easily as two separate sentences. The fact that they are written as one will increase the grade level, so count such compound sentences as two sentences when applying a formula.

Formulas use the number of "hard words," generally defined as having three or more syllables, to determine readability. Use your own discretion in determining what is or is not a "hard word." Consider not counting commonly used words such as "television" or "automobile." If the same long word appears more than once in a single sample, count it only once. The repetition will generally aid readability, while counting it more than once will result in a higher grade level score. Consider not so much whether a word is hard or long, but whether it fits the context. A carburetor is a carburetor and any attempt to call it something else would be ridiculous and demeaning to the reader.

Use readability formulas to determine a range of difficulty rather than a static grade level. For example, in the bibliographies of Chapters 6, 8, and 9 the books were categorized in the following broad groupings:

Beginning new reader: grades 1–3
Intermediate new reader: grades 4–6
Advanced new reader: grades 7–8

Designating books according to these categories, which are deliberately vague, will allow students, teachers, and librarians a wider latitude within which to find appropriate and appealing reading materials. Remember, too, that the information reading technique and assisted reading technique—two teaching methods described in Chapter 3—enable students, with the help of tutors, to read books they are not yet ready to read independently.

One of the most commonly used readability formulas for assessing books for adult new readers is the Gunning Fog Index. It involves a six-step analysis.

1. Select a sample and count off 100 words. (Count to the end of the sentence closest to the one-hundredth word, so you may have 98 words, 102 words, etc.) If the piece is long enough, choose two or three samples, near the beginning, middle, and end.
2. Count the number of sentences in each 100-word sample. Determine the average sentence length by dividing the number of words by the number of complete sentences. Round off the number to the nearest tenth.
3. Count the number of words with three or more syllables to determine the number of "hard" words. Do not count proper nouns, easy compound words, or verb forms in which the tense ending forms the third syllable.
4. Find the percentage of hard words as follows:

$$\frac{100 \times \text{number of hard words}}{\text{number of words}} = \text{percentage of hard words}$$

Again, round off to the nearest tenth.
5. Add the percentage of hard words (step 4) to the average sentence length (step 2), then multiply this sum by .4. The resulting product is the reading grade level.

Example:
Number of words: 104
Number of complete sentences: 8
Average sentence length (104/8):   13
Number of hard words: 2
Percentage of hard words (100 × 2/104):   1.9
% of hard words + average sentence = sum × .4 = grade level
                    length
   1.9   +   13   = 14.9 × .4 = 5.9 or 6.0

6. Compute the score for the other two 100-word samples, then find the average grade level.[3]

Selecting Books for Adult New Readers

Reading level is only one factor that affects a book's suitability for adult new readers. The selection committee must consider other, more subjective, criteria as well. Following is a discussion of those criteria, along with several questions to consider for each category.

The Appearance of the Book

In general, choose books that have an "adult" look, an appealing cover, and good quality paper with adequate spacing of print. Some specific questions to consider are

1. Print size—including spacing between words and between lines

   Is the book physically easy to read?
   Is the print sufficiently large for new readers whose eyes are not practiced at reading print?
   Is the print so large that the book looks "childish"?

2. Illustrations

   Are photographs or drawings relevant to the text?
   Do they extend the information given in the text?
   Are they adult in character?
   Are they clearly labeled and organized?

Do they invite browsing, or do they give the book a cluttered look?

3. Captions

   Are they as easy to read as the text?
   Are they sufficiently separated from the text to present an uncluttered look?

4. Diagrams—including charts, graphs, etc.

   Are they clear and uncluttered?
   Are they visually appealing?
   Are explanations clear?
   Do they add to the text?

5. Overall appearance

   Is the book small enough not to discourage a new reader?
   Is the cover appealing?
   Does it look like an "adult" book?
   Do the title and cover accurately represent the contents?
   Is paper of sufficient quality that print doesn't show through to the back of a page?

The Language of the Book

Readability levels are one consideration here, but so are the more subjective observations you can make by examining a book in hand. Some specific questions to consider are

1. Sentences

   Are sentences mostly short but with sufficient variation to make the language interesting?
   Are most sentences written in the active rather than passive voice?

2. Vocabulary

   Does the author use precise words, even if they are difficult, or substitute easier words that may create a condescending tone?

Are difficult words explained either in the text or in a glossary?

If jargon or colloquial expressions are used, are they appropriate, and are they explained?

3. Writing Style

Does the writing read like natural speech or does it sound as though it has been written to accommodate a controlled vocabulary list?

Does the writer use concrete examples to explain the concepts?

Does the meaning stand out clearly, or is it obscured by unnecessary words?

If dialogue is used, does it sound natural or contrived?

Is the writing engaging and fluent? Is it enjoyable to read aloud?

Are there references to children as the intended audience?

For either fiction or nonfiction, is the tone moralistic or judgmental?

Are chapters generally short, and do they lead logically from one to the next?

Is the title informative or misleading?

The Subject Matter

Books for adult new readers cover a wide range of topics. Fictional accounts of adults facing problems, such as illiteracy, joblessness, difficulties with spouses or children, unexpected changes, and the like, are popular. So are nonfiction biographies of celebrities and accounts of major historical events, especially those that focus on one particular aspect of a subject, such as a book about the attack on Pearl Harbor rather than one that gives a general overview of World War II.

In general, a chronological narrative is easiest to follow. Techniques such as flashbacks confuse new readers. Also a list of characters should be long enough to provide variety, but not so long as to be confusing.

Consider the audience to whom a book will appeal. Some books will appeal to a general audience, a cross-section of the new reader population; others will appeal to specific audiences, such as women, young adults, or particular ethnic groups. Some books will appeal to students of English as a foreign language. Some books can be read on multiple levels. For example, photo-documentaries can be read for the pictures alone or for both pictures and text. Some books may be too hard for beginning readers to read independently but are good books for tutors to read aloud. Make sure your collection has a good balance to attract as many new readers as possible.

Some specific questions to consider are

1. Fiction

   Are the characters true-to-life and well developed?
   Do the characters or situations reflect any stereotypes of race, age, sex, religion, etc.?
   Is the setting appropriate to the story? Is it well described and easy to imagine?

2. Nonfiction

   Is the information substantial or superficial?
   Has the author selected information judiciously or tried to pack too much into a limited text?
   Does the text include helpful features, such as maps, a glossary, an index, etc.?
   Is the information accurate and current?
   Does the author distinguish between fact and theory?
   Does the author recognize different points of view?
   Are generalizations supported by facts?
   Are the author's qualifications for writing on the topic explained?
   Does the writing suggest that the author really cares about the subject?

Building a Comprehensive New Readers' Collection

Collections for new readers should be rich and diverse, reflect-ing the range of subject matter available throughout the gen-eral collection of the library. They should include workbooks in both basic skills and coping skills as well as a wide range of titles offering general information and leisure reading opportunities.

Workbooks in Basic Skills and Coping Skills

Librarians may be concerned that putting workbooks in the new readers' collection merely duplicates what is already available in the Adult Basic Education or literacy program. In this situation, however, duplication is a real service because literacy programs are not well funded. They purchase only a limited number of the many workbooks available on the market. Also, in most Adult Basic Education programs, books do not circulate, so students cannot take books home to practice unless they purchase copies themselves. The library's new readers' collection can supplement and extend the resources of the local literacy programs by providing additional copies of workbooks used in the programs as well as copies of other workbooks. Visit the local Adult Basic Education and literacy programs to determine what workbooks are used there and what other skill-building materials would be helpful additions to the library's new readers collection.

A good collection for new readers will include workbooks offering practice in the basic skills of reading, English, and math, as well as materials for the General Education Development (GED) test and pre-GED practice books. The collection should also contain workbooks covering various life-coping skill categories, such as health and family matters, community resources, consumer education, money management, job skills, and other topics essential to functional literacy.

General Information Books

Adult new readers missed much of the subject matter taught in elementary and high school because of their inability to read or because they dropped out early. As a result, they feel they know much less than adults who can read. Although they want to learn about the world around them, just as other library patrons do, their desire to learn is complicated by their lack of confidence as well as by their limited reading ability. It is important, therefore, to include in a new readers' collection books covering topics such as politics, history, travel, religion, economics, science, technology, the arts, popular culture, biography, and sports and recreation. Many books on these topics have been published recently for adult new readers. Consult the bibliographies listed at the end of this chapter for suggested titles.

As suggested in previous chapters, many nonfiction works written for children can also be used with adults. The New True Book series of titles about science and technology and the World at War series, both published by Childrens Press, are but two examples. Many nonfiction children's books discuss their subjects in clear, readable language that is informative and not juvenile. Tutors and librarians must exercise discretion when choosing children's nonfiction for adults. Some students will eagerly read children's books that teach them something they want to know, while others may dismiss them out of hand. For those students who are willing to use them, selected children's books can expand the subject coverage and strengthen the quality of the adult new readers' collection.

Leisure Reading Materials

Some adult students will relish the opportunity to read books just for fun. Others will be slow to choose reading as an activity of leisure, since for them reading requires work. Tutors and librarians need to encourage leisure reading as much as possible. Reading aloud to students during each lesson from stories, poems, or other works is one way to entice students into more frequent reading. Exposing them to a wide selection of possibilities in the new readers' collection at the library will also help students develop a habit of reading.

As with books of nonfiction, you want the new readers' collection of leisure reading materials to reflect the range of formats and subjects available in the general collection. Include books of poetry, fiction, and humor. Numerous works have been published for the new reader audience, and they are listed and annotated in the resources suggested at the end of this chapter. In addition, consider duplicating some titles from the children's department, especially anthologies of poetry that are suitable for adults as well as children, and some of the crossover books suitable for new readers suggested in Chapter 8. Consider also including adult "picture books," such as collections of photographs or paintings, travel books, and photodocumentaries.

Organization

Adult new readers' collections must be visible, attractive, and easily accessible to new readers, many of whom feel uncomfortable in the library. Most public libraries shelve materials for adult new readers separately from the general collection. Some name their collections "The Learning Center," "The Reading Corner," or similar names that indicate the general nature of the collection but do not emphasize the reading level of the books. Others use more specific names such as the Adult Basic Education Center.

Using a somewhat different approach, some libraries group skill-building materials together, regardless of difficulty, and label them according to the skill area rather than the reading level. These collections may focus on life-coping skills, such as buying and maintaining a car, or on basic skills, such as reading and math. Such arrangements attract to the display all library patrons seeking the specific information, not just adult new readers. The same concept applies to separate collections of romances and popular science fiction titles that are easy to read but that attract patrons interested in the genre, not the reading level.

Many libraries with new readers' collections have adopted a specific adult new reader logo that can be used in a variety of ways. The logo can identify all announcements published by the library concerning new reader events and materials. It can designate the location of the adult new readers' collection. Printed on small labels and placed on the spines of books, the logo can identify new readers' books housed in special collections, or it can indicate books that are considered acceptable for new readers but filed within the general collection. Labeling books from the adult new readers' collection with the logo also gives the library a means of tracking the materials for purposes of circulation statistics and reshelving.

User Evaluation

All library activities and collections need to be evaluated, and the adult new readers' collection is no exception. Librarians, literacy tutors, and literacy students should be involved in the process together. Librarians can monitor the circulation of all adult new reader materials. They can also establish a mechanism by which tutors and students contribute reviews of books in the collection. These reviews can be filed in file boxes (at least five by eight inches to allow room for enough information) or printed on eight-by-ten-inch sheets of paper and filed in three-ring binders. Photocopies of the reviews can be filed under several headings, including author, title, and subject (use the subject headings assigned in the library's catalog but modify them to more natural language when necessary). Keep the file boxes or notebooks near the adult new readers' collection. In all visits to Adult Basic Education centers and contacts with literacy programs, librarians can invite students and tutors to contribute reviews and to use the reviews of others to select books.

Tutors, for their part, should share reviews they write with their students, and then encourage the students to write their own. Discussing the books in classes or tutoring sessions will help the students think about the books more critically and write more thoughtful reviews. Teachers can also show more advanced students how to use the file of reviews kept at the library to select their own books. A sample form for reviewing books in the new reader's collection appears in Appendix F.

In addition to helping patrons find books, the file of reviews can help the selection committee weed the collection and make additional purchases. The selection committee can also make some kind of suggestion box available near the new readers' collection so patrons can recommend additional titles or request books on subjects not covered in the collection.

The adult new readers' collection is an important introduction to the library for many adult literacy students. The quality, diversity, depth, and accessibility of the collection will influence the students' perceptions of the library as a whole. If students feel welcome and stimulated, they are more likely to explore other resources in the library and become enthusiastic, confident library users.

Resources for Selecting Books for Special Collections

Adult Literacy Resource Institute, c/o Roxbury Community College, 1234 Columbus Ave., Boston, MA 02120.

    This literacy program sponsors a "Publishing for Literacy" project that publishes the writings of new readers. Write to it for information and a list of available titles.

Bayley, Linda. *Opening Doors for Adult New Readers: How Libraries can Select Materials and Establish Collections.* Syracuse, N.Y.: New Readers Press, 1980.

    Bayley's small book discusses the organizational details of setting up a new readers' collection.

Buckingham, Melissa Forinash, comp. *Reader Development Bibliography.* Philadelphia: Free Library of Philadelphia, 1986.

    Buckingham's excellent annotated bibliography categorizes books according to leisure reading interests, coping-skill area, or nonfiction subject. An introductory chapter on choosing low reading level materials for adults is very helpful.

Laubach, Robert S., and Kay Koschnick. *Using Readability: Formulas for Easy Adult Materials.* Syracuse, N.Y.: New Readers Press, 1977.

    In this brief but useful book the authors look at readability from two perspectives: evaluating the reading level of books and promoting the writing of more readable books. They examine the Gunning Fog Index and the Fry Readability Graph, two formulas frequently used for adult new reader materials. Also discussed are more subjective elements of writing, such as sentence structure and clarity of style. Several exercises will help readers develop an intuitive feel for readability.

LiBretto, Ellen V., comp. and ed. *High/Low Handbook: Encouraging Literacy in the 1990s.* New York: R. R. Bowker, 1990.

    Although intended for teachers, librarians, and others working with reluctant teenage readers, the discussions on evaluating and selecting books can also be helpful to anyone working with adult new readers. The well-annotated bibliography of books for reluctant readers contains many potential crossover titles that may be suitable for some adult literacy students.

Literacy Volunteers of New York City. 121 Ave. of the Americas, New York, NY 10013.

    This adult literacy program publishes *New Writers' Voices,* a series of publications containing the writings of new readers. Write to it for a catalog and ordering information.

Lyman, Helen Huguenor. *Library Materials in Service to the Adult New Reader.* Chicago: American Library Assn., 1973.

This extensive, ground-breaking study on the interests of adult new readers has played a major role in the development of new readers' collections in public libraries.

National Council of Teachers of English, Committee to Revise High Interest-Easy Reading. *High Interest Easy Reading.* 5th ed. Urbana, Ill.: NCTE, 1988.

This bibliography lists more than 400 books recommended for reluctant readers in junior and senior high school. The list contains many crossover titles that may appeal to adults. The annotations are informative and the categorization by easily understood terms such as war experiences, ethnic experiences, and technology are particularly helpful.

Pursell, Frances Josephson, comp. *Books for Adult New Readers.* 6th ed. Cleveland, Ohio: Project: LEARN, 1991 (available from New Readers Press).

This excellent annotated bibliography, produced by librarians and literacy workers at a highly successful adult literacy program, categorizes books according to general fiction areas, such as mystery or science fiction, and numerous nonfiction subject areas, such as biography, reading, religion, history, and travel. It also includes a chapter on periodicals for new readers and software for literacy programs.

Ryder, Randall J., et al. *Easy Reading: Book Series and Periodicals for Less Able Readers.* 2d ed. Newark, Del.: International Reading Association, 1989.

This is a bibliography of book series written for reluctant middle and high school students and adult literacy students. The introductory chapter discusses questions of readability and interest level.

11 _____

Using the Library for Lifelong Learning

The library was on Sixth Avenue and Ninth Street on the
south slopes of the Brooklyn hills and for a long time in
my young life it was the true center of the world.[1]

Pete Hamill

As stated earlier, simply learning how to read is not enough. We
want our adult literacy students to become proficient readers
who use reading to learn new things all through their lives—to be
lifelong learners. If adult literacy students are to participate actively in a life of reading and learning—at whatever level they are
able—they need to know how to use all the resources and information services available at the public library.

While books are the library's most visible business, they are
not its only business. Libraries collect information in other formats: audio recordings, video recordings, and computerized materials. Libraries also collect other forms of print: newspapers
and magazines, pamphlets, maps, even pictures. Libraries are
also information centers, providing resources and services to
help people find whatever information they seek.

This chapter suggests ways to help literacy students become
lifelong learners familiar with all the resources and services offered by the public library. It reviews the range of resources
beyond the circulating book collection available to library users,

discusses the library as an information center, and identifies the skills new readers need in order to use the library well. Throughout the chapter sample activities are provided to help students learn the skills necessary to be competent and efficient library users.

A Note to Tutors: This review of library skills and resources is addressed primarily to tutors helping students learn to use the library. The best way to teach literacy students how to use the library is to weave "library exercises" into the pattern of tutoring sessions, rather than to present an isolated unit on library skills. For example, if a student really likes a book she has read, you might suggest that together you look in the library's catalog to find other books by that same author. Such an activity can lead to lessons on the organization of a library catalog, rules for alphabetizing names (Where do I find "Mc" names? for example), or the use of pseudonyms. Familiarize yourselves with the library so you can connect the experiences, needs, and questions of your students to appropriate library resources as situations arise. Responding to the "teachable moment" by introducing your student to a resource that answers an immediate need will heighten the impact of that resource.

Most of the exercises suggested in this chapter are aimed at intermediate and advanced new readers. However, even beginning level new readers can start learning about using the resources of the entire library. They can use many of the nonprint materials, for example. They can also use, with your help, basic information sources such as telephone books and newspapers.

A Note to Librarians: As you read the following sample activities, think of specific materials in your library that literacy tutors will want to know about. Plan user-instruction activities geared to tutors and their students. Consider offering a workshop on the use of library resources to literacy tutors as part of the basic literacy-training program. Many tutors will not be familiar with the range of resources available at the library, especially computerized resources, so they will welcome your guidance.

Nonbook Library Resources

Public libraries of all sizes are increasing their collections of nonbook materials. The following discussion reviews library materials that are not books but are commonly found in public libraries and suggests activities to introduce these materials to adult new readers.

Audiovisual Materials

Audiovisual materials can be used for educational or entertainment purposes, just as books are. They offer literacy students a chance to use library resources that don't discriminate between patrons who read and those with limited reading ability. Teachers can also use many of the library's audiovisual materials to support and extend classroom presentations and to individualize instruction.

Records, Tapes, and Compact Disks

Most public libraries circulate records, cassette tapes, and compact disks (CDs). Many of these materials are musical recordings that literacy students, new to the library, may not realize are available for circulation. Borrowing music to enjoy at home or in the automobile can help literacy students come to see themselves as library users.

In addition to music, however, many recordings (especially those on cassette tapes and, to a limited degree, on the records still available) are of the spoken word. These materials include recordings of speeches or of historical events, poetry and short story readings, recordings of plays and radio shows, and discussions of nonfiction topics such as parenting, black history, nutrition, or sports. Such recordings can enhance classroom instruction for Adult Basic Education and General Education Development (GED) test students and serve as supplementary materials for students working in individualized settings.

There is also a growing list of books on tape, including readings of both adult and children's books. Available titles that may interest literacy students include popular novels, many of which became movies, such as Pat Conroy's *Prince of Tides;* books that inspired television series, such as Ernest Gaines's *The Autobiography of Miss Jane Pitman;* classic mysteries, such as *The Maltese Falcon* by Dashiell Hammett; and books of popular commentary, such as Erma Bombeck's *At Wit's End* or Robert Fulghum's *All I Really Need to Know I Learned in Kindergarten.*

SAMPLE AUDIO RECORDING ACTIVITIES

1. Recordings of the spoken word can spark numerous language experience exercises. Find tapes or records that relate to a particular time, place, or event your student is interested in. Have him listen to the tape, then ask him to give his reaction, recall his own version of the time or place, or imagine what he would have done in the circumstances described. Write down his comments, then help him read his own words.

2. Use recordings of historical speeches, readings from important documents, or accounts of major events in classes preparing for the social studies section of the General Education Development test. Ask students to discuss what they have heard or to write answers to questions based on the information in the recordings to give them practice answering the kinds of questions they will find on the test.

3. Use materials similar to those suggested in activity 2 to stimulate discussions of history, culture, and vocabulary with students studying English as a second language or preparing for citizenship.

4. Use recordings of poetry or plays with students preparing for the General Education Development reading exam. Again, have students write answers to questions based on information they've listened to. Use similar materials with students who need practice listening to spoken English.

5. Encourage students to borrow books on tape to listen to in their cars or at home. Tutors and students might borrow the same tape to listen to individually, then discuss it during tutoring sessions. Such discussions develop the same thinking and language skills that discussions of written works will require later in the progression toward literacy.

6. Have students follow along in the written version of a poem, story, or speech they listen to on tape or record.

7. Have students read aloud with the tape or record to practice fluency.

Movies and Video Cassettes

Many libraries now offer video cassettes, some for entertainment and some for educational purposes. Here is another opportunity for new readers to use the library frequently and comfortably without any acknowledgment of their level of reading skills. Libraries display videos in a variety of ways, but the arrangement at the Main Library of the Columbus Metropolitan Library is particularly advantageous to new readers: It shelves nonfiction videos according to call number and clearly labels each shelf section with popular headings such as travel, history, biography, etc. This arrangement enables patrons to find videos in subject areas of interest without having to look them up through subject headings in the library's catalog. The library also displays all the videos, including adult entertainment and children's videos, face out on the shelves, thus making them easier to recognize by the pictures on the container.

Instructional videos offering advice on numerous topics from house repairs to exercise programs are popular in library collections. Some collections also include videos that provide instruction in the basic skills of reading, writing, English, and math, many of which are specifically prepared for adult literacy students. These videos provide literacy students opportunities to review basic skills in the privacy of their homes. The journal *Booklist*, published by the American Library Association, periodically offers an annotated list of videos for literacy. Ask to review this list with your librarian and suggest some reviewed videos for library purchase.

SAMPLE VIDEO CASSETTE ACTIVITIES ⎯⎯⎯⎯⎯⎯⎯⎯⎯⎯⎯⎯⎯

1. Many children's books, including some of the best of the genre, have been dramatized on video. Suggest that students who are parents watch these videos with their children and discuss the story, the characters, the emotions engendered, and the quality of the language and illustrations. Although videos should never be a substitute for reading the books themselves, the experience of sharing the stories seen on video can help new readers learn to discuss ideas presented in books, as we hope they will do when they eventually read to their children. Seeing the stories portrayed

on video also gives new readers a familiarity with the story and its language, which will aid subsequent reading.

2. Show videos on topics of current events, history, biography, or nature in Adult Basic Education classes or to groups of students in a literacy program to spark discussion and lead to subsequent writing exercises. Such activities would be especially helpful to students preparing for the science and social studies sections of the GED exam.

Computer Software

Computers are everywhere, including in the library. Many public libraries, especially large ones, make computers and software programs available for public use. Word processing and spreadsheet programs are popular, as well as computer-assisted instruction for a range of topics. Computer programs that teach basic reading skills may provide good practice of the basic skills students need to master to become independent readers. While computer-based reading lessons can never replace a teacher who understands the particular needs and interests of individual students, they do offer students the opportunity to practice basic skills in a format that affords privacy and familiarizes the student with the most prevalent tool of our modern age. If your library does not offer computer programs that teach basic reading skills, ask the librarian to consider doing so. Some libraries also offer educational computer games.

Libraries are also computerizing their catalogs. Most large libraries have already done so, and smaller ones are following the trend. As students become familiar with the varied resources of the library, they will want to learn how to use its catalog. Mastering the library's catalog, if it is computerized, offers literacy students another opportunity to improve their computer literacy skills. In cases where the computerized catalog is new to the tutor as well, tutor and student can learn to use the new system together. (Learning to use the library's catalog is discussed more fully later in this chapter.) For literacy students seeking to improve their job skills and become computer literate, the library offers a friendly environment in which to become familiar with many applications of computers at no cost.

SAMPLE COMPUTER ACTIVITIES _____

1. If computer facilities are available at your local library, help your student learn to use a word processing program. Suggest that beginning level students copy language experience stories they have learned to read and build vocabulary lists. Encourage more advanced students to write letters or write and edit their own stories. Using a computer keyboard to write stories can be particularly beneficial to beginners because it involves their tactile and kinesthetic senses in the learning experience. The eye-hand motor coordination needed to locate the correct letter on the keyboard and the sensory feedback that comes from pushing the keys reinforces neurologically the basic skills beginning readers are learning, enabling them to "feel" the words as well as to see, hear, and speak them.

2. If your student is interested, consider playing a computer game as a supplementary exercise. Reading instructions and following a sequence of activities in the context of using a new and popular "toy" may prove to be an effective and fun exercise for some students.

Magazines and Newspapers

Public libraries collect magazines and newspapers. The number of magazine subscriptions will vary according to the size of the library, but in general you will find news magazines, such as *Time* and *Newsweek*; popular culture magazines, such as *Good Housekeeping* and *People*; educational magazines, such as *National Geographic* and *Smithsonian*; magazines featuring specific sports or hobbies, such as *Bicycling, Knitters,* and *Popular Mechanics*; basic science and medicine journals, such as *Scientific American* and *The Journal of the American Medical Association*; and even children's magazines, such as *Sesame Street* and *Cricket*.

Magazines and newspapers offer pictures, interesting stories, articles on popular topics, cartoons, recipes, project instructions, and other features that make them a versatile teaching resource. They contain information presented in a variety of formats from cartoons with few words to critical essays, offering students at all reading levels a chance to practice basic skills. Dailies and periodicals can be used in the classroom to augment specific lessons or to suggest ideas for discussions and writing assignments. Browsing through magazines and newspapers in the library is also a pleasant way for students to become accustomed to being there and often leads to more extensive use of the library as a whole. Some libraries circulate magazines, especially back issues, making it easier to use them in tutoring sessions. Check with the librarian to find out your library's circulation policy. Most public libraries carry both local and at least some out-of-town newspapers.

SAMPLE MAGAZINE AND NEWSPAPER ACTIVITIES

1. With beginning readers, develop exercises in which students look for letters or newly learned words in headlines and titles.

2. Choose a few short articles, photocopy them, then separate the headlines from the stories. Ask the students to read the stories and match them with the correct headlines.

3. For students who are interested in sports, the newspaper is a virtual reading textbook. Help students learn to read charts from a daily examination of the box scores and league standings of professional teams. Develop vocabulary activities, such as having student list all the words used in headlines to indicate a team won a game (beat, nip, rout, whip, trounce, shut out, etc.). Have students scan a full-length article for details, such as who won, what was the score, who were the pitchers, who scored the winning run, who committed an error, whether it was a close game or one team dominated, etc. Encourage students to develop a critical sense by distinguishing between reports of a game and editorial comments about the state of the sport in general, perhaps by having students write their own commentary in reply to an editorial selection.

4. Collect cartoons from both newspapers and magazines. With cartoons that continue over a series of blocks, separate the blocks and ask students to put them in the correct sequence. With cartoons presented in a single block, ask students to imagine they are trying to explain the cartoon to someone who hasn't seen it, or ask them to explain why the cartoon is—or is not—funny or provocative.

5. Have students collect recipes they like. Develop a vocabulary list of cooking terms and measurements. Ask students to write a recipe for a dish they cook frequently.

6. If a student is planning a long driving trip, have her consult the weather map in the daily newspaper to determine what kind of weather she can expect along the way. Have her determine the temperature range in both her home city and the destination city, then compare the two. Have her find the time of sunrise and sunset, and ask her to figure out how many hours she will have to travel in daylight, making sure she considers any time zone changes.

7. Have students examine the advertisements that appear in news-papers and magazines. Encourage them to look critically at the ads by asking questions such as: What is the relationship between what is pictured and what is being sold? Are there different ways to interpret the text of the ad? What are the most important words of the ad? How effective is the ad?

8. Read letters to the editor or to columnists such as Ann Landers. Ask your students to write a reply.

Microfilm and Microfiche

In addition to current newspapers, libraries also maintain collec-tions of old newspapers, sometimes going back many years. They are generally stored on microfilm or microfiche. In the following example, a student uses old newspapers to answer a question of interest, and at the same time he learns about doing historical research using a technology common to public libraries.

SAMPLE MICROFILM ACTIVITY

A student who is interested in baseball might enjoy looking through old newspapers to verify particular facts. Let's say he wants to know the starting pitchers for the sixth game of the 1975 World Series. He knows the game occurred in October of that year, but not the specific date. Take him to the newspaper section of the library and help him find copies of either the local newspaper or a major paper, such as *The New York Times,* for several days in October 1975. Have him read the directions for setting up the microfilm in the reader, helping him whenever necessary. Help him find the sports section of the paper, then have him scan through as many days' papers as necessary until he finds the information he is looking for.

Citations to articles in magazines and newspapers are also accessible now through computerized databases. Many libraries make these systems available to the public. While the computer programs are "user friendly," they are not simple. However, they do offer access to a powerful source of information, as well as additional opportunities for advanced new readers to use sophisticated computer applications. Such computerized databases are discussed later in this chapter.

The Pamphlet File

Most libraries have pamphlet files—some call them vertical files. They are collections of pamphlets, leaflets, booklets, and other materials not cataloged and shelved with the books. The material is filed by subject; in some large libraries, each department may have its own pamphlet file. The pamphlet file is a very useful but often overlooked information source. Even longtime library users don't use the pamphlet file because they are not aware that it exists or because the file cabinets look too "official" to be open to the public. They are for public use, however, and they contain a wealth of information covering a broad range of topics. Government publications, manufacturer's information about specific products, and informative booklets published by national organizations of all kinds are among the sorts of things you will find in a pamphlet file.

Pamphlets often serve as a first source of information on a particular subject. For example, much basic patient information about various diseases is distributed in pamphlet form, often by government health agencies or by organizations such as the American Heart Association. Although this information is somewhat superficial, it gives an introductory overview of a topic and, more importantly, lists names and addresses of other sources of information. If your student is looking for information about a potentially complicated or difficult topic, consider the pamphlet file as a starting place. Use the information reading technique (described in Chapter 6) as a means of helping the student read and understand the information.

The Picture File

Many public libraries maintain picture files. These are files, arranged by subject, of pictures clipped from popular magazines and other sources. Most libraries circulate the materials in the picture files. Subjects covered will vary from one library to another, but most picture files will include pictures showing major countries and cities; pictures of popular sports and hobbies; pictures of famous personalities in politics, sports, and the arts; and pictures of events of historic or cultural interest. These pictures can be used with Adult Basic Education students to stimulate writing exercises and language experience stories. They can also be used with English as a Second Language students to spark discussion on current events or cultural practices or to enhance vocabulary exercises.

Information and Reference Services

Pubic libraries do not just lend books and other materials; they also provide information. The reference service offers walk-in patrons and telephone callers answers to a vast number of questions ranging from the important—"Who is my state representative?"—to the trivial—"Who played second base for the Indians in 1954?" Introducing Adult Basic Education students to the library's reference services is yet another way to familiarize them with the library and its services. The possibility of calling the library to ask questions, and thus preserving anonymity, may be especially appealing to literacy students. In the reference department, literacy students will also find such useful items as telephone books from cities across the country, road maps for local areas as well as distant cities and states, dictionaries for English and other languages, and numerous encyclopedias, almanacs, and other reference books.

Incorporate these reference resources into your tutoring activities whenever possible. Take your student to the reference section of the library and show her the format of the materials and how they are used. Encourage her to do as much of the "looking up" as possible to give her both confidence and skill in using the materials.

Dictionaries

All dictionaries define words, but their individual contents vary considerably from one to another. Unabridged dictionaries, such as *The Random House Dictionary of the English Language,* offer a comprehensive, inclusive list of the words of a language; abridged dictionaries select from that list the most commonly used words or as many words as seem appropriate to the intended audience. *The American Heritage Dictionary,* for example, published by Houghton Mifflin, is an abridged dictionary that is particularly noted for its clear definitions and its quotations illustrating how words are used. Houghton Mifflin also publishes a *Children's Dictionary* and *The American Heritage Student's Dictionary,* geared toward students in sixth through ninth grades. Both of these dictionaries are based on *The American Heritage Dictionary.* Most dictionaries also include pronunciation guides, notes on the etymology or origin of words, and information on usage, such as whether a word is obsolete, colloquial, or vulgar. Finally, dictionaries offer a range of other features, usually found in the back of the book, including lists of famous names, lists of places, lists of presidents, and small atlases.

Dictionaries can also be highly specialized. For example, there are dictionaries of rhyming words, of slang, of abbreviations, and of synonyms. There are also subject dictionaries that define words used in a particular subject area, such as science or medicine. Exploring some of these dictionaries with adult literacy students can be fun and can also introduce students to the many tools that help readers and writers use words well.

Encourage your students to develop the dictionary habit early in their reading instruction. Any library offers numerous dictionaries spanning a range of levels of difficulty. Ask your local librarian to help you identify a dictionary that is suitable for your students, and help them learn to use it. The resource section at the end of this chapter lists a few examples of the many possible choices.

SAMPLE DICTIONARY ACTIVITIES _____

1. Determine which dictionary would be most appropriate for your student. Your librarian can help you make this selection. Introduce your student to the dictionary by browsing through it together. Look up a few familiar words, examine the parts of entries, such as the pronunciation and examples of usage, and look through the back of the book to see what other features are included.

2. Have your student keep a vocabulary notebook. Encourage him to list all words he encounters that are unfamiliar, whether he finds them in his reading or hears them on the radio or TV or in conversation. Then have him look up the words in the dictionary, giving him help with spelling and alphabetical order, if necessary, to ease the task without weakening the learning experience for him. Encourage him to write the appropriate definition for the context in which he found the word. Have him copy the sentence in which he encountered the word or describe the situation in which he heard it.

3. Have your student look up the same word in a student dictionary, an abridged dictionary, and an unabridged dictionary. Have him write the primary definition found in each source and note variations in the additional information given by each dictionary.

Specialized Dictionaries

Specialized dictionaries offer opportunities for fun and informative exercises. The following activities involve use of specialized dictionaries.

SAMPLE SPECIALIZED DICTIONARY ACTIVITIES _____

1. Have your students choose five rhyming words from a dictionary of rhyming words, then try to write a poem—a nonsensical one will do—that uses all five words.

2. Together with your student, keep a running list of slang expressions or colloquialisms, such as "in the catbird seat" or "graveyard shift." Then have the student find the definitions in a dictionary of slang and write each expression in a sentence.

3. Ask the student to page through the daily newspaper and list all the abbreviations she can find. Then have her look up the meanings of those abbreviations in a dictionary of abbreviations. For those abbreviations that have multiple meanings, have the student match the abbreviation with the most probable meaning, judging from its context in the newspaper.

Encyclopedias

Encyclopedias are good references sources for answering specific questions, such as "When did Arizona become a state?" or "Who invented television?" They also offer a broad overview of many topics, so they can be a good starting place for a student who wants to learn about a subject completely new to him.

Some encyclopedias are multivolume works, such as the comprehensive *Encyclopedia Americana* or the somewhat less scholarly *Academic American Encyclopedia,* which is geared toward high school and college students. Both are published by Grolier Education Corporation. Other encyclopedias are more concise reviews of general knowledge in one or two volumes, such as *The Lincoln Library of Essential Information,* published by Frontier Press.

Several multivolume encyclopedias are published for children. One of the most popular is *The World Book Encyclopedia,* published by World Book Inc. Geared to middle- and junior-high school students, *World Book* provides extensive up-to-date information in a format that is very suitable for adults.

Special-subject encyclopedias cover one general topic in great detail. Subjects covered range from science to rock and roll. Depending on their particular interests, literacy students may be surprised to discover encyclopedias such as *Baseball Encyclopedia,* published by Collier Macmillan; *Blacks in American Film and Television: An Encyclopedia,* published by Garland; or *The Encyclopedia of Pop, Rock, and Soul,* published by St. Martin's Press.

Some encyclopedias are intended for a scholarly audience, others for a more general readership, and still others for students from elementary through college levels. Several titles could easily be shelved either in the children's department or the adult department, or both.

SAMPLE ENCYCLOPEDIA ACTIVITIES _____

1. Suppose your student is particularly interested in rock and roll music. Ask her to think of some questions or information she might like to look up, such as the relation between rock and roll and rhythm and blues, the year a particular singer started his career, or the name of the first record recorded by an artist who subsequently became very famous. Then go to the reference department together to find the answers to her questions. You might begin by reading a general article on rock and roll in a general encyclopedia, such as *The Academic American Encyclopedia* or *The World Book Encyclopedia,* depending on the student's reading level. Then go to a specialized encyclopedia, such as the *Encyclopedia of Pop, Rock, and Soul.* Discuss the different levels of information presented. Ask the student to evaluate the authority of the information given, based on her previous knowledge. If she disagrees with any of the information she finds (and it's important that she understand that books are not always completely accurate or up-to-date), help her find other sources to check.

2. Give your students a list of statements about some topics that interest them. Ask them to verify the statements and note for each statement what reference source they used to check the information.

Other Reference Books

In addition to the books mentioned, the reference department of a library will have numerous other information sources including familiar ones, such as telephone books from around the country and atlases, which give facts and figures about countries, states, and cities as well as numerous and highly detailed maps. Perhaps less familiar, but equally informative, are almanacs, which are compendiums of economic, political, geographic, demographic, and meteorologic facts as well as chronologies of the events of any one year; directories that provide names and addresses for businesses and organizations; and compilations of facts, such as the *Guinness Book of Records,* that provide fascinating if not essential information about the range of human activity.

_____ SAMPLE REFERENCE BOOK ACTIVITIES _____

1. If your student is planning a long driving trip, help him consult an atlas to plan the route. Have him make note of any major cities he will travel through to reach his destination. Ask him to find the geographical size and the population for those cities, perhaps graphing the information. Have him figure out the mileage from start to finish and plan convenient places to stay overnight if the trip requires more than one day's driving.

2. If a student has a need to find information about a particular medical problem, look with her at the *Encyclopedia of Associations* to find an association that provides information and support for families affected by this problem.

3. Students who grow some of their own vegetables might be interested in looking at previous years' almanacs to chart the weather patterns for the growing season.

4. Whenever your students need help for immediate problems, consider using your local *Yellow Pages* to help them find the store or service that will meet their needs. Always ask them to suggest the headings to look under first. Point out that the indexing principles used by the *Yellow Pages* are the same as those used in the library's catalog and in periodical indexes (both discussed following). The more practice they get "subject searching" in the phone book, the more easily they will understand the principles of subject indexing applied to library information.

5. If your students have friends or relatives living in other cities, ask them to look up the addresses and phone numbers in the telephone directories found in the reference department. This exercise gives students practice with alphabetical order; it can also lead to discussions and practice exercises for spelling rules and exceptions, as illustrated by the various spellings of some names. If they are capable, have them look up the street addresses in the zip code directory, then write letters to their friends or relatives.

The resources of the library's reference department can provide quick answers to students' questions or whet their appetites for more extensive inquiry into a topic. Take your students to the reference department whenever they have a question or interest that can be addressed there. Ask the reference librarian at your local library to give a presentation to tutors discussing books from the reference collection, highlighting those that might be particularly interesting or useful to new readers. Ask the librarian to include works from the children's reference area that are suitable for adults. If you are familiar with the library's basic reference resources and aware of the extent of information available, you can incorporate useful activities into your instructional sessions that can help to extend students' understanding as well as give them practice and confidence in using all the resources of the public library.

What Students Need to Know about the Library

To use a library effectively for lifelong learning, students need to know a few facts and some basic skills:

1. Students should recognize that libraries are comprehensive information resources, providing access to information in print and in audiovisual and computerized formats.
2. Students should know that librarians are increasingly able to gain access to information and materials available at other locations. For example, they can request books not available on site from other libraries through interlibrary loan, or they can answer questions by searching electronic databases over telephone lines.
3. Students should know that librarians are trained to help people find information as well as to select books, and they should feel comfortable asking librarians for help.
4. Students should recognize library terms, such as call number, fiction, nonfiction, catalog, reference, etc.
5. Students should be able to use the library catalog to find books by author, title, or subject.
6. Students should understand that classification systems, most commonly the Dewey Decimal System, are used to arrange library collections by subject.

7. Students should be able to read call numbers so that books that have been identified in the catalog can be found on the shelves.

8. Students should be able to read and understand the essential information contained in the catalog record, including subject headings.

9. Students should be able to use basic reference sources, such as dictionaries, encyclopedias, and almanacs.

10. Students should be able to understand and use periodical indexes in print and electronic formats.

The following sections deal more specifically with two of the main sources of information in a library: the library catalog and periodical indexes.

Using the Library Catalog

Literacy students often become acquainted with the library through the new readers' collection. Initially, they may choose books only from this collection. As students' reading abilities and familiarity with the library increase, they will want to find other books. To do so efficiently, adult literacy students need to use the library's catalog.

Some libraries still maintain their catalogs on three-by-five cards filed in drawers, but card catalogs are quickly giving way to computerized catalogs, even in smaller libraries. Whether the information is on a file card or on a computer, however, the terminology and basic format are the same. While a card catalog may be reassuringly familiar to those not yet introduced to computer catalogs, the computers offer two advantages that are a great boon to library research: They are faster, and they allow the user to search the catalog in many ways. For example, you can search by title, by author, or by subject, as you can in a card catalog; but in many systems you can also search by a combination of author and title, by keywords if you can't remember an exact title, or by Boolean searching, which means combining terms such as *Steinbeck* and *mice* to find an entry for John Steinbeck's *Of Mice and Men.*

Computerized library catalogs also give literacy students—and sometimes their tutors—a chance to practice computer skills and to learn an application of computer technology that many long-time library users have yet to master. If tutor and student learn together, the shared learning experience can boost a student's confidence.

Things to Know about Library Catalogs

1. Although the information contained on computerized catalogs is standardized, the software packages that provide access to those data vary from system to system and from library to library. Be sure to read the instructions for your local system to find out what kind of searches are possible.
2. Many computerized systems have two records for each book. One record gives the title, author, call number, and availability, that is, whether or not the book is on the shelf and which branches hold copies (if the library is a multibranch one). The other record, called a catalog or bibliographic record, gives all the information available on the old catalog card, including title, author, call number, publisher, copyright date, size and number of pages, and subject headings.
3. Books are indexed in a catalog under title, author or editor (when there is one), and subject headings. Most books are listed under more than one subject heading.
4. Reading subject headings on the catalog record suggests additional subject headings to search for books on a topic. Following is a sample catalog record:

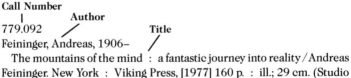

Call Number
| **Author**
779.092   /   **Title**
Feininger, Andreas, 1906–   /
   The mountains of the mind : a fantastic journey into reality / Andreas Feininger. New York : Viking Press, [1977] 160 p. : ill.; 29 cm. (Studio Book)

SUB: 1. Photography, Artistic 2. Nature photography
           ＼ **Subject Headings** ／

Students and tutors who have used this book, for example, can search under the subject headings photography, artistic, or nature photography to find other books.

5. If you have a book in hand and you want to find others on the same topic, look on the back of the title page. Many books contain what is called Cataloging-in-Publication data supplied by the Library of Congress. This information resembles a catalog card and lists the subject headings under which that book would be indexed. Then look up those subject headings to find other books. Following is a sample of Cataloging-in-Publication data:

Library of Congress Cataloging-in-Publication Data

Author ——————— Feininger, Andreas, 1906–
Title ————————— The mountains of the mind.
(A studio book)
Subject Headings ——— 1. Nature photography.   2. Photography, Artistic.
I. Title.
TR721.F44   779′.092′4   76-51762
ISBN 0-670-49129-2   └——— Dewey Decimal Number

The following suggested activities will help your students learn to use the library catalog. Remember to develop activities for your students based on their abilities and particular interests. Library activities that lead students to the books and information they want or have immediate need for will have a lasting impact.

———————— **SAMPLE LIBRARY CATALOG ACTIVITIES** ————————

1. If your student enjoys watching videos, have her list a few titles, then search the library catalog to find out if the library holds those titles. Then have her find the movies on the shelves.

2. After your student has finished a book he's enjoyed, have him look up the author in the library catalog. If other books by that author are available, have him find them on the shelves.

3. Assume, for example, that a student has expressed an interest in learning about labor unions. Suggest that together you look for some books on the topic in the library catalog. First, ask the student to think of subject headings under which this topic may be found. Then have him search under the subject headings. In many cases, if the subject heading is not the accepted one, the computer will present alternatives. For example, if you look in the catalog under

the heading "labor unions" you will be told to "see trade unions," which is the official subject heading. The catalog will also suggest that you "see also labor movement" and other related terms that may lead to books of interest. If you get no helpful responses to the subject headings you enter, ask the librarian to help you select the correct term. Once a student has found some books under the subject heading, ask him or her to retrieve those books from the shelves.

Using Periodical Indexes

Periodical indexes lead researchers to articles by particular authors or about particular subjects that have appeared in magazines and newspapers. To be indexed, an article is read by professional indexers (or in some cases by computers) and assigned subject headings that reflect the major topics of the articles, in much the same way that books are assigned subject headings. The *Readers' Guide to Periodical Literature* is perhaps the best known index to articles from popular magazines and newspapers.

Although periodical indexes might be generally associated with students doing reports and term papers for their classes, they are also frequently used by the general public. Library patrons use periodical indexes to help them choose a new car, to pursue various hobbies, or to satisfy their curiosity about numerous topics. The indexes are relatively easy to use, once you understand the general principle of subject indexing and become familiar with the formats and abbreviations used to identify articles. Introducing intermediate and advanced new readers to periodical indexes will give them access to a major source of information.

Increasingly, periodical indexes are available in computerized versions as well as in print. Computerized indexes employ the same general indexing principles, but are faster and cover a wider range of sources. Computerized indexes also offer users the opportunity to do what is called Boolean searching. This simply means that the user can tell the computer to find only those articles that discuss a specified combination of concepts. For example, if you were using a print index to find articles on the recycling of plastics, you would have to look under the subject heading "recycling" and then read through the titles to find articles that are specifically about the recycling of plastics. Using a computerized index, you can tell the computer to retrieve only those articles that deal specifically with the recycling of plastics. *Newspaper Index* and *Infotrac* are two popular computerized indexes to magazines and newspapers.

Students do not have to be proficient in using a printed index before learning to use the computerized version. The computerized indexes are "user friendly," which means that they take the user through the process step by step, offering choices, called "menus," at various stages of the search to lead him from telling the computer what he wants to choosing from among the articles the computer retrieves. But user friendly doesn't necessarily mean simple, so the more the user understands about the basic principles of indexing the more successful he is likely to be. Looking up articles under subject headings in the print indexes first allows the student to see the structure of the database, to see articles listed under specific subject headings. Visualizing this arrangement when using the computer index will help the student understand the choices the computerized menus offer and increase the likelihood that his search for articles relevant to his topic will be successful.

Using computerized indexes is obviously one more way students can practice computer skills and master yet another application of computer technology, enhancing their efficiency as learners as well as their prospects for employment in a technological society. There are many different computerized indexes intended for general use found in public libraries. Check the reference department of your library to see what computerized indexes they have available.

_____ SAMPLE PERIODICAL INDEX ACTIVITIES _____

1. If a student talks about buying a car, suggest that she do some research in recent consumer magazines to compare prices, repair records, and relative safety. Suggest that she go to the reference department and ask the librarian to help her choose an index that will contain references to articles on buying cars. Help her as needed, but let her do as much of the asking and searching as possible, so she will gain both confidence and skill.

2. If a student has a particular interest in a certain musician, he might enjoy looking for articles about that person, including reviews of recent recordings and concerts.

The activities suggested in this chapter are intended to help literacy students learn to use all the varied resources of the public library. This is a tall order for tutors as well as for students. Not all literacy students will reach the point of researching topics through periodical indexes, but many students can reach that point if given sufficient assistance and encouragement. And all literacy students deserve to know the extent of knowledge and information available to them through the public library. Even if they don't develop the skills to use many resources themselves, they can request help from librarians, tutors, family members, or friends, and they can encourage others, particularly their children, to use this remarkable resource.

In this rapidly changing world, the library changes, too. The public library of today is a very different place than it was even ten years ago, and it will inevitably be different again in another ten years. So much change presents library users with a challenge but also with extraordinary opportunities. For librarians and literacy teachers, the challenge is to make all the riches of the library accessible and understandable to adults just beginning their quest for lifelong learning, and all the potential opportunities that quest can bring.

Resources for Using the Library for Lifelong Learning

Cheyney, Arnold. *Teaching Reading Skills through the Newspaper.* 2d ed. Newark, Del.: International Reading Assn., 1984.

> Cheyney offers numerous suggestions for using the newspaper to teach various reading skills.

Felkor, Bruce L. *How to Look Things Up and Find Things Out.* New York: William Morrow, 1988.

> This highly readable book is intended for the general public. It discusses methods and sources for finding information on a wide range of topics.

Gates, Jean Key. *Guide to the Use of Libraries and Information Sources.* New York: McGraw-Hill Book Co., 1989.

Gates focuses on the organization, arrangement, effective use, and diversity of materials available in any public library. The first chapter offers a brief but informative history of books and libraries.

Heitzman, Wm. Ray. *The Newspaper in the Classroom.* 2d ed. Washington, D.C.: National Education Association, 1986.

Suggestions for using the newspaper to teach reading, including critical thinking skills, are presented.

Horowitz, Lois. *Knowing Where to Look: The Ultimate Guide to Research.* Cincinnati, Ohio: Writer's Digest Books, 1984.

Written in a highly readable style for a general audience by a reference librarian, this book discusses numerous sources of information and illustrates their uses.

Soule, Jennifer A. *The Adult New Reader Learns the Library: Curriculum Ideas for Librarians and Adult Educators.* Chicago: American Library Assn., 1990.

Soule's very helpful guide takes tutor and student through all library resources and services. She offers numerous suggestions for learning activities specifically geared to adult new readers.

Part Four

BRINGING IT
ALL TOGETHER

12

Building a Literacy Coalition

> Since my family did not own many books or have the money for a child to buy them, it was good to know that solely by virtue of my municipal citizenship I had access to any book I wanted... from the branch library I could walk to in my neighborhood.[1]　　　Philip Roth

According to the *Oxford English Dictionary*, the original root of the word *coalition* is the Latin word *coalere*, meaning "to sustain and nourish." That seems a particularly apt image of what a library does for literacy students: sustains and nourishes their developing reading skills and their participation in a life of reading and learning. For this to happen, however, librarians and literacy providers need to work closely together. They also need significant support and assistance from the community at large.

Recognizing the need for collaborative efforts, library staff and literacy workers across the country are forming coalitions. In modern usage, the *Oxford English Dictionary* defines *coalition* as "the growing together of separate parts" or "a fusion of parties, principles, and interests." It is this kind of coalition that librarians and literacy providers aim to build for literacy. It must be a fusion of parties: the public library, adult literacy programs, and the community at large. It must be a fusion of principles: a strong belief in the value of learning for each individual and the importance to a free society of a literate, informed, inquisitive citizenry. It must be a fusion of interests: the interests of students who need excellent, well-funded literacy programs to help them learn how to read; the interests of literacy teachers, who seek to provide the best learning opportunities for their students; the interests of the public library, which aims to collect, preserve, and make available to all the rich resources of our culture; and the interests of the community, which works to use, build upon, and transmit that culture to future generations.

Forming the Library Literacy Connection

Community literacy programs and the public library form the core of the literacy coalition. Literacy programs teach adult students how to read or improve their reading. Libraries offer students opportunities to apply developing reading skills to a wide range of materials. Working together, librarians and literacy teachers strengthen each other's efforts and increase opportunities for students to succeed. Let's look at some specific activities library and literacy program personnel can undertake to advance literacy.

What Library Staff Can Do

Librarians should visit local Adult Basic Education and literacy programs regularly. They should become familiar with the staff and students and with the general operation of the programs in their community. During their visits to the literacy program, librarians can promote the library literacy connection in numerous ways. They can:

> Explain the new readers collection. Tell students where it is, what it contains, and how they may use or borrow the materials.
> Identify and encourage use of materials from the general collection that are appropriate for literacy students. Include photodocumentaries, collections of paintings and photographs, poetry, audiovisual materials, newspapers, magazines, pamphlets, and other materials.

Read stories and poems to classes and talk to students about specific books.

Poll students' interests for suggestions of books or topics to add to the library's collection.

Invite students to read and review books being considered for the new readers' collection.

Distribute library-card applications.

Place rotating deposit collections in Adult Basic Education centers, for volunteer literacy programs, and on bookmobiles. Include a sampling of all kind of materials for new readers.

Build a collection of resource materials for tutors, including training manuals from other programs as well as a comprehensive collection of books on reading, literacy, and adult education.

Participate in tutor training sessions by preparing information packets, giving library tours, and discussing the various library resources available to new readers.

Conduct short, welcoming library orientations for students and tutors when they first come to use it (or when the student feels sufficiently comfortable). Highlight services and collections new readers may want to use.

Maintain an accessible file of reviews of books for new readers.

Publish periodic bibliographies of books for new readers and distribute them to literacy programs.

Add copies of books to the new readers' collection from the general adult collection or the children's collection that are appropriate for new readers.

Label books that are shelved in other sections but that are appropriate for new readers with a literacy logo to make them easily identifiable to tutors and literacy students.

Display easy-to-read pamphlets from the library's pamphlet file. Consider giving them away if multiple copies are available.

Develop a picture file and encourage its use among literacy teachers.

Refer potential students to the local literacy program.

Make library space available for classes or tutoring sessions.

Invite authors of books that are popular with new readers to discuss their writing and to speak to a larger community about writing and literacy.

Serve as a clearinghouse for literacy information. This can include maintaining a bulletin board with information about local literacy programs; distributing flyers, brochures, and other information sources about literacy programs; and maintaining a file of literacy activity nationwide.

What Literacy Tutors Can Do

Teachers not only teach, they serve as role models for learners. Teachers can encourage library use among students by talking about books they are reading and by linking classroom activities with library books. Tutors can also:

Take classes or individual students to the library and have the librarian show them the various books and resources available.

Read stories or poems to classes for brief periods each day. Mention similar books that are available in the library.

For higher level classes, illustrate or supplement specific lessons with a range of books and other materials from the library. For example, enrich a history lesson by reading from a collection of letters from a person studied in the lesson.

Create a library corner in the classroom with a changing display of books, pamphlets, and other relevant materials. Highlight materials and information that students might not expect to find in a library.

Bring newspapers, magazines, books, and other materials related to current events to the class to help stimulate discussions as well as reading and writing activities. Consider including items from the library's picture file.

Ask students for specific questions or general topics they would like to investigate. Bring library books that pertain to the students' questions and interests to the class.

Review lists of newly published books for adult new readers with library staff. Make specific recommendations for library purchase.

Encourage students to write book reviews.

Distribute library-card applications.

Invite the local librarian to serve on a board of advisors or other such group.

Learn as much as possible about the library: how it is funded, who governs it, and how it views its mission. Advocate services for new readers whenever appropriate.

What Library Staff and Literacy Tutors Together Can Do

Share ideas for collaborative efforts to improve literacy.

Develop a jointly sponsored family literacy program. Librarians can offer workshops discussing children's literature, reading to children, or various parenting skills. Literacy tutors can help students learn to read children's books that students will later read to their children.

Conduct training activities to acquaint each other with each agency's services and to develop skills necessary to implement and evaluate jointly planned programs.

Share promotional materials (flyers, bookmarks, posters, etc.) describing services of each other's agencies; include the other agency on your mailing list for newsletters and other communications.

Sponsor a speaker's bureau through which library staff and literacy tutors can speak to social service agencies and community organizations about literacy services for adults.

Recruit volunteers to carry out specific tasks planned by joint library-literacy efforts.

Develop a literacy component of library programs planned for a general audience. One example of a library program that could accommodate a literacy component is Voices and Visions, a poetry reading and discussion project sponsored in part by the National Endowment for the Humanities.

Establish a new readers' book discussion club. Librarians can make multiple copies available.

Encourage students' writing by publishing and disseminating collections of their works.

Reaching Out to the Community at Large

The public library and local literacy programs are at the heart of the literacy coalition. But illiteracy affects all aspects of a community, and all segments of that community should be involved in efforts to reduce it. Consider inviting into the coalition representatives from the business community, social welfare organizations, vocational rehabilitation programs, youth groups, senior citizen agencies, employment services, refugee groups, churches, correctional institutions, local universities, and the local media. This larger coalition can address issues that are fundamental to the success of a literacy program but that are often beyond the scope of any one literacy program working alone. In particular, a broad-based community literacy coalition can address two issues crucial to the success and viability of any program: funding and the recruitment and retention of students.

A successful literacy program needs solid, long-term financial support. For too many programs, funding is sporadic and insufficient. Staff must spend their time gathering whatever crumbs of financing are available, often competing with other worthy agencies. Changing this situation will require significant change in the way government and business view education. Whether these changes will be forthcoming is unknown and unpredictable at this point. What is clear is that significant changes will occur only if the literacy community speaks loudly and frequently about the needs of literacy students. Many voices speak louder than one. Broad-based literacy coalitions, representing all segments of a community, can put literacy on the government and business agenda better than any one program director acting alone.

Other than funding, the most significant problem literacy programs face is recruiting the most needy students and keeping them in the program once they have started. As explained in Chapter 2, many potential students are wary of institutionalized or "school-like" programs. They often mistrust persons from outside their social environment. Others are fearful or ashamed of their inability to read and afraid of failing one more time.

For students who do begin a literacy program, staying with it can be harder than admitting the problem in the first place. Drop-out rates in Adult Basic Education and literacy programs can exceed 50 percent. The task of learning to read is hard and requires immense time, effort, and commitment. For adult students, their efforts are inevitably complicated by pressures from a job, or the lack of one, family responsibilities, physical disabilities, and nagging self-doubt.

Stong community support can help literacy students enter and remain in literacy programs. For that to happen, however, the coalition must include persons who come from the same economic and social circumstances as the students. These community members can reach potential students through local churches, social organizations, and personal contact. They can gain the trust of potential students and recruit other community members to serve as tutors or supporters of literacy.

What the Community-Wide Literacy Coalition Can Do

Organize public relations efforts including newsletters, press releases, business breakfasts, and read-athons at local shopping areas (to name just a few methods that have been tried).

Raise the issue through all local media: letters to the editor, editorials in the local newspapers, radio talk shows, and public lectures.

Research funding opportunities and write grant applications.

Lobby legislators, both national and local, to provide substantial, long-term support for literacy programs.

Create an ongoing dialogue in the community about literacy and educational issues in general.

Organize a committee of teachers, librarians, students, and community writers and scholars to write materials for new readers. Resources such as *Thinking Is a Basic Skill* (listed at the end of this chapter) offer guidelines for groups writing for new readers.

Sponsor community oral history projects involving new readers as well as other members of the community.

Expand the base of volunteer tutors to include management and workers from area businesses, work-study students from local colleges, senior citizens, and retired workers.

Establish an advocacy group of students and former students and involve them in planning, implementing, and promoting activities to support literacy programs.

Organize and maintain ancillary services to support literacy programs, such as child care, transportation, and employment counseling.

Recruit community members to serve as mentors for literacy students.

Encourage businesses to support literacy by allowing released time for students and tutors to work together, by making on-site tutoring available, and by providing incentives for workers who agree to improve their basic skills.

Arrange large-scale public events including members of the arts, entertainment, and sports communities to support the efforts of literacy programs and students.

Working together, members of the literacy coalition will sustain and nourish adult literacy students. No one agency can do the job alone. Literacy programs teach students how to read. Public libraries offer students the opportunity to practice newly acquired reading skills by reading books that provide information important to their everyday lives, books that entertain or amuse them, and books that invite them to explore a world of knowledge and ideas beyond their current understanding. The community at large supports literacy students by providing substantial, long-term funding for literacy programs and jobs for students who improve their skills. Sustained and nourished by this coalition, adult new readers will not only learn how to read, they will become enthusiastic readers and lifelong participants in our learning society.

Resources for Building Literacy Coalitions

Chisman, Forrest P. *Leadership for Literacy: Agenda for the 1990's.* San Francisco: Jossey-Bass Publishers, 1990.

Several contributors discuss the current status of literacy programs, trends for the future, and ways in which government officials, educators, and community leaders can strengthen literacy activities in the coming decade.

Davis, Nancy Harvey, and Pam Fitzgerald. "Literacy Clearinghouse." *Library Journal,* a monthly column.

Every month this column offers practical advice, examples of programs that work, reviews of new materials, and other timely and useful information on literacy activities and the public library.

Fineman, Marcia Pollack. "Project: LEARN—Adults Become Readers." *Library Journal* 112 (1 March 1987): 45–46.

Fineman describes the book-discussions clubs sponsored by Cleveland's Project: LEARN and the Cuyahoga County Public Library. Write for a "Leaders' Packet for Adult New Readers' Book Clubs" to Cuyahoga County Public Library, 4510 Memphis Ave., Cleveland, OH 44144.

Johnson, Debra Wilcox, Jane Robbins, and Douglas L. Zweizig. *Libraries: Partners in Adult Literacy.* Norwood, N.J.: Ablex Publishing Corp., 1990.

This book explores the library's role as a partner in adult literacy. It includes a review of the literature, 1979–1988, a survey of various types of libraries regarding their involvement in literacy, and case studies of model programs.

Johnson, Debra Wilcox, and Jennifer A. Soule. *Libraries and Literacy: A Planning Manual.* Chicago: American Library Assn., 1987.

This manual is intended for libraries deciding whether or in what way to participate in literacy activities in their communities. It gives an overview of the problem of illiteracy and discusses all aspects of a library's involvement including building collections, working with literacy providers, publicizing literacy activities, and evaluating programs.

Kozol, Jonathan. *Illiterate America.* Garden City, N.Y.: Anchor Press/ Doubleday, 1985.

Kozol describes the social and economic costs of illiteracy and offers a bold plan to mobilize illiterate adults, their teachers, and advocates to effect substantial and pervasive changes in the instructional programs that serve adult literacy students.

Lawson, V. K. *Thinking Is a Basic Skill: Creating Humanities Materials for the Adult New Reader.* Syracuse, N.Y.: Literacy Volunteers of America, 1981.

Lawson discusses an innovative project, sponsored in part by the National Endowment for the Humanities, in which humanities scholars were recruited and trained to write books for new readers in their areas of expertise. It contains much useful information about writing for new readers.

Lyman, Helen H. *Literacy and the Nation's Libraries.* Chicago: American Library Assn., 1977.

A standard in the field, Lyman's book is a thorough review of the role of libraries in literacy activities. The author makes a strong case for library involvement, reviews the characteristics of adult learners, and examines numerous ways librarians can serve adult literacy students.

National Partners for Libraries and Literacy. American Library Association, Public Information Office, 50 E. Huron St., Chicago, IL 60611.

This is an organization of libraries, literacy providers, and numerous other organizations interested in furthering literacy.

Quezada, Shelley, comp. and ed. *Strengthening the Literacy Network.* Proceedings of a National Forum for State Libraries, May 20–22, 1990. Boston: Massachusetts Board of Library Commissioners, 1990.

Speakers at this forum addressed the role of libraries in literacy, the federal role in promoting literacy and libraries, workforce literacy, and other significant issues. Speakers included Gary Strong, State Librarian of California; Marilyn Gell Mason, Director of the Cleveland Public Library; and Senator Paul Simon, author of the National Literacy Act.

Appendix A

Common Sight Words

The New Instant Word List
by Edward Fry

According to Dr. Fry, the first 10 words in this list make up 24 percent of all written material, the first 100 words make up about 50 percent of written material, and the 300 words in total represent about 65 percent of all words written in English.[1]

Many of these words present a particular challenge to adult literacy students. Some are easily reversed or differ in only one letter. Others are phonetically irregular. Students need many opportunities to read and write these words in order to master them.

The First Hundred

Group 1a	Group 1b	Group 1c	Group 1d
the	or	will	number
of	one	up	no
and	had	other	way
a	by	about	could
to	word	out	people
in	but	many	my
is	not	then	than
you	what	them	first
that	all	these	water
it	were	so	been
he	we	some	call
was	when	her	who
for	your	would	oil
on	can	make	now
are	said	like	find
as	there	him	long
with	use	into	down
his	an	time	day
they	each	has	did
I	which	look	get
at	she	two	come
be	do	more	made
this	how	write	may
have	their	go	part
from	if	see	over

Common suffixes: *s, ing, ed*

The Second Hundred

Group 2a	*Group 2b*	*Group 2c*	*Group 2d*
new	great	put	kind
sound	where	end	hand
take	help	does	picture
only	through	another	again
little	much	well	change
work	before	large	off
know	line	must	play
place	right	big	spell
year	too	even	air
live	mean	such	away
me	old	because	animal
back	any	turn	house
give	same	here	point
most	tell	why	page
very	boy	ask	letter
after	follow	went	mother
thing	came	men	answer
our	want	read	found
just	show	need	study
name	also	land	still
good	around	different	learn
sentence	form	home	should
man	three	us	America
think	small	move	world
say	set	try	high

The Third Hundred

Group 3a	Group 3b	Group 3c	Group 3d
every	left	until	idea
near	don't	children	enough
add	few	side	eat
food	while	feet	face
between	along	car	watch
own	might	mile	far
below	close	night	Indian
country	something	walk	real
plant	seem	white	almost
last	next	sea	let
school	hard	began	above
father	open	grow	girl
keep	example	took	sometimes
tree	begin	river	mountain
never	life	four	cut
start	always	carry	young
city	those	state	talk
earth	both	once	soon
eye	paper	book	list
light	together	hear	song
thought	got	stop	leave
head	group	without	family
under	often	second	body
story	run	late	music
saw	important	miss	color

Appendix B

Word Lists for Initial Consonant Sounds

b	hard c /k/	soft c /s/	d	f
bait	cake	celery	damp	face
bat	can	cell	dark	fall
bed	cap	cent	day	far
bend	car	center	dear	farm
best	carry	century	deep	fast
better	cash	certain	dent	father
bill	coat	citizen	did	feel
boat	cold	city	dinner	first
born	come	civic	dish	fit
build	cow		do	fly
burn	cry		done	for
butter	cup		door	found
buy	cut		down	full

hard g /g/	*soft g* /j/	*h*	*j*	*k*
gain	gender	had	jail	kale
game	gene	hair	jam	keep
garden	gent	hand	jar	keg
gate	gentle	hat	jelly	kept
gave	giblets	have	jet	kettle
get	ginger	he	job	key
gift	giraffe	head	join	kick
give	gist	hill	joke	kill
go		him	joy	kind
gold		hire	jump	king
gone		hold	June	kiss
good		home	just	kite
got		hot		kitten

l	*m*	*n*	*p*	*q*
lady	man	name	paid	qualm
lake	many	near	paint	quarter
lap	may	need	pan	quell
late	me	never	paper	question
let	meet	new	part	quiet
letter	men	next	party	quilt
light	milk	nice	pass	quit
like	mine	night	pen	quite
listen	most	none	people	quota
little	move	noon	person	quote
look	much	north	pick	
lost	must	not	pig	
love	my	now	port	
			pull	
			put	

r	s	t	v	w
race	said	table	van	walk
rain	same	tail	vast	warm
ran	sat	take	very	water
rat	save	talk	view	went
real	say	tall	visit	will
red	see	tap	voice	window
rest	seen	tell	vote	work
ride	set	ten		
right	sing	tent		
ring	sit	time		
river	soap	to		
road	soda	told		
roller	soft	too		
room	some	took		
run	sue	top		

x	y	z
Xerox	yard	zebra
xylophone	year	zip
	yellow	zipper
	yes	zone
	yet	zoo
	you	
	your	

Appendix C

Vowel Patterns

Words marked with an asterisk (*) are pronounced differently according to their use in a sentence.

Short Vowel Patterns

Short a

-ab	-ack	-ad	-ag	-am
cab	back	ad	bag	am
dab	hack	bad	gag	dam
gab	jack	cad	hag	ham
jab	pack	dad	lag	jam
lab	rack	fad	nag	ram
nab	sack	had	rag	yam
tab	tack	lad	sag	
		mad	tag	clam
blab	black	pad	wag	slam
flab	slack	sad		dram
slab	crack		brag	gram
crab	track	clad	drag	tram
drab	shack	glad	flag	swam
grab	whack	shad	shag	
scab	smack		snag	
	snack		stag	
	stack			

-amp	*-an*	*-and*	*-ang*	*-ank*
camp	an	and	bang	bank
damp	ban	band	fang	rank
lamp	can	hand	gang	sank
ramp	fan	land	hang	tank
champ	man	sand	rang	yank
clamp	pan	bland	sang	blank
cramp	ran	gland	tang	plank
tramp	tan	brand	clang	crank
stamp	van	grand	slang	drank
	clan	stand		frank
	plan			spank
	scan			thank
	span			
	than			

-ap	*-ash*	*-asp*	*-ass*	*-ast*
cap	ash	asp	bass	cast
gap	bash	gasp	lass	fast
lap	cash	hasp	mass	last
map	dash	rasp	pass	mast
nap	gash	clasp	brass	past
rap	hash		grass	vast
tap	mash		class	blast
chap	rash		glass	
clap	sash			
flap	clash			
slap	crash			
snap	trash			
trap	smash			
	stash			

-at	*-atch*	*-ath*	*-ax*
at	catch	bath	ax
bat	hatch	path	lax
cat	latch	wrath	tax
fat	match		wax
hat	patch		flax
mat	thatch		
pat			
rat			
sat			
slat			
that			

Short e

-ead	-eck	-ed	-eg	-elf
dead	deck	bed	beg	elf
head	heck	fed	egg	self
lead*	neck	led	keg	
read*	peck	red	leg	shelf
		wed	peg	
bread	check			
dread	speck	bled		
tread		fled		
spread		sled		
thread		shed		
		sped		

-ell	-elp	-elt	-em	-en
bell	help	belt	hem	den
dell	kelp	felt	them	hen
fell	yelp	melt	stem	men
hell		welt		pen
quell	whelp			ten
sell		smelt		
tell				glen
well				then
yell				when
shell				
smell				
spell				
swell				

-end	-ent	-ept	-ess	-est	-et
bend	bent	kept	less	best	bet
end	dent	wept	mess	nest	get
lend	lent			pest	jet
mend	rent	crept	bless	rest	let
send	sent	slept	chess	test	met
	tent	swept	dress	vest	net
blend				west	pet
spend	went				set
trend				chest	wet
	spent			crest	yet
				quest	

Short i

-ib	*-ick*	*-id*	*-ift*	*-ig*
bib	kick	bid	gift	big
fib	lick	did	lift	dig
rib	nick	hid	rift	fig
crib	pick	kid	sift	jig
glib	sick	lid		pig
	tick	rid	drift	rig
	wick		shift	wig
		grid	swift	
	brick	skid		brig
	trick	slid		swig
	chick			twig
	thick			
	click			
	flick			
	slick			

-ilk	*-ill*	*-im*	*-in*	*-inch*
bilk	bill	dim	bin	cinch
milk	fill	him	din	inch
silk	gill	rim	fin	pinch
	hill		in	winch
	ill	brim	kin	
	kill	grim	pin	clinch
	mill	trim	sin	
	pill	skim	tin	
	rill	slim	win	
	sill	swim		
	till	whim	chin	
	will		shin	
			thin	
	chill		grin	
	drill		skin	
	grill		spin	
	quill		twin	
	spill			

-ing	*-ink*	*-int*	*-ip*	*-ish*
bing	ink	hint	dip	dish
ring	link	lint	hip	fish
sing	mink	mint	lip	wish
wing	pink	tint	nip	
zing	rink		rip	swish
	sink	flint	sip	
bring	wink	print	tip	
cling		squint	zip	
fling	brink			
sling	drink		chip	
sting	clink		ship	
swing	slink		whip	
thing	stink		flip	
	think		slip	
			grip	
			trip	
			quip	
			skip	
			snip	

-iss	*-ist*	*-it*	*-itch*	*-ive*
hiss	fist	bit	ditch	give
kiss	list	fit	itch	live*
miss	mist	hit	pitch	
		it	witch	
bliss	twist	kit		
		lit	stitch	
		mitt	switch	
		pit		
		sit		
		wit		
		grit		
		quit		
		slit		
		skit		
		spit		

-ix

fix
mix
six

Short o

-ob	-ock	-od	-og	-oll
cob	cock	cod	bog	doll
fob	dock	God	cog	loll
gob	hock	nod	dog	moll
job	lock	pod	fog	
mob	mock	rod	hog	
rob	pock	sod	log	
sob	rock			
		clod	clog	
blob	clock	plod	frog	
slob	flock	shod	smog	
knob	crock	trod		
snob	frock			
	shock			
	smock			
	stock			

-on	-ond	-ong	-ot	-ox
con	bond	bong	cot	box
don	fond	gong	dot	fox
non	pond	long	got	lox
on		song	hot	ox
	blond		not	sox
	frond	prong	pot	
		wrong	rot	
		strong		
		thong	blot	
			clot	
			plot	
			slot	
			shot	
			spot	
			trot	

Short u

-ough	-ove	-ub	-uck	-ud
enough	above	cub	buck	bud
rough	dove	dub	duck	cud
tough	love	hub	luck	mud
		nub	muck	
slough	glove	pub	puck	stud
	shove	rub	suck	thud
		sub	tuck	
		tub		
			chuck	
		club	shuck	
		grub	cluck	
		scrub	pluck	
		snub	stuck	
		stub	struck	
			truck	

-udge	-uff	-ug	-ull	-um
fudge	buff	bug	cull	bum
judge	cuff	dug	dull	gum
nudge	huff	hug	gull	hum
	muff	jug	hull	mum
grudge	puff	lug	lull	rum
sludge		mug	mull	sum
	bluff	pug	null	
	gruff	rug		chum
	scuff		skull	drum
	snuff	chug		glum
	stuff	drug		plum
		thug		slum
		slug		scum
		smug		strum
				swum

-umb	*-ump*	*-un*	*-unch*	*-ung*
dumb	bump	bun	bunch	hung
numb	dump	fun	lunch	lung
	hump	gun	punch	rung
crumb	jump	nun		sung
plumb	lump	pun	brunch	
thumb	pump	run	crunch	clung
	ump	sun		flung
				stung
	clump	shun		strung
	plump	spun		swung
	slump	stun		wrung
	chump			
	thump			
	grump			
	stump			

-unk	*-up*	*-us*	*-ush*	*-usk*
bunk	cup	bus	gush	dusk
dunk	pup	us	hush	husk
hunk	sup		lush	musk
junk	up	plus	mush	tusk
		thus	rush	
chunk				
drunk			blush	
flunk			flush	
shrunk			plush	
skunk			slush	
			brush	
			crush	
			shush	
			thrush	

-ust	*-ut*	*-uzz*
bust	but	buzz
dust	cut	fuzz
just	gut	
lust	hut	
must	jut	
rust	nut	
	rut	
crust		
	shut	
	smut	
	strut	

Long Vowel Patterns

Long a

-ace	-ade	-age	-aid	-ail
ace	fade	age	aid	bail
face	jade	cage	laid	fail
lace	made	page	maid	hail
mace	wade	rage	paid	jail
pace		sage	raid	mail
race	blade	wage		nail
	glade		braid	pail
brace	grade	stage		quail
grace	trade			rail
trace	shade			sail
place	spade			tail
space				
				frail
				trail
				snail

-aim	-ain	-aint	-ait	-ale
aim	gain	faint	bait	ale
maim	lain	paint	gait	dale
	main	quaint	wait	gale
	pain	saint		hale
	rain		trait	kale
	vain			male
				pale
	brain			sale
	drain			tale
	grain			vale
	train			
	chain			scale
	plain			shale
	slain			whale
	stain			stale

-ame	*-ane*	*-ape*	*-ase*	*-aste*
came	cane	ape	base	baste
dame	lane	cape	case	haste
fame	mane	gape	vase	paste
game	pane	nape		taste
lame	sane	rape	chase	waste
name	vane	tape		
same	wane			chaste
tame		drape		
	crane	grape		
blame	plane	scrape		
flame		shape		
frame				
shame				

-ate	*-ave*	*-ay*	*-aze*	*-eigh*
ate	cave	bay	daze	neigh
date	gave	day	faze	weigh
fate	nave	gay	gaze	
gate	pave	hay	haze	sleigh
hate	rave	jay	maze	
late	save	lay	raze	
mate	wave	may		
rate		nay	blaze	
sate	brave	pay	glaze	
	crave	ray	craze	
crate	grave	say	graze	
grate	shave	way		
plate	slave			
slate		clay		
skate		play		
state		fray		
		gray		
		pray		
		tray		
		spray		
		stray		

-eight

eight
weight

freight

Long e

-e	-ea	-each	-ead	-eak
be	pea	beach	bead	beak
he	sea	each	lead*	leak
me	tea	peach	read*	peak
we	flea	reach	plead	weak
she	plea	teach		bleak
		bleach		creak
				freak
				speak
				streak
				squeak

-eal	-eam	-ean	-eap	-east
deal	beam	bean	heap	beast
heal	ream	dean	leap	east
meal	seam	lean	reap	feast
peal	team	mean	cheap	least
real	cream	wean		
seal	dream	clean		
veal	gleam	glean		
zeal				
squeal				
steal				

-eat	-ee	-eech	-eed	-eef
beat	bee	beech	deed	beef
eat	fee	leech	feed	reef
feat	see		heed	
heat	tee		need	
meat	wee		seed	
neat	free		weed	
peat	tree		bleed	
seat	flee		breed	
cheat	glee		creed	
cleat	thee		freed	
pleat	three		greed	
treat			speed	
wheat			steed	
			tweed	

-eek	-eel	-eem	-een	-eep
leek	eel	deem	keen	beep
meek	feel	seem	queen	deep
peek	heel	teem	seen	jeep
reek	keel		teen	keep
seek	peel			peep
week	reel		green	seep
			sheen	weep
cheek	creel		screen	
creek	steel			creep
sleek	wheel			sheep
				sleep
				steep
				sweep

-eet	-ief	-y
beet	brief	bunny
feet	grief	carry
meet	chief	funny
	thief	marry
fleet		sunny
sleet		
greet		
sheet		
sweet		
tweet		

Long i

-ice	-ide	-ie	-ife	-igh
dice	bide	die	life	high
ice	hide	lie	rife	nigh
lice	ride	pie	wife	sigh
mice	side	tie		
nice	tide	vie	knife	thigh
rice	wide		strife	
vice				
	bride			
slice	pride			
spice	glide			
twice	slide			
	stride			

-ight	-ike	-ild	-ile	-ime
fight	bike	mild	bile	dime
light	dike	wild	file	lime
might	hike		mile	mime
night	like	child	pile	time
right	mike		rile	
sight	pike		tile	chime
tight			vile	climb
	spike			slime
bright	strike		smile	crime
fright			while	grime
flight				prime
knight				

-ind	-ine	-ipe	-ire	-ise
bind	dine	pipe	dire	rise
find	fine	ripe	fire	wise
hind	line	wipe	hire	
kind	mine		ire	
mind	nine	gripe	mire	
rind	pine	snipe	sire	
wind*	tine	stripe	tire	
	vine	swipe	wire	
blind	wine			
grind			spire	
	shine			
	whine			
	spine			
	swine			
	twine			

-ite	-ive	-y	-ye
bite	dive	by	dye
kite	five	my	eye
mite	hive		lye
quite	live*	cry	rye
rite		dry	
site	chive	fry	
	drive	pry	
spite	strive	fly	
white	thrive	ply	
write		sly	
		shy	
		thy	
		why	
		sky	
		spy	
		sty	
		try	

Long o

-o	-oach	-oad	-oal	-oam
go	coach	goad	coal	foam
ho	poach	load	foal	loam
no	roach	road	goal	roam
so	broach	toad	shoal	
pro				

-oan	-oast	-oat	-obe	-ode
loan	boast	boat	lobe	bode
moan	coast	coat	robe	code
roan	roast	goat	globe	mode
groan	toast	moat	probe	ode
		oat		rode
		bloat		strode
		float		
		gloat		
		throat		

-oe	-oke	-old	-ole	-olt
doe	coke	bold	dole	bolt
foe	joke	cold	hole	colt
hoe	poke	fold	mole	dolt
toe	woke	gold	pole	jolt
woe	yoke	hold	role	molt
	bloke	mold	stole	volt
	choke	old	whole	
	smoke	sold		
	spoke	told		
		scold		

-ome	-one	-ope	-ose	-ost
dome	bone	cope	hose	host
home	cone	dope	nose	most
tome	hone	hope	pose	post
chrome	lone	lope	rose	
	pone	mope		
	tone	nope	chose	
	zone	pope	those	
		rope	close*	
	clone			
	drone	grope		
	prone	scope		
	phone	slope		
	shone			
	stone			

-ote	-ove	-ow
note	cove	bow*
quote	dove*	low
rote	rove	mow
tote	wove	row
vote		sow*
	clove	tow
wrote	drove	
	grove	blow
		flow
		glow
		slow
		crow
		grow
		know
		show
		snow

Long u

Note: The sound represented by /oo/ as in *cool* is sometimes considered part of this grouping.

-ew	*-ude*	*-ue*	*-uke*	*-ule*
dew	dude	due	cuke	mule
few	nude	rue	duke	yule
hew	rude	sue	nuke	
new				
pew	crude	blue		
	prude	clue		
blew		flue		
flew		glue		
slew		true		
chew				
brew				
crew				
drew				
grew				
knew				
stew				

-une	*-use*	*-ute*
dune	fuse	cute
June	muse	jute
tune	use	lute
prune		mute
		brute
		chute
		flute

r-Controlled Vowel Patterns

/**ar**/

-ar	*-arch*	*-arge*	*-ark*	*-arm*
bar	arch	barge	bark	arm
car	march	large	dark	farm
far	parch	charge	hark	harm
jar	starch		lark	charm
par			mark	
tar			park	
scar			shark	
spar			spark	
star			stark	

-arn	*-arp*	*-arsh*	*-art*
barn	carp	harsh	art
darn	harp	marsh	cart
yarn	tarp		dart
	sharp		mart
			tart
			chart
			smart
			start

/er/

-er	*-erm*	*-ern*	*-ir*	*-ird*
her	berm	fern	fir	bird
per	germ	tern	sir	gird
	term	stern	stir	third
			whir	

-irl	*-irt*	*-ur*	*-urn*
girl	dirt	cur	burn
swirl	flirt	fur	turn
twirl	shirt	blur	spurn
whirl	skirt	slur	
	squirt	spur	

/or/

-oar	*-oard*	*-oor*	*-or*	*-ord*
boar	board	door	for	cord
oar	hoard	floor	nor	ford
roar			or	lord
soar				sword

-ore	*-ork*	*-orm*	*-orn*	*-ort*
bore	cork	form	born	fort
core	fork	norm	corn	sort
fore	pork		horn	tort
gore		storm	morn	
more	stork		torn	short
ore			worn	sport
pore				
sore				
tore				
wore				
chore				
score				
swore				

-orth	*-our*
forth	four
north	pour

Other Vowel Patterns

/au/ as in *all*

-all	*-alk*	*-aught*	*-aul*	*-aunch*
all	balk	caught	haul	haunch
ball	talk	naught	maul	launch
call	walk	taught		paunch
fall				
gall	chalk			staunch
hall	stalk			
mall				
tall				
wall				
small				
stall				

-aunt	*-ause*	*-aw*	*-awl*	*-ought*
gaunt	cause	caw	awl	bought
haunt	pause	jaw	bawl	fought
jaunt		law		ought
taunt	clause	saw	brawl	sought
vaunt			crawl	
		claw	shawl	brought
		flaw		thought
		draw		

/oo/ as in *cool*

-oo	-ood	-ool	-oom	-oon
boo	food	cool	boom	boon
coo	mood	fool	doom	coon
goo		pool	loom	goon
moo	brood	tool	room	loon
too			zoom	moon
woo		drool		noon
zoo		school	bloom	soon
		spool	gloom	
shoo		stool	broom	croon
			groom	spoon
				swoon

-oop	-oose	-oost	-oot	-ooth
coop	goose	boost	boot	booth
hoop	loose	roost	hoot	tooth
loop	moose		loot	
	noose		moot	
droop			root	
troop			toot	
scoop				
sloop			scoot	
snoop			shoot	
stoop				
swoop				

-ove
move
prove

/oo/ as in *book*

-ood	-ook	-ould	-ull	-ush
good	book	could	bull	bush
hood	cook	would	full	push
wood	hook		pull	
	look	should		
stood	nook			
	took			
	brook			
	crook			
	shook			

/oi/ as in *boy*

-oice	*-oil*	*-oin*	*-oint*	*-oise*
voice	boil	coin	joint	noise
choice	coil	join	point	poise
	foil	loin		
	oil			
	soil	groin		
	toil			
	broil			
	spoil			

-oist	*-oy*
foist	boy
hoist	coy
joist	joy
moist	soy
	toy

/ou/ as in *ouch*

-ouch	*-ound*	*-ouse*	*-out*	*-outh*
couch	bound	house	bout	mouth
ouch	found	louse	gout	south
pouch	hound	mouse	out	
vouch	mound	souse	pout	
	pound		rout	
	round	grouse		
	sound		scout	
			shout	
	ground		spout	
			stout	
			trout	

-ow	*-owl*	*-own*
bow*	cowl	down
how	fowl	gown
cow	howl	town
now	jowl	
vow	owl	brown
wow	yowl	crown
		drown
plow	growl	frown
	prowl	clown

Appendix D

Consonant Blends and Digraphs

Initial Consonant Blends

-*l* Blends

bl-	*cl-*	*fl-*	*gl-*	*pl-*	*sl-*
black	class	flag	glad	place	slate
blade	clay	flat	glare	plan	slave
blame	clean	flew	glass	plane	sled
blew	clear	flight	gleam	plant	sleep
blind	climb	float	glean	plate	slept
block	clock	flood	glee	play	slid
blood	close	floor	glint	player	slip
bloom	clothes	flour	gloom	please	slipper
blow	cloud	flower	glove	plenty	slop
blue		fly	glow	plow	slow

-r Blends

br-	*cr-*	*dr-*	*fr-*	*gr-*
brake	crack	draw	free	grade
brave	crawl	dream	freeze	grain
bread	cream	dress	fresh	grape
brick	creek	drew	friend	grass
bridge	crib	drink	fright	gray
bright	crop	drive	frog	great
bring	cross	drop	from	green
brother	crowd	drove	front	grew
brought	crumb	drum	frost	ground
brown	cry	dry	fruit	group

pr-	*tr-*
press	track
pretty	trade
price	train
pride	tramp
prime	trap
print	tree
prize	trick
proud	trip
prune	truck
	true

s- Blends

sc-	*sk-*	*sm-*	*sn-*	*sp-*
scamp	skate	smack	snail	space
scan	sketch	small	snake	spade
scant	ski	smart	snap	spark
scar	skid	smell	sneeze	speak
scare	skimp	smile	snip	spear
scarf	skin	smoke	snipe	spell
scold	skip	smooth	snooze	spice
score	skirt	smudge	snow	spill
scout	skunk		snub	spot
scull	sky		snug	spur

st-	*sw-*
stack	swan
stage	swat
stamp	sweat
star	sweater
steal	sweep
steam	sweet
step	swept
stiff	swim
stock	swing
stunt	

Three-letter Blends

scr-	*spl-*	*str-*
scram	splash	strain
scratch	splat	strait
scream	spleen	strand
screech	splendid	strange
screen	splendor	streak
screw	splice	street
scrounge	splint	strike
scrub	split	string
scruff	splotch	strung
scrunch	splurge	

Consonant Digraphs

ch-	*-gh*	*-ng*	*-nk*	*ph-*
chain	enough	bang	bank	phantom
chair	rough	long	brink	phase
change	tough	rang	drink	phone
charge		sang	link	photo
charm		sing	pink	phrase
check		sling	rank	
chest		song	rink	
child		string	spank	
chill		wing	thank	
church		young	think	

sh-	th- (voiceless)	th- (voiced)	wh-	wr-
shelf	thank	that	whale	wrap
shell	thaw	the	what	wreath
shin	thick	their	when	wreck
shine	thigh	them	where	wren
ship	thin	then	whether	wring
shoe	thing	there	which	write
shoot	think	these	while	wrong
shout	third	they	white	wrote
shut	thorn	though	whizz	wrung
shy	thumb	thy	why	wry

Appendix E

Rules for Syllabication

1. A word with one vowel sound has one syllable.

    eight   wild

2. A compound word is divided between the individual words.

    ball/park   break/fast

3. A prefix is usually a separate syllable.

    re/move   un/tie

4. A suffix is usually a separate syllable.

    dead/ly   dark/ness

5. Usually when a root word ends with *d* or *t*, the *-ed* ending is a separate syllable. When the root word does not end with *d* or *t*, the *-ed* ending does not form another syllable.

Root word ending with *t*	Root word ending with *d*	Root word not ending with *d* or *t*
lift/ed	round/ed	walked
rest/ed	tend/ed	pitched

6. Generally, divide syllables between double consonants or two different consonants.

sud/den   win/ter
c/c   c/c

7. When a word contains a long vowel-consonant-vowel pattern (vcv), usually divide syllables after the long vowel (v/cv).

clo/ver   pa/per   ri/val   ti/ny
v/cv   v/cv   v/cv   v/cv

8. The consonant letter in front of *le* usually goes with the le syllable.

sim/ple   star/tle

9. Certain letters must not be separated.

oi as in *boil/ing*	*ow* as in *cow/ard*
ou as in *scour/ing*	*ng* as in *sing/er*
ew as in *re/new/al*	*tw* as in *be/tween*
br as in *em/brace*	*pl* as in *im/pli/cit*

Appendix F

Sample Evaluation Form
for Adult New Reader Materials

Following is a sample evaluation form for adult new reader materials. Encourage tutors, librarians, and—most importantly—students to write reviews of books they read and share them with other tutors and students.

EVALUATION FORM FOR
ADULT NEW READER MATERIALS

CATEGORY: (leisure reading, coping skills, etc.)

_____

CALL NO.: _____

LOCATION: (special collection, adult nonfiction, vertical file, etc.)

TITLE: _____   no. of p. _____

AUTHOR: _____   PUBLISHER: _____

SERIES: _____   DATE & EDITION: _____

BOOK_____ (hardcover_____ paperback_____ workbook_____ teacher's ed_____)

PAMPHLET_____ AUDIOVISUAL_____ (video_____ cassette_____ software)

PRIMARY SUBJECT(S):	READING LEVEL:_____	PLOT/SUMMARY/ CRITICAL COMMENTS
_____	SUITABILITY FOR ADULTS (theme, treat-	_____
_____	ment, language, etc.	_____
_____	Note appeal to any	_____
_____	particular audience.)	_____
	_____	_____
SPECIFIC SKILLS TAUGHT: (if any)	_____	_____
	_____	_____
_____	_____	_____
_____	_____	_____
_____		_____
_____		_____
_____	QUALITY OF ILLUSTRATIONS AND	_____
SPECIAL FEATURES:	OTHER FEATURES	_____
(glossary, review ques-	(include any charts,	_____
tions, maps, etc.)	graphs, etc.)	_____
_____	_____	_____
_____	_____	_____
_____	_____	_____
_____	_____	_____
_____	_____	REVIEWER:_____
_____	_____	DATE:_____

Notes

Introduction

1. Anonymous literacy student quoted in Gary Strong, "Adult Illiteracy: State Library Responses," *Library Trends* 35 (Fall 1986): 243.

Chapter 1   The Role of the Library in Promoting Literacy

1. James Madison, *The Writings of James Madison,* vol. 9 (New York: Putnam, 1900–10), 103.

2. "The Public Library: Democracy's Resource. A Statement of Principles" (Paper available from the Public Library Association, c/o the American Library Assn., 1982).

3. *Adult Functional Competency: A Summary* (Austin, Tex.: Div. of Extension, Univ. of Texas, 1975), p.6, ED114 609.

4. Daniel Boorstin, *Books in Our Future: A Report from the Librarian of Congress to Congress* (Washington, D.C.: Congress of the United States, Joint Committee on the Library of Congress, 1984), 7–8.

Chapter 2 A Profile of Adult Literacy Students

1. An adult literacy student from the Ohio State University Right to Read Program.

2. Malcolm S. Knowles, *The Modern Practice of Adult Education: Andragogy versus Pedagogy* (New York: Association Press, 1970), 39.

3. Anne Eberle and Sandra Robinson, *The Adult Illiterate Speaks Out: Personal Perspectives on Learning to Read and Write* (Washington, D.C.: National Institute of Education, 1980), 8.

4. Knowles, *Practice of Adult Education,* 44.

5. Knowles, *Practice of Adult Education,* 46.

6. George W. Eyster, *Recruiting Disadvantaged Adults* (Morehead, Ky.: Morehead State University, 1975), 4–6.

7. Eberle and Robinson, *The Adult Illiterate Speaks Out,* 2.

8. Eberle and Robinson, *The Adult Illiterate Speaks Out,* 5.

Chapter 3 Methods of Teaching Reading

1. Richard Wright, *Black Boy: A Record of Childhood and Youth* (Cleveland: The New World Publishing Company, 1945), 218.

2. Helen H. Lyman, *Reading and the Adult New Reader* (Chicago: American Library Assn., 1976), 21.

3. Edward V. Jones, *Reading Instruction for the Adult Illiterate* (Chicago: American Library Assn., 1981), 79.

4. Mike Rose, *Lives on the Boundary: The Struggles and Achievements of America's Underprepared* (New York: The Free Press, 1989), 109.

5. Frank Smith, *Reading without Nonsense,* 2d ed. (New York: Teachers' College Press, 1985), 5.

6. An adult literacy student at the Ohio State University Right to Read Program, 1977.

7. Paula Schneiderman and Marguerite Crowley, *Tutor Training Handbook* (The Ohio State University Right to Read Program, unpubl.), 25–26.

8. *Your Social Security Rights and Responsibilities: Disability Benefits* (Baltimore, Md.: Department of Health and Human Services, Social Security Administration, 1986), 9.

9. Jones, *Reading Instruction for the Adult Illiterate,* 96.

10. Frank C. Laubach, Elizabeth Mooney Kirk, and Robert S. Laubach, *Laubach Way to Reading,* Skill Book 2 (Syracuse, N.Y.: New Readers Press, 1981), 2–3.

11. John C. Adams, *Building Word Power* (Austin, Tex.: Steck-Vaughn Co., 1975), 4.

12. Harley A. Smith and Ida Lee King Wilbert, *Practice in Reading* (Austin, Tex.: Steck-Vaughn Co., 1974), 5.

13. The four stages of literacy development are adapted from similar schemes developed by Herbert Kohl in *Reading, How to* (New York: E. P. Dutton & Co., 1973), 22–118, and Helen Lyman in *Reading and the Adult New Reader* (Chicago: American Library Assn., 1976), 18–19.

Chapter 4 Teaching Literacy Skills

1. *Life and Times of Frederick Douglass* (New York: Collier Books, 1962), 79.

2. Frank Smith, *Reading without Nonsense,* 2d ed. (New York: Teachers' College Press, 1985), 66–68.

3. Smith, *Reading without Nonsense,* 66–68.

4. Smith, *Reading without Nonsense,* 85–87.

5. V. K. Lawson, *Thinking Is a Basic Skill: Creating Humanities Materials for the Adult New Reader* (Syracuse, N.Y.: Literacy Volunteers of America, 1981), 1.

6. Benjamin Bloom, ed., *Taxonomy of Educational Objectives: Handbook 1, Cognitive Domain* (New York: David McKay Co., 1956), 62–193.

Chapter 5 Language Experience Lessons in the Library

1. Annie Dillard, *The Writing Life* (New York: Harper & Row, 1989), 72–73.

2. John Loengard, *Life Classic Photographs: A Personal Interpretation* (Boston: New York Graphic Society Books, Little, Brown & Co., 1988), 8.

3. Andreas Feininger, *The Mountains of the Mind: A Fantastic Journey into Reality* (New York: The Viking Press, 1977), 7.

Chapter 6 Information Reading Lessons in the Library

1. Barbara Tuchman, as quoted in *Books in Our Future: A Report from the Librarian of Congress to Congress* (Washington, D.C.: Congress of the United States, Joint Committee on the Library, 1984), 26.

2. *Betty Crocker's Kitchen Secrets* (New York: Random House, 1983), 25.

3. Neil Isaacs and Dick Motta. *Sports Illustrated Basketball* (New York: Harper & Row, 1981), 36–38.

4. Richard Whittingham, *The White Sox: A Pictorial History* (Chicago: Contemporary Books, 1981), 80.

5. G. C. Skipper, *D-Day,* World at War series (Chicago: Childrens Press, 1982), 14–17.

6. Jack Rummel, *Langston Hughes,* Black Americans of Achievement series (New York: Chelsea House Publishers, 1988), 38.

7. *Betty Crocker's Kitchen Secrets* (New York: Random House, 1983), 72.

8. Bill James, *The Baseball Book 1990* (New York: Villard Books, 1990), 156.

Chapter 7   Using Poetry with Adult New Readers

1. Robert Frost, *The Road Not Taken: A Selection of Robert Frost's Poems,* Louis Untermeyer, sel. (New York: Henry Holt & Co., 1985), 240.

2. Maya Angelou, "Willie," in *And Still I Rise* (New York: Random House, 1978), 28.

3. Bill Moyers, "The Power of the Word," quoted in *Airfare: The Magazine of the WOSU Stations* 10 (Oct. 1989): 8.

4. Lucille Clifton, "A Simple Language," in *Black Women Writers,* ed. by Mari Evans (New York: Anchor Press/Doubleday, 1984), 137.

5. Lucille Clifton, "4 daughters," in *Next: New Poems* (Brockport, N.Y.: BOA Editions Limited, 1987), 30.

6. Kenneth Koch and Kate Farrell, *Sleeping on the Wing: An Anthology of Modern Poetry with Essays on Reading and Writing* (New York: Random House, 1981), 17.

7. Langston Hughes, "Winter Moon," in *The Dream Keeper* (New York: Alfred A. Knopf, 1986), 4.

8. Robert Frost, "Dust of Snow," in *Complete Poems of Robert Frost* (New York: Holt, Rinehart, and Winston, 1949), 270.

9. William Carlos Williams, "Young Woman at a Window," in *The Complete Collected Poems of William Carlos Williams (1906–1938)* (Norfolk, Conn.: New Directions, 1938), 228.

10. Florence Howe and Barbara Danish, "Experiment in the Inner City," in *Somebody Turned on a Tap in These Kids: Poetry and Young People Today,* ed. Nancy Larrick (New York: Delacorte Press, 1971), 110–111.

11. Marc Kaminsky, *What's Inside You It Shines Out of You* (New York: Horizon Press, 1974), 52.

12. Kenneth Koch, *I Never Told Anybody: Teaching Poetry Writing in a Nursing Home* (New York: Random House, 1977), 13–14.

13. Koch, *I Never Told Anybody,* 70.

14. Kaminsky, *What's Inside You,* 73.

15. Kenneth Koch, *Wishes, Lies, and Dreams: Teaching Children to Write Poetry* (New York: Random House, 1970), 22.

16. Koch, *I Never Told Anybody,* 11.

17. Richard Wilbur, interviewed by David Dillon, in *American Poetry Observed: Poets on Their Work,* ed. Joe David Bellamy (Urbana, Ill.: University of Illinois Press, 1984), 286–287.

18. Koch, *I Never Told Anybody,* 109.

19. Nikki Giovanni, "Because," in *Cotton Candy on a Rainy Day* (New York: Wm. Morrow & Co., 1978), 47.

20. Bob Kaufman, "Response," in *Black Out Loud: An Anthology of Modern Poems by Black Americans,* ed. Arnold Adoff (New York: Macmillan, 1970), 76.

21. Reed Whittemore, "The Party," in *City in All Directions,* ed. Arnold Adoff (New York: Macmillan, 1969), 71.

22. Alice Walker, "Good Night, Willie Lee, I'll See You in the Morning," in *Good Night, Willie Lee, I'll See You in the Morning* (New York: Dial Press, 1979), 12.

23. Robert Hayden, "Those Winter Sundays," in *I Am the Darker Brother: An Anthology of Modern Poems by Black Americans,* ed. Arnold Adoff (New York: Macmillan, 1968), 10.

24. William Carlos Williams, "This Is Just to Say," in *Selected Poems of William Carlos Williams* (New York: New Directions Paperbook, 1969), 55.

25. William Carlos Williams, "Complete Destruction," in *The Complete Collected Poems of William Carlos Williams (1906–1938)* (Norfolk, Conn.: New Directions, 1938), 84.

26. William Carlos Williams, "The Great Figure," in *The Complete Collected Poems,* 100.

27. Langston Hughes, "Juke Box Love Song," in *I Am the Darker Brother* (New York: Macmillan, 1968), 14.

28. Seamus Heaney, "Scaffolding," in *Poems 1965–1973* (New York: Farrar, Straus & Giroux, 1980), 38.

29. Alice Walker, "He Said," in *Good Night, Willie Lee,* 12.

Chapter 8   The Uses of Literature

1. John D. MacDonald, *Reading for Survival* (Washington, D.C.: Center for the Book, 1987), frontmatter, unpaged.

2. Alex Haley, *Roots* (Garden City, N.Y.: Doubleday, 1979), a brief summary.

3. Eliot Wigginton, *Sometimes a Shining Moment: The Foxfire Experience* (Garden City, N.Y.: Anchor Press/Doubleday, 1985), a brief summary.

4. Robert Coles, *The Call of Stories: Teaching and the Moral Imagination* (Boston: Houghton Mifflin, 1989), 30.

5. Anna Bishop, *Beyond Poindexter Village: The Blackberry Patch* (Columbus, Ohio: Public Library of Columbus and Franklin County, 1982, unpubl.), unpaged.

6. May Swenson, "Irving Frajans," in *First-Person America,* ed. Ann Banks (New York: Alfred A. Knopf, 1980), 124.

7. Studs Terkel, "Roy Schmidt," in *Working* (New York: Pantheon Books, a Division of Random House, 1972), 104.

8. Marc Kaminsky, *What's Inside You It Shines Out of You* (New York: Horizon Press, 1974), 160–161.

9. Milton Meltzer, *The Black Americans: A History in Their Own Words* (New York: Harper & Row, 1984), 36–37.

10. James Baldwin, *If Beale Street Could Talk* (New York: Dial Press, 1974), 3–4.

11. Maya Angelou, *All God's Children Need Traveling Shoes* (New York: Random House, 1986), 3.

12. Pete Hamill, *The Gift* (New York: Random House, 1973), 3–4.

13. Pete Hamill, "D'Artagnan on Ninth Street: A Brooklyn Boy at the Library," *New York Times Book Review* (26 June 1988), 48.

Chapter 9 Using the Children's Collection

1. Jim Trelease, *The New Read-Aloud Handbook* (New York: Penguin Books, 1989), xv.

2. C. S. Lewis, "On Three Ways of Writing for Children," in *Children and Literature: Views and Reviews,* ed. Virginia Haviland (Glenview, Ill.: Scott, Foresman, 1973), 233.

3. Maurice Sendak, *Where the Wild Things Are* (New York: Harper & Row, 1984), a brief summary.

4. Robert McCloskey, *Make Way for Ducklings* (New York: Viking Penguin, 1941), unpaged.

5. John Burningham, *Mr. Gumpy's Motor Car* (New York: Thos. Y. Crowell, 1976), unpaged.

6. Dorothy Butler, *Babies Need Books* (New York: Atheneum, 1982), viii.

7. Napa City–County Library, 1150 Division St., Napa, CA 94559–3396.

8. The Family Reading Project, Vermont Council on the Humanities, Box 58, Hyde Park, VT 05655.

Chapter 10 Special Collections for New Readers

1. Michael Brennan, "All I Really Need to Know I Learned in the Library," *American Libraries* 23 (Jan. 1992), 38.

2. Melissa Forinash Buckingham, comp., *Reader Development Bibliography* (Syracuse, N.Y.: New Readers Press, 1982), 71.

3. Robert S. Laubach and Kay Koschnick, *Using Readability: Formulas for Easy Adult Materials* (Syracuse, N.Y.: New Readers Press, 1977), 13–15.

Chapter 11   Using the Library for Lifelong Learning

1. Pete Hamill, "D'Artagnan on Ninth Street: A Brooklyn Boy at the Library," *New York Times Book Review* (26 June 1988), 48.

Chapter 12   Building a Literacy Coalition

1. Philip Roth, "The Newark Public Library," in *Reading Myself and Others* (New York: Farrar, Straus & Giroux, 1975), 176.

Appendix A   Common Sight Words

1. Edward Fry, "The New Instant Sight Word List," *The Reading Teacher* (Dec. 1980), 285–288.

Author-Title Index

Marguerite Crowley Weibel directed the educational program of The Ohio State University Right to Read program and developed the Library Learning Centers of the Columbus Metropolitan Library. She has tutored adult literacy students individually, taught writing and reading classes for new readers, and led numerous tutor training workshops. Ms. Weibel has Master's degrees in adult education and library science and is currently librarian and instructor at The Ohio State University Libraries.